Librar
& Democracy
The Cornerstones of Liberty

Nancy Kranich
Editor

AMERICAN LIBRARY ASSOCIATION
Chicago and London
2001

Cover and text design by ALA Production Services

Composition by ALA Production Services

Printed on 50-pound white offset, a pH-neutral stock, and bound in 10-point coated cover stock by Batson Printing

The paper used in this publication meets the minimum requirements of American National Standard for Information Sciences—Permanence of Paper for Printed Library Materials, ANSI Z39.48-1992. ∞

Library of Congress Cataloging-in-Publication Data

Libraries and democracy : the cornerstones of liberty / [edited by] Nancy
   Kranich.
      p.   cm.
   ISBN 0-8389-0808-X
   1. Libraries and society—United States. 2. Libraries and state—United
States. 3. Information policy—United States. 4. Freedom of information—
United States. 5. Internet access for library users—United States.
I. Kranich, Nancy C.
Z716.4 .L459 2001
021'.0973—dc2p1   2001022974

Printed in the United States of America.

50 04 03 02 01   5 4 3 2 1

Contents

Preface

> Libraries are . . . essential to the functioning of a democratic society . . . libraries are the great symbols of the freedom of the mind.
> —*Franklin D. Roosevelt*

Democracies need libraries. An informed public constitutes the very foundation of a democracy; after all, democracies are about discourse—discourse among the people. If a free society is to survive, it must ensure the preservation of its records and provide free and open access to this information to all its citizens. It must ensure that citizens have the resources to develop the information literacy skills necessary to participate in the democratic process. It must allow unfettered dialogue and guarantee freedom of expression. Libraries deepen the foundation of democracy in our communities.

Libraries are for everyone, everywhere. They provide safe spaces for public dialogue. They disseminate information so the public can participate in the processes of governance. They provide access to government information so that the public can monitor the work of its elected officials and benefit from the data collected and distributed by public policy makers. They serve as gathering places for the community to share interests and concerns. They provide opportunities for citizens to develop the skills needed to gain access to information of all kinds and to put information to effective use.

Ultimately, discourse among informed citizens assures civil society. In the United States, libraries have greeted the self-determination of succeeding waves of immigrants by offering safe havens and equal access to learning. They continue this mission today. Indeed, libraries ensure the freedom to read, to view, to speak, and to participate. They are the cornerstone of democracy.

Introduction

L ibraries serve the most fundamental ideals of our society as uniquely democratic institutions. As far back as the mid-nineteenth century, libraries were hailed as institutions that schooled citizens in the conduct of democratic life. This symbiotic relationship between libraries and democracy is often celebrated. Grandiose statements abound espousing the importance of libraries to democracy—a concept most Americans take for granted. Yet very little is written that explicitly discusses the meaning of libraries as cornerstones of democracy. In 1947, Sidney Ditzion published *Arsenals of a Democratic Culture* (ALA), which was among the first books to address the foundations of the relationship between libraries and democracy. Almost fifty years later, Arthur Hafner included a chapter on democratic ideals in his book *Democracy and the Public Library* (Greenwood, 1993).

Now, with the dawn of the information age, the relationship between libraries and democracy demands our attention more than ever. This book, *Libraries and Democracy,* focuses on the role libraries play in advancing deliberative democracy. Democracy is no simple construct. President Lyndon B. Johnson believed in voting as the crux of democracy. At the end of the century, President Bill Clinton held governance to be the dominant feature of democracy. Perhaps the most comprehensive view was held by President Franklin D. Roosevelt, who considered democracy to be the opportunity for everyone to participate in all aspects of society.

I set out to collect essays representing a broad array of perspectives on the role of libraries in supporting democratic participation and an informed citizenry. Contributed by widely recognized experts on a range of topics, these essays elaborate on the relationship between libraries and democracy. In section I, Stielow, Schement, and McCook provide us with a historical and theoretical overview of the role of libraries in a democracy. Fred Stielow updates the classic Ditzion text, providing a context from which we can dissect the myth from the reality of the symbolic role American libraries play throughout the world. Jorge Reina Schement views democracy in terms of participation and challenges libraries to support equitable services in order to ensure a fair as well as just information society. Kathleen de la Peña McCook also focuses on equitable services by reviewing the historical development of public libraries and their commitment to leaving no one behind.

In the second section, Durrance, McCabe, and Marcoux address the contributions of libraries to civil society. Joan Durrance and her colleagues demonstrate how libraries provide information to help citizens thrive in their local communities. Ron McCabe discusses civic librarianship and its support for American participation in the democratic process following several decades of extreme individualism. Betty Marcoux describes the importance of information literacy skills for citizens to thrive and participate in the information society of the twenty-first century.

Modern democracy cannot be considered without taking into account the role of technology. Libraries promote democracy well beyond their local communities by utilizing new technologies. In Section III, Kranich, Kretchmer, and Pitman discuss the challenges libraries face in extending their traditional roles of serving the information needs of all people. My essay considers the impact of the Internet on widening the gaps between the haves and have-nots in our communities, endangering our democratic values. Susan Kretchmer analyzes the Internet controversy in libraries at the intersection of old and new technologies. Technology has also affected the way we exercise our right to vote, which is the topic of my essay on libraries and the electoral process. Randy Pitman explores the role of video as an influence on democratic values.

Beyond local communities, libraries promote democracy through public policy. With the growing importance of information in the national and international policy arenas, librarians advocate more accessible, available, and affordable information. In Section IV, Heanue, Blanton, McMasters, Kretchmer, and Vaidhyanathan map out perspectives on the public's information rights, many of which are now hotly contested. Anne Heanue describes how access to government information continues to present major challenges to the library community. Tom Blanton relates recent struggles over ethics and power, along with the roles they play in determining who will control public access to information. Paul McMasters' and Susan Kretchmer's articles argue the merits of the struggle to protect our democratic freedoms under the First Amendment. On yet another policy front, Siva Vaidhyanathan explains how the balance between creators and users of intellectual property has tilted toward the powerful, thereby threatening the key role of copyright in fueling the production of information products, the engines of democracy.

The essays in Section V by Cole and Billington chronicle the important role of the Library of Congress in both American and international democracy building. John Cole recounts how the Library has served national democratic goals throughout its two-hundred-year history. Then, James Billington,

Librarian of Congress, discusses his vision for moving the Library beyond its traditional mission to promote international understanding and democracy.

Working together, librarians actively participate in political deliberation that addresses the interests and concerns of communities. Library associations provide the opportunity to multiply and amplify individual voices so librarians can present their collective views and values effectively. In the final section, Schuman, Gordon, and Belfrage review advocacy roles that promote democratic participation. Patricia Glass Schuman articulates the key role of librarians in promoting the public's right to know. Bill Gordon and Joneta Belfrage describe the role of library associations as advocates for democracy; Gordon presents the point of view of ALA and Belfrage the role of the Swedish Library Association.

The twenty essays in this collection take different views on the impact libraries have on democracy. The tendencies and tensions of American society, first described by Alexis de Tocqueville in *Democracy in America* in 1835, are represented and reflected in these essays about the role libraries play in our democracy. In fact, the essays themselves reflect the character of democratic discourse. Librarians must now carry this extraordinary legacy into the twenty-first century if libraries are to continue to serve as the cornerstone of democracy.

I. Historic and Theoretical Overview of the Role of Libraries and Democracy

Reconsidering *Arsenals of a Democratic Culture*
Balancing Symbol and Practice

Frederick Stielow

> Libraries are directly and immediately involved in the conflict which divides our world, and for two reasons; first, because they are essential to the functioning of a democratic society; second, because the contemporary conflict touches the integrity of scholarship, the freedom of the mind, and even the survival of culture, and libraries are the great tools of scholarship, the great repositories of culture, and the great symbols of the freedom of the mind.
>
> —*Franklin D. Roosevelt*

The stirring tones of President Franklin D. Roosevelt helped introduce a landmark of library history. In *Arsenals of a Democratic Culture,* Sidney Ditzion outlined the complex mixture behind the birth of the American public library. His text has stood the test of time. While subsequent scholarship has improved our specific knowledge about this nineteenth-century American innovation, Ditzion set the stage and touched on every significant issue about that topic. Equally important, his work remains the point of departure for understanding the role of libraries and democracy across the modern era.[1]

The Invention of Tradition

Ditzion first focused on the second quarter of the nineteenth century. As subsequent historians have explained, this was a time when the United States realized that the great experiment of the American Revolution had succeeded. But, the democracy was still very new and in need of supporting mechanisms.

3

Americans looked back to find their origins and went forward with democratic traditions and romantic trappings for future generations. The young nationalists hearkened to the wisdom of the Constitution and supported hagiographic treatments that deified the Founding Fathers. Territorial expansion across the continent became our Manifest Destiny.[2]

Avoiding the static national monuments of Europe, states and local communities stepped forth with active local initiatives. Civic celebrations, especially centered on the Fourth of July, became patriotic mainstays in almost every town and village. The most important efforts, however, were reserved for education. Reformers such as Horace Mann presented a case for mandatory public schooling that consciously built on the democratic rhetoric of the era. Their cause reflected a national consensus on the "democratic premise," which Ditzion described as taking hold by 1850:

> The concepts of republicanism, risen from the enlightenment, advertised in the Revolution, strengthened in the philosophy of Jeffersonianism, and practiced in the era of Jacksonian democracy, were by mid-century deeply engraved upon the popular mind. The doctrines of human rights, political equality, and residence of authority in the whole people, had become firmly fixed in the professed American credo.[3]

The public school campaign would itself redefine an essential portion of the American myth. The new entitlement to education quickly became institutionalized as an inalienable right. The same rhetoric would be borrowed to frame the case for developing the most democratic social service ever conceived—a parallel educational innovation for adults in the form of local libraries for all the people.

Building on the positive historical concepts of the temple of knowledge, proponents still had to democratize the image of the library away from an elitist and academic bastion. Instead, it was to be reinvented as a place of advancement for all the people—a physical confirmation of the values of the Revolution. Proponents sang the praises of a pure democratic spirit in support of the general welfare. To speakers at the dedication of the Boston Public Library, the first public library and a model for much of what followed, the new American library was to become a civic treasure—"our intellectual and literary common." It would be open to "the rich and the poor . . . the high and the lowly born, the masses who wield the hammers of toil, and the unenvied few who are reared in affluence and ease."[4]

Ditzion could not deny the New England orientation and culture conceits of the conceivers, who viewed the public library as a needed social service and moral defense against the dangers of an ignorant electorate. Similar reasoning played a role in early support for state libraries and the Library of Congress. As the unpublished preamble to the groundbreaking Massachusetts Library Law summarized:

> Whereas, a universal diffusion of knowledge among the people must be highly conducive to the preservation of their freedom, a greater equalization of social advantages, their industrial success, and their physical, intellectual, and moral advancement and elevation. . . . [T]here is no way that this can be done so effectively as by the formation of Public Libraries . . ."[5]

Despite their biases, proponents understood that their ideal would call for compromise. Hence, rationales included the importance of physical convenience and economic advantages for a practically minded citizenry. As Ditzion argued, flexible and individualistic Americans could employ the "democratic premise— and could modify, distort, or even pervert it to suit the requirements of widely varying points of view."[6] Such pragmatists recognized that their situation had not been perfected and came replete with contradictions. Even the benign paternalism of the Revolution needed to be altered toward more democratic principles by Jacksonian-era drives for participatory government. Strict Calvinistic doctrines of moral worth and Puritanical order were giving way to romantic Unitarianism, which featured the "democratic perfectibility" of the Transcendentalists. The country could blend doctrines of moral stewardship and self-improvement along with new beliefs in scientific advancement, industrialization, and the cultural nationalism of the period. Aristocrats and the common man understood that their democratic melting pot would need future refinement. In Ditzion's words:

> The major ideological currents of this period were directed toward producing a unified nation based on the free informed choice of individuals rather than on measures of indoctrination in behalf of any particular group. As it happened there was a fairly close identity among the requirements of national prosperity, the needs of the new dominant industrial class, and the tenets of flourishing individualistic philosophies. Divisive tendencies, having their origins in prejudices of race, section, nationality, creed and class, were present indeed. It was hoped that these could be eased, or perhaps erased by establishing agencies of enlightenment for adult and youth alike.[7]

The public library was thus conceived as a logical and flexible creation. It would evolve over time and help Americans to perfect their system and themselves. To Ditzion, the idea appeared almost naturally as part of the evolution of the United States: "The tax-supported public library not only answered the criteria inherent in the democratic premise but also offered an instrument as responsive to varying social requirements as democracy itself."[8]

From Tradition to Practice

With the democratic ideal of the public library in place, Ditzion's main task was to describe the social and economic factors that framed actual development during the second half of the century. The range was immense. Ditzion mentions such overlapping and occasionally conflicting elements as:

- The advances and lower costs in paper and printing technology, which ushered in a communications revolution and mass culture.
- The struggle for cultural leadership between New England and the economically burgeoning Mid-Atlantic States.
- The Social Gospel and humanitarian ideas of social uplift to fight the perceived evils of the city and industry.
- The desires of industrialists for a better-conditioned work force, including "Americanizing" foreign laborers.
- The rise of wealthy philanthropists, which would be epitomized by Andrew Carnegie and the Gospel of Wealth.
- Developments in adult education that reached to lyceums, young men's institutes, Chatauqua, and the university extension movement.
- A portion of what later historians would call the "feminization of American culture," in which paternalism and the democratic push for women's rights helped create an acceptable new work arena for middle-class women and domesticated the library.
- The tolerance and support of publishers and then booksellers to an agency that seemingly threatened their profits.
- The role of the public library as a social service that marked a community's passage from the frontier into civilization.
- The transit of leadership from trustee founders to a newly professionalizing group of librarians.

As epitomized by their choice of the centennial year of 1876 to launch the American Library Association (ALA), the first generation of American practitioners retained the ability to use democratic symbols. Yet, the new leadership also faced significant challenges in trying to reach their democratic ideal. The first and still continuing battle was to secure reliable public funding. Ditzion puts this especially in light of the financial success of the public school movement. The second was the need to secure patrons—a volunteerism unlike the mandatory nature of the schools. Libraries simply had to respond to the voters. According to Ditzion, service called for synthesis:

> The concept of service, which took hold early in the history of free libraries, was one of the accommodations to the mass of voters by whose mandate and for whose benefit the libraries were being run. . . . The desires and convenience of readers were the sole criteria for selecting, arranging, and listing books. Libraries were built where they would be most accessible to the greatest number of readers. Hours of operation were determined in accordance with needs of the majority of the population.[9]

As his narrative closes at the turn of the twentieth century, we see the American system at work. An agency begun exclusively for adult education was being open to children and family entertainment. Women had risen to the forefront. Libraries were responding with reduced fines and popular literature along with such innovations as children's rooms and interlibrary loans. The institution was open to the presence of technical manuals, newspapers, and even Sunday opening hours. Previously sacrosanct stacks were even democratized for public browsing. Whatever the original intent, the democratic process was taking hold.

Understanding Ditzion in His Context

The reader should understand that historical analyses are often as instructive about the times, scholarly milieu, and makeup of the writer as the era being described. Michael Harris and Dee Garrison, for example, could later challenge Ditzion's interpretation for capitalistic leanings and an overly male-centered treatment, which would likely not have been recognized at the time of its writing.[10] Ditzion's scholarship certainly reflects the book's origins as a dissertation for the Department of History at Columbia University. Written under the direction of Merle Curti, it can be classified as part of the so-called progressive history movement. Ditzion was part of a chain of studies on the American mind that began with Vernon Parrington and the multi-volume *Main Currents in American Thought*.[11] According to Richard Hofstadter, progressive historians—most notably Parrington, Charles Beard, and Frederick Turner—tended toward activism. They were driven to democratize history and use it as a tool to reform the remaining contradictions within the nation. Such scholars were "eager to make up for the past failure of historians to deal with the interests of the common man and with the historic merits of movements of reform. They attempted to find a useable past . . . to make history an active instrument of self-recognition and self-improvement."[12]

Similarly, Ditzion reflected the civilized nature of the nation and state of the library field of his era. The country had completed its search for order and closed off its frontier before Ditzion's birth. The pioneering library movement of the nineteenth century had given way to widespread professional education and the added stimulus of Carnegie's largesse. Instead of an experimental social service, Ditzion grew up with libraries as the expected sign of a modern, progressive American community. In addition, Ditzion himself was trained as a librarian. A former classicist, he had earned a bachelor's in 1934 from the Columbia University School of Library Service and his master's from City College in 1938. He had been indoctrinated into a field that was far more mature than the one he described. By his era too, American libraries had taken on a new international role, faced their major intellectual contradiction, and were becoming involved in an ideological struggle against fascism.

Extending the Mission to the World

Thanks largely to the emergence of the Library of Congress (LC) and ALA— the two bodies that are prominently featured in the rest of this volume— American libraries would take on a position of international leadership soon after the close of Ditzion's period of study. Herbert Putnam seems to have played the pivotal position in this transformation. With Putnam at its helm, LC would rise to technical dominance in such areas as book processing and cataloging. Equally important, Putnam helped extrapolate the "American library" from the community-centered ideal of the public library to a more generalizable international symbol for democracy.

Putnam had assumed his position during the jingoist cries of the Spanish American War, but World War I provided him with the major venue to remake the image of the American library for the world. With the war, Putnam was appointed director general of Library War Services for the United States. Under his leadership, librarians rallied around the flag and actively asserted the scientific professionalism of their "accelerated library movement." As suggested by Theodore Koch's 1919 volume *Books in the War: The Romance of Library*

War Service, the patriotic lure and need to export American ideals was irrepressible.[13]

Putnam had also opened the door for an active partnership and expanded role with the then fledgling ALA. The latter became one of the "Seven Sisters"—quasi-official agencies that provided social services for the troops. Carl Milam, Putnam's major assistant and successor at Library War Services, would attempt to continue the wartime momentum for American libraries at ALA. In 1919, Milam took charge of ALA's Enlarged Program with its pronouncedly All-American propaganda thrust for American libraries. From 1920 to 1948, he would serve as the ALA's chief administrative officer and the major force in its historical development. Under Milam, ALA would help to rebuild foreign libraries destroyed in the war and continue to provide library services to occupation troops and the Merchant Marines. It would even contribute to a new symbol of democracy with the creation of the American Library in Paris.[14]

In the 1930s, a very different set of circumstances would arise. Milam emerged at the head of a group of library hawks against the ideological specter of fascism. Following the German invasion of Poland in 1939, the ALA would abandon most of the trappings of neutrality. The association quickly commissioned two bibliographies on the *Dangers to Democracy.* Looking back to the halcyon days of WWI, it also formed a Committee on Mobilization and War Services Plans. And, acting in keeping with Milam's patriotic fervor, ALA belatedly moved to resolve the major theoretical impediment to the library's democratic mission—a change that merits a brief aside.

Intellectual Freedom

Although noting a paucity of resources, Ditzion had argued for a nineteenth-century commitment to intellectual freedom. He found that "a certain amount of circumspection, tempered by a goodly amount of willing conformity, . . . usually provided the library administration with sufficient fortification against moralistic raids."[15] More recent scholarship suggests the reality of a democratic contradiction for these early "apostles of culture" and their "library hostesses." Ditzion's reports of circumspection and conformity were really indicative of an initial professional commitment to censorship.

As others and I have suggested, exclusion was an accepted part of the library climate of opinion and professional duties. This status would substantially change only after World War I. Only then would librarians face the challenge of popular literature of questionable value and their own democratic

responsibilities to present full and complete information to the people. As previously suggested, however, ALA's official posture was not fully altered until
the 1930s in response to the threats from fascism and such affronts as the Nazi
book burnings of May of 1934—events that occurred as Ditzion was entering
the field. Even so, the formal embrace of intellectual freedom was delayed until
after the start of warfare with the invasion of Poland. It appeared in December
of 1939 with the adoption of the Library Bill of Rights. That crucial document
for the library's future devotion to the First Amendment may only have passed
as a part of wartime fervor. It was deliberately conceived to counter enemy
propaganda and to "mobilize all educational and cultural resources for the
preservation and improvement of American Democracy."[16]

WWII and FDR

The influence of World War II on Ditzion's book about the nineteenth century
is inescapable. According to the vita in the text, the author was working at the
City College of New York at the start of the war. Born in 1908, he may have
been a trifle old for frontline service, but took leave in 1943 to teach physics
at the college. The following year, he engaged in "war work in a research and
production capacity for an optical laboratory."

Ditzion's wartime views also appear influenced by the transcendent figure
of Franklin Delano Roosevelt. FDR was the president during most of the librarian's formative years as an adult. Roosevelt's understanding of the importance
of ideas and democratic symbols during his battle against the Depression
played a significant and still underappreciated role in bolstering libraries and
archives. He signed the legislation that created the National Archives and used
his considerable status to launch the first presidential library at Hyde Park.
Although the president earned professional ire by selecting Archibald
MacLeish to succeed Putnam as director general of Library War Services, the
choice brought unprecedented national and international prestige to the field
and LC. MacLeish would even pen the opening quotation of this essay for
Roosevelt to present to the ALA's national convention in 1942.[17]

In keeping with library sentiment, Roosevelt and MacLeish saw the
Second World War as much a conflict for the mind as one on the battlefield. To
MacLeish, this front against fascism was totally necessary: "We will either educate the people of this republic to know and therefore to value and therefore to
preserve their own democratic culture or we will watch the people . . . trade
their democratic culture for the nonculture, the obscurationism, the supersti-

tion, the brutality, the tyranny."[18] Or, as Roosevelt put it in the other quotation at the start of Ditzion's work and probable inspiration for its title:

> In our country's first year of war, we have seen the growing power of books as weapons. . . . This is proper, for a war of ideas can no more be won without books than a naval war can be won without ships. Books, like ships, have the toughest armor, the longest cruising range, and mount the most powerful guns. I hope that all who write and publish and sell and administer books will . . . rededicate themselves to the single task of arming the mind and spirit of the American people with the strongest and most enduring weapons.

Following Pearl Harbor, the ALA's Committee on Mobilization and War Services Plans quickly morphed into the War Services Committee. ALA also sought ties with LC, which would lead the government's wartime library activities. As John Cole later demonstrated, the resulting union produced a Victory Books campaign that eventually delivered 120 million books to soldiers as weapons in the war of ideas. MacLeish established a Division of Wartime Communications to look at public opinion and propaganda efforts. The war also provided new opportunities for librarians within American defense. One still largely hidden role would place them as active agents within the intelligence community and the world of spying. MacLeish used his position to introduce librarians and library techniques to intelligence analysis. He even dedicated staff and a portion of LC to Col. William Donovan to start the OSS (Office of Strategic Services). The process resulted in the birth of modern military intelligence and still ongoing advances in information science.[19]

In contrast to the country's behavior in World War I, the United States would not retreat from a proactive institutional base with the end of hostilities. The all-encompassing manner of WWII produced the most significant democratic posturing since the Civil War. I suggest that this included a switch in the presentation of the democratic ideal. For a century the library had served to help perfect the American system. But, wartime success against fascism provided certitude that the democracy had matured. The United States was the perfect beacon for the world. In addition to providing a pragmatic tool to help nations democratize, the American library would provide information on the end model for their journey. Thus, library officials worked together to help restock war-damaged libraries. The government would not abandon the war of ideas. It continued to fund military libraries and instituted a series of American reading rooms overseas. To paraphrase library historian Gary Kraske, the profession's embrace of a missionary role for democracy was institutionalized as part of a new form of American cultural diplomacy.[20] Such a role is even evident in Curti's phrasing for the foreword to Ditzion's monograph:

> With the growing interest abroad in American civilization, we can be sure that this book will find a place in the collections of the cultural attaches in our legations and embassies, and that foreign librarians and students of American civilization will make good use of it in broadening and deepening their knowledge of more of the most distinctive and influential agencies of our cultural life.[21]

Conclusions

Ditzion's patriotism and progressive belief in the American system obviously colored his text, but did not prevent a balanced treatment. He distinguished the theoretical conceits of the proponents of this most democratic social service from the reality of the library's evolution:

> Librarians, for all their self-interest and tendency to overrate their own role in the movement, really believed in the mission of their institution. Their contribution, especially in the last quarter of the nineteenth century was considerable. . . . In achieving their ends, they drew heavily upon democratic and humanitarian values. . . . Both the institution and its methods were conceived . . . as a contribution toward the self-realization of the broad masses of the people.[22]

To me, the value of the library for democracy goes beyond physical use and holdings. Nationalistic proponents reconfigured the idea of library into a new type of voluntary civic agency in support of the general welfare. In the late nineteenth century, librarians and the American people took that vision and pragmatically molded it to fit their times. The reconstruction has never stopped. It would take on different forms in the early twentieth century, for example, and return wholeheartedly to its mythic roots during World War II. Such changes did not deny the continuity of the underlying tradition—the American library emerged as a sign of the United States on a par with apple pie, motherhood, and the flag. In addition to actual services and clientele, this institution must thus be judged in relation to its external or semiological factors. At the local level, it would evolve into the most visible civic statement and monument to a democratic way of life. Internationally, the concept of the American library would come to serve as a powerful cultural symbol and visible goal for all democratic societies. And the current Information Age offers us the distinct possibility of achieving its mythic promise as a "virtual arsenal" for democracy.

Notes

1. Sidney Ditzion, *Arsenals of a Democratic Culture* (Chicago: ALA, 1947). Jesse Shera's "The Foundations of the Public Library" (Ph.D. diss., University of Chicago, 1942) was the other landmark historical study of the World War II era and was cited by Ditzion for its synthesis of the pre-public-library period and precedents. Interestingly, Shera would serve as Col. Donovan's librarian at the O.S.S. during the war.
2. Historians have produced a growing series of studies on civic celebrations and the rise of nationalistic symbols in the Era of Good Feelings, which followed the War of 1812. The seminal work in this line remains Wesley Frank Craven's *The Legend of the Founding Fathers* (Ithaca, N.Y.: Cornell, 1956). As exemplified by the long struggle to erect the Washington Monument, any embrace of fixed monuments would date to later in the century.
3. Ditzion, *Arsenals of a Democratic Culture*, 51–52.
4. Quoted in Ditzion, *Arsenals of a Democratic Culture*, 22.
5. Ibid., 18–19.
6. Ditzion, *Arsenals of a Democratic Culture*, 51.
7. Ibid., 75–76.
8. Ibid., 51.
9. Ibid., 174.
10. Michael Harris, "The Purpose of the American Public Library," *Library Journal* 98 (Sept. 1973): 2509–14; Dee Garrison, *Apostles of Culture: The Public Librarian and American Society* (New York: Free Press, 1979).
11. Merle Curti, *The Growth of American Thought* (New York: Harper, 1943), provides the most significant influences; Ditzion cites only vol. 2, Vernon Parrington, *Main Currents in American Thought* (New York: Harcourt Brace, 1930).
12. Richard Hofstadter, *The Progressive Historians* (New York: Knopf, 1968), xvi–xvii. By the 1940s, the progressive school was being replaced by a consensus school of historiography.
13. Theodore Koch, *Books in the War: The Romance of Library War Service* (Boston: Houghton Mifflin, 1919); Arthur Young, *Books for Sammies* (Pittsburgh: Beta Phi Mu, 1981).
14. Peggy Sullivan, *Carl Milam and the American Library Association* (New York: Wilson, 1977), 54–77; Frederick Stielow, "Censorship in the Early Professionalization of American Libraries, 1876 to 1929," *Journal of Library History* 18 (1983): 37–54.
15. Ditzion, *Arsenals of a Democratic Culture*, 185.

16. Milam would actually be quite willing to sacrifice this ideal and embrace censorship during the war.

17. Frederick Stielow, "Librarian Warriors and Rapprochement: Carl Milam, Archibald MacLeish, and World War II," *Libraries and Culture* 25 (1990): 513–33; Franklin Roosevelt, "A Message to the 64th Annual Conference of the ALA," *ALA Bulletin* 36 (1942): 422.

18. Archibald MacLeish, "Libraries in the Contemporary Crisis," in Eva Goldschmidt, *Champions of a Cause* (Chicago: ALA, 1971), 21–22.

19. Stielow, "Librarian Warriors and Rapprochement."

20. John Cole, ed., *Books in Action: The Armed Services Editions* (Washington, D.C.: LC, 1984); Gary Kraske, *Missionaries of the Book; The American Library Profession and the Origins of United States Cultural Diplomacy* (Westwood, Conn.: Greenwood Pr., 1985).

21. Merle Curti, "Foreword," Ditzion, *Arsenals of a Democratic Culture*, viii.

22. Ditzion, *Arsenals of a Democratic Culture*, 193.

Imagining Fairness

Equality and Equity of Access in Search of Democracy

Jorge Reina Schement

> There is not, *perhaps,* a single library in America sufficiently copious
> to have enabled Gibbon to have verified the authorities for his immor-
> tal *History of the Decline and Fall of the Roman Empire.*
> —*attributed to Fisher Ames*

Revolutionary hero and Federalist Fisher Ames delivered a public address in
1809 that condemned American scholarship as greatly inferior to that conducted in Europe. He further charged that Edward Gibbon could not have written his *History of the Decline and Fall of the Roman Empire* had he searched all
of the university libraries in the United States because, taken together, they did
not hold all of the works cited by Gibbon. This accusation inflamed John Quincy
Adams, who was in the audience and proud of the feats of his father's generation. Determined as always, Adams set out to prove Ames wrong and, in the end,
his search proved Ames right. The shame was too much for Adams. Stung into
action, he purchased every work referred to in *The Decline and Fall.* All were
imported and given to the public library in Quincy, Massachusetts, so that no
future American Gibbon would be so stymied in the search for knowledge.[1]

The sixth president of the United States, John Quincy Adams remains
one of the great public intellectuals of the young republic.[2] His adventure
with Gibbon sought to achieve for American scholarship what had been
achieved for American nationalism—independence and equality within the
world community. Despite Adams' American penchant for mixing altruism
with self-interest—after all, he placed his national donation in his hometown
public library—he typifies the commitment of the nation's founders to create
a society where opportunity exists for all. Witness this excerpt from a letter
by Thomas Jefferson explaining the role of libraries as guarantors of equal
opportunity:

15

> Books constitute capital. A library book lasts as long as a house, for hundreds of years. It is not, then, an article of mere consumption but fairly of capital, and often in the case of professional men, setting out in life, it is their only capital.[3]

These three short sentences comprise a minute portion of an astounding body of correspondence encompassing the Revolution's best minds.[4] Jefferson himself sparred with all comers, especially with John Adams, father of John Quincy, until Jefferson's death on the same day as the elder Adams—July 4, 1826, during the presidency of the younger Adams. In those four decades, American intellectuals imagined a new country and a new society. They did so by examining every aspect of their social world and proposing new structures, new organizations, and new relationships. So, while this snippet can be read as a brief opinion on the value of books to an accountant, it should actually be read as something far more consequential. The question of the social value of library books, and by association libraries, is a part of the question of access in the pursuit of democracy.

In this essay, I pull Adams' resolution and Jefferson's dissection into the information age, a transition that manifests continuity and discontinuity. To begin with, the ideals of access and participation persist as firmly today as they did in the town-square, yeoman-farmer, plantation-democracy of Adams', Ames', and Jefferson's day. Yet if the ideals endure, the nation's social fabric has not. In an information society of nearly one-third of a billion people, democratic participation requires access to mediated channels and often takes place between parties whose only shared experience may come from membership in the same network. Scale alone, not to mention demographic, technological, or economic change, confronts democratic discourse with a profound challenge—how can we assure access for all?

Gaps in the Promise of Democracy

The emergence of the Internet released the pent-up optimism of technology sages and futurists. For most of two decades, they augured and foretold the Saturday evening of the future where children play *Star Wars* on a giant screen while Dad feeds his sports mania by firing instructions through his keyboard to multiple reflective partitions. Presumably, the family is nuclear and the technology convivial.[5]

When the Internet finally arrived, it brought a future at once foreseen and unexpected. Futurists could point to households so technologically affluent that they more than fulfilled the fantasies of twenty years past. Yet the future isn't what it used to be.[6] Seven percent of households still lack technology as simple as a telephone. True, some households achieve access to the network through spectacular configurations of technology.[7] At the same time, however, social researchers reveal a bewildering mosaic of the population beyond the vista of the super connected. For example, minority households below median income lag behind majority households in telephone penetration, even when they have the same income. Whereas minorities lag behind whites in PC ownership, Latinos appear to exhibit the highest purchasing rate. When African-Americans subscribe to cable services, they are more likely to purchase premium channels; and, in those households with telephones, African-Americans are more likely to purchase advanced telephone services. Elderly households are more likely to subscribe to a telephone than are young households with children, even in the same income bracket. Women, who for decades ceded the technological territory of computers to men, now equal men in access to the Internet. And, contrary to predictions of an increasingly homogenized culture where everyone consumes the same narrow media fare, proliferating channels set loose diverse tastes and choices. Even on prime time TV, the top ten choices for whites intersect those of African-Americans by one program only—Monday Night Football."[8]

So, while the information-age city on the hill opens its promenades and bazaars to the technologically blessed, others are kept at the gate.[9] In the secular language of democracy, that gate has entered policy discourse as the digital divide. Its essence resides in the traditional American concern over the existence of social gaps. That gaps of this sort fix our attention shouldn't surprise us. Early on in America's first declaration of national identity comes the phrase, "all men are created equal"; the document goes on to proclaim unalienable rights for all men, among which are "Life, Liberty, and the pursuit of Happiness."[10] Americans have built their edifice of democracy by interpreting this phrase as freedom and justice for all and, over the centuries, increasing the emphasis on *all*. Consequently, from time to time, national attention focuses on those Americans who might not have access to the same opportunities as their fellow citizens. The resulting discourse takes on the supposition of a "gap."[11]

Americans now carry these convictions with them into the information age. As a basic assumption, they firmly believe that access to information and communications technologies is the primary policy tool for enabling all citizens to participate in those economic, political, and social activities fundamental to a democratic society that is also a good society. Within this logic, an accessible National Information Infrastructure (NII) is the essential ingredient for overcoming social fragmentation and enabling participation. In the information age, communication creates society; in essence, the NII creates the weave that holds us all together. Hence, when Americans observe or imagine that some are falling behind, it gives pause because it endangers the promise of democracy—thus our anxiety over gaps, especially information gaps.

Information Equality versus Information Equity

If a society claims to derive its legitimacy from "the consent of the governed," then it must offer each member the opportunity to participate in the activities of public life.[12] To acknowledge the existence of conditions where some enjoy the opportunity to participate while others experience exclusion, full or partial, is to challenge the very claim to democracy that defines America. Yet in spite of high-minded claims, the ideal of equal access succeeds or founders on the reality; that is, on whether all citizens experience the same access to the means of participating in the discourses that guide governance. Of course, attempting to carry out any ideal in a world replete with constraints and complications invites humility and the lowering of expectations. After all, no great ideal is fully attainable. Even so, the ideal of democracy sets a high bar. In the second half of the twentieth century, for example, some white Americans rejected lesser status for African-Americans.[13] In effect, they raised the standard, reaffirming a commitment to achieve the ideal of democracy in the real world—an achievement for a democracy that began by limiting the vote to white males and registering slaves as three-fifths of a person. Still, the real world cannot be put off. In an information society inhabited by more than a quarter of a billion individuals, the goal of access as the prerequisite to participation poses singular challenges. Where citizens rarely know more than a handful of neighbors, have little direct personal experience with most national issues, and learn about these issues from mediated sources, access to information and channels of communication becomes the gateway to democracy.

Enter scale and technology. From a half a day's walk and meeting with neighbors coming together to the sedentary consumption of electronic images punctuated by telecommunications, the repercussions of a growing population coupled with the impact of information technologies have transformed democratic participation beyond the wildest eighteenth-century dream. In this latter day Digital Age, the availability of information and the technology to process it determine the reality of access. In other words, the ideal remains constant while new realities pose new challenges. So, having committed to equal access for all, how can we make it fair? In general, Americans have conceptualized fair access along two courses.

Equality of Access

Having begun from the assumption that all men are created equal, the logical derivation of this postulate requires that access be made available on even terms to all, thereby promoting equality of access to channels of communication and sources of information. This view derives from the concept of fairness as uniform distribution, where all are entitled to the same level of access and can avail themselves of this access if they so choose. This is the version of fairness—as uniform distribution—that Americans hold most dearly and comfortably. They have enshrined it from the Constitution to children's playgrounds where receiving one extra piece of candy evokes the cry "Not fair!" from a child's playmates; perhaps the most easily understood civic values are those that connect with fundamental experiences. Even so, that simple determination of fairness, so easy to understand, leads to difficult realities.

A colloid of policies—some rooted in the industrial era, others stemming from the information age—endeavor to make real the idea of equal access as uniform distribution. For example, in a complex society, functional access requires skills learned in school, especially literacy; thus, by extrapolation, if all are to experience access, then education must be provided for all as well. Consequently, amidst the many expectations heaped on them, public schools and libraries reflect in their missions the commitment to be open to all as an equal opportunity to achieve equal access. Similarly, Universal Service, once a policy aimed at ensuring that all telephone companies interconnect with each other, evolved into a policy assuring that all Americans receive the opportunity to connect to the national telecommunications network.[14] In the 1990s, the idea of universal service as uniform distribution took on a new dimension. The Education Rate, or E-Rate, established the premise that all schools, libraries, and rural hospitals should have access to the Internet.[15] Accordingly, public institutions whose core identities embrace equal access for all have themselves received the promise of equal access.

Most Americans support the idea that equal access suggests fairness because it promises the same access for everyone; surely, their continued endorsement of these policies underscores their comfort. And, complex histories notwithstanding, each of these public institutions sustains a commitment of access to all. Yet each also endorses a different, less comfortable conceptualization of fairness.

Equity of Access

The founders may have believed that all men are created equal; nonetheless, their elaborate formulations attempting to guarantee equality of access acknowledge their apprehension of the impediments to moving from ideal to reality.[16] Ninety years after the writing of the Constitution, the end of the Civil War and a churning industrial revolution exposed a society rapidly stratifying into poles of advantage and disadvantage. And, though some interpreted these disparities as God sent, or as nature's will to reward the fittest, the obvious consequences of privilege and exclusion threatened the promise of equal access to the discourses necessary for democratic participation.[17] By the eve of the twentieth century, America comprised an intricate society defined by its divides: rural/urban; black/white; foreign born/native born; working/middle/upper class; and, in the Southwest, Mexican/Anglo.[18]

In such circumstances Americans asked an old question with a new twist: "How can equal access for all exist if any group of Americans lacks the wherewithal necessary to achieve access?" In other words, though equality of access promises a level playing field, the promise fails when some Americans lack the knowledge, income, equipment, or training necessary to play the game. Thus, to continue the pursuit of a democratic ideal where all enjoy access to those public discourses through which participation becomes sovereignty, government must seek to overcome the obstacles to access experienced by affected groups, whether they be farmers, immigrants, workers, or former slaves. So delicate is the balance that failure to do so invalidates any claim to equality of access and, without equality, there can be no fairness. However, this is a new "fairness"; not fairness as uniform distribution, rather it is fairness as justice— that is, not equality of access, but equity of access. For just as there can be no fairness without equality, there can be none without justice.

History selects this view. The event that established the exclusion—i.e., slavery, native land dispossession, rural isolation, gender discrimination— requires remedies to redress the historic conditions that prevented or diminished access. So simple yet so unsettling, this interpretation of fairness sits uncomfortably with most Americans. Because the historic event underlies the disparity in access, it provokes revisions as some accept the diagnosis of unfairness but others reject it. The historic event provokes controversy. Depending on the interpretation imposed on the event, it may strengthen or weaken the claim of need. Witness the enduring lack of consensus on the motivations of the Confederacy for secession and war. Did the South fight for states' rights or for slavery—and who should merit compensation, the states or the former slaves and their descendents? Similarly, consider competing theories to explain poverty. Do the poor lack opportunities or do they lack motivation? Were we to attempt to list competing explanations for groups lacking access, the list would be long indeed. The point is that the goal of equity in pursuit of equal access depends on how we judge the event in question.

Equity-as-fairness-as-justice traces its lineage to progressive liberal philosophy. In this view, society should commit resources to overcome obstacles and barriers experienced by groups in order to maximize their opportunities for access. Franklin D. Roosevelt's New Deal and Lyndon B. Johnson's Great Society, as presidential themes, owed much to valuing fairness as justice. When libraries offer literacy programs, when schools offer courses in English as a second language, and when foundations target scholarships to students from poor families, they operationalize a belief in equity of access as fairness and as justice. Similarly, rural telecommunications cross-subsidies and the E-Rate establish their political legitimacy by appealing to equity of access as fairness and as justice. Clearly, the desire for equity draws its strength from the same deep source as that which feeds the desire for equality. Yet Americans remain ambivalent when asked to endorse policies aiming to achieve equity of access.

Equality against Equity

Policies that stress fairness as uniform distribution tend to succeed with Americans because they appear to entitle everyone, and thus, reinforce Americans' dominant construction of fairness as equality. Social Security and Medicare fall into this category. Similarly, the E-Rate, despite efforts to thwart it, has survived precisely because it benefits a large constituency. Indeed, so strong is the E-Rate's association with fairness as equality that it has survived every effort to diminish it, even relabeling it the "Gore Tax."[19]

Conversely, policies aiming to achieve equity face recurring challenges as "unfair." Affirmative Action, Lyndon Johnson's attempt to overcome generations of discrimination against women and minorities, became the law of the land without achieving the approval of Americans who saw it as "unfair." They found it unfair because it appeared to favor some over others, and thus it negated the concept of fairness as equality and as uniform distribution. Regardless of how many doors Affirmative Action opened to women and minorities, to many it seemed unfair and therefore worthy of opposition. Similarly, subsidy programs like Link-Up America and Lifeline, which assist poor households' access to telephone service, face resistance because they are seen as unfair.[20] To a cynic, it appears as though Americans will gladly accept a government subsidy for themselves, but should it go to someone else instead, they will resent it as "unfair." To someone committed to policies promoting equity as well as equality, this paradox poses a Herculean challenge.

Public Support of Fairness as a Challenge to Librarians

In such a world, librarians must tread carefully to achieve equality with equity; no matter the magnitude of the challenge, there can be no other social compact for librarians. In the twenty-first century, public librarians will achieve access for all, solely by fusing the concepts of fairness as uniform distribution with fairness as justice. If access policies concentrate solely on the objective of equality without reference to equity, their achievements will be flawed because those struggling to catch up will fall farther behind. After all, we entered the twenty-first century concerned about a "digital divide" resulting from a cluster of gaps that leave some Americans on the down side of the information age. Nonetheless, if access policies concentrate solely on the objective of equity by targeting groups who need special programs to improve their opportunities for access, they will likely reap the backlash of the many who resent such programs as unfair.

In the inevitable debates over acceptable access, librarians will need to position their programs within the range of what Americans consider fair. The E-Rate should serve as an exemplar as it incorporates the value of fairness as equality as uniform distribution by inviting all libraries to apply for the discount while it also supports fairness as equity as justice by increasing the discount for poorer libraries. The writers of the library subsidy clause won the support of the broader public by offering a policy that stressed equality and folded within it a commitment to equity.[21] The lesson? Librarians must first communicate the message that their libraries are open to all and available to everyone, even to those with no interest. Granted, such a stance seems overly easy to uphold since it reflects traditional values among librarians, but it is essential and must be constantly reinforced. To neglect this message invites the charge that libraries are not equally available to all and, therefore, not deserving of support because they are unfair. Beyond equal access, they must simultaneously pursue strategies seeking to effect equity. Targeted programs, such as literacy training or services in languages other than English, must be fully integrated into the library's larger mission and communicated as such. Sooner or later, if they stand apart, such programs will attract criticism as an "unfair" use of public funds. While these accusations may sound like trivial grumbling, over time they diminish public confidence. Thus, insofar as policies aim to achieve equality of access, they must also assimilate more narrowly focused policies that aim to achieve equity. Ultimately, there can be no equality without justice.

Raising an Identity from the Decline and Fall

I am charmed by the story of Fisher Ames' outraged denunciation and John Quincy Adams' blushing embarrassment. That the first thought his discovery worth publicizing and that the second responded with such alacrity speaks volumes about the founding generation's belief that their new country should be second to none. More important, though, it also embodies the lessons of equality and equity. Ames molded his charge around the critique that *all* American scholars were deprived of the advantage enjoyed by Gibbon in his English libraries; thus, Ames' condemnation hinges on a lack of equal access. For his part Adams was stung into purchasing the books cited in Gibbon's footnotes by his desire to redeem an insufficiency and bring it up to a level even with his measure of civil society—the essence of equity. True, my example may seem a tempest in a teapot, but bear in mind that equal and equitable access to information forms the basis for democratic discourse and, consequently, participation (Gibbon's judgment of the last Romans provides plenty of lessons for citizenship).[22] From the beginning, the inventors of democracy in America intuited the fundamental nature of that relationship and took it beyond theory.

Can we, their heirs, forge a robust democracy for the information age? We can if we recognize that democratic discourse ascends from the little things: from wanting the address of a polling station, from sending the mayor an e-mail, from tracking down a footnote—and from recognizing that access to that discourse is the sine qua non of democratic participation.[23] For democracy to derive its just powers from the consent of the governed, a communicative process must thrive. That process demands much of us for it demands that we ensure equal and equitable access for all.

Notes

1. *North American Review* 71 (1850): 186.
2. I confess to a technical interpretation in the interest of literary expedience. I live in the United States *of America*. A technicality, though I retain the sensibilities

brought here by my Mexican ancestors who came from the United States of Mexico. In speech and in my writings, I most often refer to my native country as *the* United States, though I maintain an awareness that these United States are not the only occupiers of the North American continent.

3.   President Thomas Jefferson to former President James Madison, Sept. 1821.

4.   When I read the individual essays and letters in this correspondence, I am some-times appalled, especially when reading opinions on the status of slaves and on proposed relations with the Indians, but, more often, my imagination soars and I am inspired to examine and question my own society and my own times.

5.   The list of futurists and their scenarios is long. For a sampling of various approaches see: A. Toffler, *Future Shock* (New York: Random House, 1970). J. Martin, *Telematic Society: A Challenge for Tomorrow* (New York: Prentice-Hall, 1981). S. Brand, *The Media Lab: Inventing the Future at MIT* (New York: Viking, 1987). National Research Council, *Realizing the Information Future: The Internet and Beyond* (Washington, D.C.: National Academy Pr., 1994).

6.   "The future ain't what it used to be," is one of the least attributed of Yogi Berra's many perceptive observations. Long-time catcher for the New York Yankees in the 1940s and 1950s, Berra is also responsible for "It ain't over till it's over," and "When you come to a fork in the road, take it." See Y. Berra, *The Yogi Book: I Really Didn't Say Everything I Said* (New York, Workman Publishing, 1998), 118–19.

7.   In this essay the term "network" refers to a system of computers interconnected for communication purposes. Thus, to transmit voice or data, one must access the "network," or "net."

8.   See L. J. Perl, *Residential Demand for Telephone Service 1983*, no. 1, National Economic Research Associates, Inc., for the Central Services Organization, Inc., of the Bell Operating Companies. J. Hausman, T. Tardiff, and A. Belinfante, "The Effects of the Breakup of AT&T on Telephone Penetration in the United States," *American Economic Review* 83, no. 2 (1993): 178–84. J. R. Schement, "Beyond Universal Service: Characteristics of Americans without Telephones, 1980–1993," *Communications Policy Working Paper No. 1*, Benton Foundation, 1994. J. R. Schement, "Thorough Americans: Minorities and the New Media," *Investing in Diversity: Advancing Opportunities for Minorities and the Media* (Washington, D.C.: Aspen Institute Publication, 1998), 87–124. J. R. Schement, A. Belinfante, and L. Povich, "Trends in Telephone Penetration in the United States 1984–1994," in E. M. Noam and A. J. Wolfson, eds., *Globalism and Localism in Telecommunications* (Amsterdam, The Netherlands: Elsevier, 1997), 167–201. M. Mueller and J. R. Schement, "Universal Service from the Bottom Up: A Study of Telephone Penetration in Camden, New Jersey," *The Information Society* 12 (1996): 273–92. J. R. Schement, "Beyond Universal Service: Characteristics of Americans without Telephones, 1980–1993," *Telecommunications Policy* 19, no. 6 (1995): 477–85. F. Williams and S.

Hadden, *On the Prospects for Redefining Universal Service: From Connectivity to Content,* Policy Research Project: The University of Texas at Austin (1991). F. Williams and S. Hadden, "On the Prospects for Redefining Universal Service: From Connectivity to Content." *Information and Behavior* 4 (1992): 49–63.

9. The metaphor of a city on a hill has long signified a utopian ideal for all to witness. John Winthrop usually receives credit in a sermon delivered in 1630 en route to America aboard the *Arabella,* "Consider that wee shall be as a Citty upon a Hill, the eies of all people are uppon us; . . ." First governor of the Massachusetts Bay colony, he seems to have been inspired by Matthew, "Ye are the light of the world. A city that is set on an hill cannot be hid." Matt. 5:14.

10. After beginning with the portentous, "When in the Course of human events," the Declaration of Independence goes on to offer the most succinct description of a democracy ever written. "We hold these truths to be self-evident, that all men are created equal, that they are endowed by their Creator with certain unalienable Rights, that among these are Life, Liberty, and the pursuit of Happiness. That to secure these rights, Governments are instituted among Men, deriving their just powers from the consent of the governed, That whenever any Form of Government becomes destructive of these ends, it is the Right of the People to alter or to abolish it, and to institute new Government, laying its foundation on such principles and organizing its powers in such form, as to them shall seem most likely to effect their Safety and Happiness."

11. The language of gaps can be potent. In his second inaugural address, Franklin D. Roosevelt took the first step of his new administration by challenging the picture of America as the land of opportunity. He looked out beyond his audience and declared, "I see one-third of a nation ill-housed, ill-clad, ill-nourished," and in so doing tapped into the terror that America's promise could not be fulfilled.

12. Perhaps the most powerful and provocative phrase of the Declaration of Independence; for, in four words, it defines democracy and the United States yet to be.

13. Separate but equal strategies meant that only whites could sit at public lunch counters, that African-Americans were forced to ride at the back of public buses and travel in their own separate, shabby railroad cars. As a child in San Antonio, I puzzled over side-by-side water fountains labeled "whites" and "colored." I encountered the ultimate insult in San Antonio's first shopping mall—separate restrooms for white men and women, but a single room for "coloreds" of both sexes.

14. "[T]o make available, so far as possible, to all of the people of the United States a rapid, efficient, Nation-wide, and world-wide wire and radio communication service with adequate facilities at reasonable charges, for the purpose of the national defense, for the purpose of promoting safety of life and property through the use of wire and radio communication, and for the purpose of securing a more effective execution of this policy by centralizing authority with respect to interstate and foreign commerce in wire and radio communication, . . ." Title I—

General Provisions, Section 1 [47 U.S.C. 151]. The provision relating to the promotion of safety of life and property was added by "An Act to amend the Communications Act of 1934, etc." Public Law 97, 75th Congress, approved and effective 20 May 1937, 50 Stat. 89. For a thorough discussion of the evolution of the concept of universal service, see M. L. J. Mueller, *Universal Service: Competition, Interconnection, and Monopoly in the Making of the American Telephone System* (Cambridge, Mass.: MIT Pr., 1997).

15. Telecommunications Act of 1996, Pub. L. 104-104, 110 Stat. 56.

16. Jefferson, primary author of the Declaration of Independence, felt strongly about the importance of an egalitarian society. In a 1785 letter he postulates, "Were I to indulge my own theory, I would wish them [Americans] to practice neither commerce nor navigation, but to stand, with respect to Europe, precisely on the footing of China. We should thus avoid wars, and all our citizens would be husbandmen." In an 1814 letter, he renewed his concern, "I fear nothing for our liberty from the assaults of force; but I have seen and felt much, and fear more from English books, English prejudices, English manners, and the apes, the dupes, and designs among our professional crafts. When I look around me for security against these seductions, I find it in the wide spread of our agricultural citizens, in their unsophisticated minds, their independence and their power, if called on, to crush the Humists of our cities, and to maintain the principles which severed us from England." S. K. Padover, ed., *Thomas Jefferson on Democracy* (New York: New American Library, 1946), 69, 85.

17. The interpretation of social disparities resulting from industrialization has drawn some of the most perceptive observers from both sides of the Atlantic. The persistently curious should begin here: T. Arnold, *The Folklore of Capitalism* (New Haven, Conn.: Yale Univ. Pr., 1937). E. D. Baltzell, *The Protestant Establishment: Aristocracy and Caste in America* (New York: Vintage Books, 1964). T. B. Bottomore, *Elites and Society* (Harmondsworth, England: Penguin Books, 1964). G. W. Domhoff, *Who Rules America?* (Englewood Cliffs, N.J.: Prentice-Hall, 1967). G. W. Domhoff, *The Higher Circles: The Governing Class in America* (New York: Vintage, 1970). G. W. Domhoff, *The Powers That Be: Processes of Ruling-Class Domination in America* (New York: Vintage, 1978). G. W. Domhoff and H. B. Ballard, eds., *C. Wright Mills and the Power Elite* (Boston: Beacon, 1968). B. Ehrenreich, *Fear of Falling: The Inner Life of the Middle Class* (New York: Harper Perennial, 1990). P. Fussell, *Class* (New York: Ballantine, 1983). A. Giddens, *The Class Structure of Advanced Societies* (New York: Hutchinson, Anchor Press, 1973). D. Gilbert and J. A. Kahl, *The American Class Structure* (Homewood, Ill.: Dorsey Pr., 1982). C. W. Mills, *White Collar* (Oxford, England: Oxford Univ. Pr., 1951). C. W. Mills, *The Power Elite* (Oxford, England: Oxford Univ. Pr., 1956). K. S. Newman, *Falling from Grace: The Experience of Downward Mobility in the American Middle Class* (New York: Vintage, 1989). F. F. Piven and R. A. Cloward, *Regulating the Poor: The Functions of Public Welfare* (New York; Vintage, 1971).

R. Sennett and J. Cobb, *The Hidden Injuries of Class* (New York: Vintage Books, 1972). T. Veblen, *The Theory of the Leisure Class: An Economic Study of Institutions* (New York: The Modern Library, 1918). T. Veblen, *The Theory of Business Enterprise* (New York: New American Library, 1958).

18. Perhaps, with such emerging diversity, it should not surprise anyone that the notion of America as a melting pot took hold in the early decades of the twentieth century. In 1908, Israel Zangwill, an English playwright, scored immense success with his play *The Melting Pot*. The play exults in America's fusion of races, "America is God's Crucible, the great Melting-Pot where all the races of Europe are melting and re-forming!" (Act 1). Even so, in light of later Nazi rhetoric, the play also sounds a darker note, "No . . . the real American has not yet arrived. He is only in the Crucible, I tell you—he will be the fusion of all races, perhaps the coming superman." (Act 1). A powerful idea, it became the explanation for the immigrant experience among a generation of social observers.

19. Republican challengers sought to discredit the E-Rate by tarring it with negative associations to the Clinton administration. Telephone companies identified it as a line item on consumer bills, hoping to foment public opposition. Because of Vice President Gore's reputation as a proponent of access, opponents dubbed it the "Gore Tax."

20. Link-Up America is a federal/state program that reduces initial connection charges, while Lifeline reduces monthly charges. At present, Link-up America and Lifeline discounts for low-income residents apply only to home phone service, not to new telecommunications services such as the Internet, though policy proposals to expand these services are in circulation. See M. Blizinski and J. R. Schement, "Rethinking Universal Service: What's on the Menu" (paper presented at the 1997 ICA Conference, Montreal, Canada, May 25, 1997). B. A. Cherry, S. S. Wildman, and A. S. I. Hammond, *Making Universal Service Policy: Enhancing the Process through Multidisciplinary Evaluation* (Mahwah, N.J.: Lawrence Erlbaum Associates), 69–83.

21. S.652, Title I, Sec. 254. (A)(6) Access to Advanced Telecommunications Services for Schools, Health Care, and Libraries—Elementary and secondary schools and classrooms, health care providers, and libraries should have access to advanced telecommunications services as described in subsection (h).

22. I chose this phrase thinking it embedded in the vocabulary of the eighteenth century. While I suspect it familiar to eighteenth-century gentlemen, the origins of this phrase extend all the way back to classical Latin, "Dorion, ridiculing the description of a tempest in the 'Nautilus' of Timotheus, said that he had seen a more formidable storm in a boiling saucepan." Athenaeus (fl. c. 200), The Deipnosophists, viii. 19.

23. "Sine qua non." From the Latin, literally, "without which nothing." More colloquially an essential element or condition. Still, I know of no phrase in English that conveys this sentiment with such finality.

Poverty, Democracy, and Public Libraries

Kathleen de la Peña McCook

A central feature of public librarianship in the United States is that librarians have worked to develop a climate of openness by defining library policies to create an institution where all are welcome. In 1990 the American Library Association (ALA) adopted the policy, "Library Services for the Poor," in which it is stated, "it is crucial that libraries recognize their role in enabling poor people to participate fully in a democratic society, by utilizing a wide variety of available resources and strategies."[1] This policy was adopted because there had been a shifting level of emphasis in the interpretation of openness since the establishment of the public library. Open doors are very different from proactive service. In this chapter the socio-economic context of poverty is explored to gain an understanding of the role librarians can play today to provide opportunity for poor people to participate in democracy. A brief review of key writing and documents that define public library service is provided to establish the historical foundation.

The administration and policy setting of public agencies supported by taxes are not well understood by most residents.[2] Roads, schools, sanitation, police and fire protection, social services, and libraries are used when needed and relatively few residents attempt to influence or change their performance except at times of perceived crisis. For the most part these public services are supported by taxes, administered by local jurisdictions, and overseen by elected or appointed technical experts.

Changing the mode of operation of any public service by external means generally only takes place by legislation or administrative action (desegregation rulings, welfare-to-work regulations, zoning changes) or when an influx of new monies is available (community policing, funds for new construction). Although such actions are the result of the political process, they are not often the result of action initiated at the local level. Efforts by residents to affect public services they receive locally are almost always in reaction to specific situations rather than contributory to changes of broader policy. For instance, a road through a neighborhood to enhance access to a big box store might bring residents to a zoning meeting only to learn that the zoning had been authorized years before. While local boards and advisory entities provide some representation that drives the shape of public service, there is evidence that the actions and advice of these groups are no more representative of "all the people" than any other form of representative government.[3] This is not to say that there is not strong sentiment by public agencies for greater civic participation, but there is a need to foster inclusiveness with more commitment, as Gates and O'Connor point out: "Working our collaborative and citizen-based efforts into the formal, local political structure will not only create policy that reflects the values of citizens but will also hasten reform of local government from that of a purely representative form to a highly participatory and dynamic decision-making structure."[4]

Agencies that operate in the public service sector must conduct self-analysis to make improvements that respond to community needs. Librarianship exemplifies a public service that carries out a sustained effort to improve services through a complex set of internal actions, association developmental activities, and participation by working members. While trustees and library board members do provide resident involvement, libraries have not been able to bring to their planning and policy deliberations a truly representative community voice.

The way in which librarians have broadened and strengthened their commitment to serving all people, by working with all people—especially poor people—to enhance participation in the democratic process is very complex. A general understanding of the origins of the public library movement and the work of librarians over the last 150 years to develop mechanisms to respond to their communities is necessary.

Origins and Development of Public Library Service Framed as Contributory to Democracy

> The modern public library in large measure represents the need of democracy for an enlightened electorate, and its history records its adaptation to changing social requirements.
>
> —*Jesse H. Shera*[5]

It was more than a century from the beginning of the establishment of a tax-supported public library in the United States to the first major histories of public library development. In the years following World War II, several major publications and actions established broad examination of the public library movement, with a special focus on the democratic philosophies that framed it. Any serious considerations of democracy and libraries must be informed with knowledge of their contents.

In *Foundations of the Public Library*, Jesse H. Shera provided well-documented analysis of the factors leading to the public library as we know it today.[6] Complex as these factors may be and somewhat open to interpretation, it is Shera's identification of the democratizing function of the public library from its very founding that is important for this discussion.[7] Shera identified four factors linking the movement for universal schooling and the movement for tax-supported public libraries:

- a growing awareness of the ordinary man and his importance to the group,
- a conviction that universal literacy is essential to an enlightened people,
- a belief in the practical value of technical studies, and
- an enthusiasm for education for its own sake.[8]

Understanding these factors has remained central to the conceptualization of public library service by the profession's leaders as it has been transmitted and reconfigured for each changing era. Exploring the contributions that the United States public library makes to support democracy is not new. The monograph *Arsenals of a Democratic Culture* by Sidney Ditzion analyzed the public library's role in supporting democracy. Ditzion noted that in the latter decades of the nineteenth century libraries continued "the educational process where the schools left off and by conducting a people's university, a wholesome capable citizenry would be fully schooled in the conduct of a democratic life."[9]

The histories by Shera and Ditzion coincided with ALA initiatives to identify the future of the public library in a time of great change. *A National Plan for Public Library Service* established two main objectives for public libraries: to promote enlightened citizenship and to enrich personal life.[10] The *National Plan* was the final part of the work of ALA's Committee on Post-War Planning and formed part of the basis for the Public Library Inquiry.

In *Librarianship and Legitimacy*, his analysis of the Public Library Inquiry (carried out and published between 1947 and 1952), Douglas Raber characterized the inquiry as a professional legitimating project and noted that the discourse of the inquiry "constituted an exercise in identity creation that relied heavily on the role of the public library as a sustaining contributor to American democracy."[11] The results of the inquiry yielded some recommendations, which if followed, would play down the role of the public library among the general public in favor of opinion leaders in the community.[12] This point was made by Robert D. Leigh, who, as director of the inquiry, wrote the general report that is the most frequently consulted overview. Leigh characterized opinion leaders as those for whom the public library was most important.[13]

These four events—the histories by Shera and Ditzion, the reports of the Committee on Post-War Planning, and the set of volumes issued by the Public Library Inquiry—provided the framework in which United States librarians worked at mid-century.[14] To gain a historical framework of the concepts linking democracy to libraries, readers are directed to these books and primary source documents as well as *Librarianship and Legitimacy*. Suffice it to say that in the general perception—both of the public and the profession in general, as the nation moved into the second half of the century—the identification of libraries with the support and promotion of democracy was strong.

Democracy for All through Libraries: Standards, Principles, Role Setting, and Transformation

> Public libraries continue to be of enduring importance to the maintenance of our free democratic society. There is no comparable institution in American life.
>
> —*Public Library Principles Task Force*[15]

As Leigh pointed out in *The Public Library in the United States*, there was political efficacy in attending to the needs of opinion leaders, for from them would come support—especially as the nation's libraries sought broader funding through federal legislation during the fifties. In a study conducted by the System Development Corporation (SDC) for the U.S. Office of Education, *The Public Library and Federal Policy*, the authors noted, "The public library community must determine whether public libraries should be principally concerned with serving the information and library needs of the sophisticated information user or whether they should try to serve the needs of all segments of the population."[16] Leigh and the SDC study bracket the third quarter of the twentieth century in terms of library direction. Between the post-World War II histories and studies and the SDC study, United States librarians could look back on the years since World War II and recognize that the profession had endeavored to expand its service base without coming to consensus on who should receive priority for service.

The Library Services Act passed in 1956 aided libraries in small towns and rural areas. Its successor, the Library Services and Construction Act passed in 1964, provided the means for bricks and mortar as well as interlibrary cooperation. Libraries also applied for and were awarded support under programs of the War on Poverty. Participation in these programs was a factor that changed the way the profession looked at its articulation of service.

While some have looked back at the demonstration projects of the War on Poverty period and decided that librarians tried to do too much, these projects nevertheless helped to foster a grassroots movement within the American Library Association that fought to expand the meaning of outreach. In 1968 the American Library Association Council voted to establish a Coordinating Committee on Service to the Disadvantaged, which became the Office for Library Service to the Disadvantaged in 1970 (and today is the Office for Literacy and Outreach Services). This is the ALA home for the Subcommittee on Library Services to Poor and Homeless People. The ALA Social Responsibilities Round Table (SRRT) held its first formal meeting in 1969. Today SRRT includes a Task Force on Hunger, Homelessness, and Poverty.

A number of publications during and after the War on Poverty shaped ideals of the library as an agent for change and contributed to the dialogue about expanded activist service during this time. Among these were the 1967 ALA survey, *Library Services to the Disadvantaged*, Margaret E. Monroe's "Readers' Services to the Disadvantaged in Inner Cities," Kathleen Weibel's *Evolution of Library Outreach 1960–1975*, Helen Lyman's *Literacy and the Nation's Libraries*, and Clara S. Jones' *Public Library Information and Referral Service*.[17] The perspective of serving poor people was passionately described and well-defined by librarians during this period.

In 1956 and 1966, over this same period (1950–1975), ALA issued two standards documents.[18] The 1966 standards came out amidst the War on Poverty and were seen as inadequate to the times. Many librarians felt that national standards could no longer reflect local community needs. In fact, the 1966 *Minimum Standards for Public Library Systems* would be the last effort at national public library standards issued by the association.[19]

The complex process of the Public Library Association (PLA) moving from the 1966 standards to a planning process in the seventies is viewed by Verna L. Pungitore as a major innovation. In her study of the adoption of the public library planning process, Pungitore examined how the set of techniques developed and promoted by PLA allowed public librarians to engage in user-oriented planning, community-specific role setting, and self-evaluation.[20] This transformation of planning for public library service replaced nationally developed standards with locally derived goals. Attempts to track a particular value or focus—such as the role of democracy—are naturally more complex as the devolution of mission to the local level makes it inappropriate to identify generalizations about all public libraries. McCook, reviewing the history of the activation of the library's clientele through the filter of standards observed that the planning process is "an iconoclastic challenge to the previous statements that tried to define the role and purpose of the public library . . . libraries are to develop services which their community needs. There are no prescriptions offered."[21]

Once PLA developed the planning process, each public library had a methodology to use at the local level to develop its own mission, goals, and objectives in collaboration with community and staff. The 1980 manual, *Planning Process for Public Libraries,* and the 1982 *Output Measures for Public Libraries* provided the tools for planning and measurement.[22] The role of the public library in serving democracy was no longer a value imbedded in a formal public library standards document, for no such document existed at the national level.

There were two documents issued by PLA during the launching of the planning process that need examination in light of this discussion: *The Public Library Mission Statement and Its Imperatives for Service* (1979), a product of the PLA Goals, Guidelines, and Standards Committee intended as a bridge between standards and the planning process, and "The Public Library: Democracy's Resource, A Statement of Principles," put together by the Public Library Principles Task Force in 1982.[23]

The *Mission Statement* was not well received. In fact, as Pungitore points out, some of the members of the committee disavowed it after it was approved.[24] However, the *Statement's* idealism reflected public librarians' desire to have an over-arching mission statement while recognizing the need to establish a new methodology for local planning. This *Statement* is an important reflection of the profession's thoughtful reaction to the ideas of *The Other America.*[25] The classic thesis (old standards), antithesis (1979 *Mission Statement*), synthesis (1982 "Statement of Purpose"/new planning process) formulation works here.

The 1982 "Statement of Purpose," "The Public Library: Democracy's Resource," was issued amidst the adoption of the new PLA planning process. It incorporated support for the planning model in its declaration. This one-page document (issued suitable for framing) identified the public library as offering access freely to all members of the community "without regard to race, citizenship, age, education level, economic status, or any other qualification or condition."[26] It is a document of synthesis for it provides a strong sense of mission yet incorporates the new process of local role identification.

By the late eighties the publications and initiatives that comprised the public library planning process were characterized as the Public Library

Development Program (PLDP). The publications issued under this designation included the *Public Library Data Service Statistical Report* and its ongoing annual successor, the *Statistical Report,* a second edition of *Output Measures for Public Libraries* (1987), *Planning and Role Setting for Public Libraries* (1987), a manual for trainers (1988), *Output Measures for Public Library Service to Children* (1992), and *Output Measures and More: Planning and Evaluating Public Library Services for Young Adults* (1995).[27]

In 1994 the PLA Committee on Planning and Evaluation commissioned a study to evaluate the effectiveness and redefine the direction of PLDP as public libraries entered the twenty-first century. The study, "An Evaluation of the Public Library Development Program" completed in 1995 recommended a revised PDLP.[28] PLA then appointed a ReVision Committee in 1996 to oversee the process in collaboration with consultants. In 1998, *Planning for Results: A Public Library Transformation Process* was published as the new PLA planning document moving from library roles to library responses. Among the changes was a new planning component highlighting the importance of community and visioning statements.[29] However, as pointed out in her analysis of the role of libraries in building communities, McCook identifies this point of connection as most crucial for public library inclusion in national community initiatives but not treated with sufficient attention.[30]

What can be seen by this summary of the move by public librarians from national standards to a planning and transformation process is an internal philosophical struggle to create a process that would reflect local community needs. This was carried out at the same time the nation, states, and local jurisdictions were struggling to find ways to enable local communities to build capacity.

The Search for Broad Mission

> Since their inception, libraries have served as pivotal community institutions upholding, strengthening, and realizing some of the most fundamental democratic ideals of our society.
>
> —*Nancy Kranich*[31]

When PLA began to move to a planning process and PLDP in place of national standards, the effort to establish a national mission for public libraries was no longer part of the PLA agenda although, as noted above, the 1979 *Mission Statement* and 1982 "Democracy's Resource" statement were surely such efforts.

Ongoing debate on the mission of the public library included Hafner's 1994 reaffirmation of the library's democratic purpose and critique of the move to popularization.[32] While PLA pulled back from a broad mission definition regarding democracy for all libraries after 1982, ALA and the National Commission on Libraries and Information Science (NCLIS) continued to provide general statements of direction. This is not a place for a sidebar on the role of ALA or other entities versus ALA's type of library divisions to speak for all libraries, but in the absence of a broad mission by PLA, such actions were inevitable.

In 1995 ALA's journal, *American Libraries,* listed "12 Ways Libraries Are Good for the Country," and included in the prefatory material the statement, "Libraries safeguard our freedom and keep democracy healthy." With a photograph of the Statue of Liberty in the background the first of the twelve ways listed was "to inform citizens," because democracy and libraries have a symbiotic relationship.[33]

The 1999 ALA Council adopted the statement "Libraries: An American Value," included it as an official public policy statement (Policy 53.8), and printed it on the cover of the association's 1999–2000 *Handbook.* This statement noted, "we preserve our democratic society by making available the widest possible range of viewpoints, opinions and ideas."[34] That same year the ALA sponsored a Congress on Professional Education that resulted in an effort to develop "A Statement on Core Values," and NCLIS passed a resolution adopting the *Principles for Public Library Service* based on the *UNESCO Public Library Manifesto.*[35] These *Principles* include the key mission that the public library will be a "gateway to knowledge," and that "Freedom, Prosperity and the Development of Society and of individuals are fundamental human values. This will be attained through the ability of well-informed citizens to exercise their democratic rights and to play an active role in society."[36]

This summary of the last fifty years of public libraries' efforts in the United States to establish standards and move to planning at the start of a new century is a history of a sustained and consistent commitment to the ideals of democracy. The language and location of this commitment may vary from document to document, but the idea of democracy emerges again and again. The expansion of the idea of service in support of democracy became even broader during the War on Poverty to delineate the heretofore left behind. This caused consternation among some that libraries were trying to do too many things. Yet others held fast to a comprehensive commitment to work with all people. This summary is intended only to provide a foundation for asserting that public librarians have remained constant in their hearts. Though much labor has gone into procedures and techniques, the essence remains a firm commitment to democratic values.

This essence is a temptation to metaphorical rhapsodizing that might seem too simple in its purity. But it cannot be helped. For librarians democracy is our arsenal, our cornerstone, our beacon, our strongest value. And a commitment to democracy leads us without a doubt to be committed to serving poor people.

Local Communities Include Poor and Working Class People

Although we profess that we are citizens of a democracy, and although we may vote once every four years, millions of our people feel deep down in their heart of hearts that there is no place for them—that they do not "count." They have no voice of their own, no organization (which is really their own instead of absentee) to represent them, no way in which they may lay their hand and their heart to the shaping of their own destinies.

—*Saul Alinsky*[37]

When we say "for the poor," we do not take sides with one social class . . . what we do is invite all social classes, rich and poor without distinction, saying to everyone: Let us take seriously the cause of the poor as though it were our own.

—*Oscar Romero*[38]

PLA has developed powerful new tools that can assist public libraries in developing service configured to the needs of the local community. ALA, at its policy levels, has reaffirmed democracy as a central library value. Citizen input and the librarian's connection to the community are crucial. This is where there lies a potential for misstep. The *total* community is not easily involved—not for community visioning, not for library visioning. Yet ALA's policy on services to the poor, specifically objective 10, says that librarians have decided collectively that we will work to make this so. The policy states, "promoting direct representation of poor people and anti-poverty advocates through appointments to local boards . . . such appointments to include library-paid transportation and stipends."

The PLA standards and planning efforts are impressive for their sustained commitment by so many, which is apparent and sincere. The best legacy these documents and processes provide is great freedom to work with communities and forge a vision. But there are many levels and layers of communities within any given community. There are homeowners, business people, professionals, and the working poor. The communities with which the librarians find themselves most often working or the communities that choose to work with the librarian are most likely not the communities that include poor people. This is not an act of commission, but an act of omission. It is hard to get poor people to the many meetings at which vision statements are formed—not just for the library, but also for the community as a whole. Poor people are simply working too hard to be able to exercise their chances to participate in the democratic process in a way that is sustained enough for their voices to be heard.

Poverty in the United States is defined by a changing income level calculated since 1969, which is adjusted each year for inflation using the consumer price indexes.[39] In 2000 the poverty threshold was calculated at $8,350 for a single person and $17,050 for a family of four. Yet this threshold is extremely inadequate for a modest standard of living. It is deceptive. It ignores the costs of childcare, differences in health insurance, and changes under the Personal Responsibility and Work Opportunity Reconciliation Act of 1996.[40]

In the 2000 report *Does a Rising Tide Lift All Boats?* labor economist Linda Barrington has constructed a series of poverty statistics that provide four major findings:

1. Poverty has risen in both the number and share of those employed full-time and year round since 1973. Gains of the 1960s ceased in the mid-1970s.
2. Long-term economic growth has had little impact on poverty among full-time workers.
3. There are great differences in the poverty experience of full-time workers living in different regions of the country and belonging to different racial/ethnic groups.
4. Ethnic minorities working full-time move in and out of poverty more often than whites.[41]

The October 2000 analysis of census data by the Center on Budget and Policy Priorities reports that 11.9 percent of all U.S. citizens still live in poverty, and the child poverty rate is 16.9 percent. This means that 32.3 million people still live below the official poverty threshold of $17,050 for a family of four. In fact, those who have remained poor have grown poorer. The poverty gap—the total amount by which the income of all poor households falls below the poverty line—has increased as the truly poor have experienced reductions in means-tested benefits that offset increases in earnings. The minimum wage still remains substantially below the levels of the 1970s in purchasing power.[42] Children are more likely than any other age group to live in poverty, with 8 percent of all American children living with incomes 50 percent below the poverty line. Additionally, it should be noted that many children (40 percent) are "near" poor and just above the poverty line.[43]

In *The State of Working America 2000–2001* it is made clear that the typical American family is working more hours and taking on higher levels of household debt, and that increases in income are based on more hours worked. Middle and lower income workers have increased time at work by 19 weeks since 1969. There is simply less free time for middle and working class families.[44] This aspect of degraded family time is also explored by Theda Skocpol in *The Missing Middle: Working Families and the Future of American Social Policy.*[45]

Without time to participate in community discussions, poor and working class people seldom have their particular needs heard in community forums. Without the tools of discourse, even if they make efforts to be heard, they still are not. Librarians striving to develop comprehensive community involvement in planning must realize that to include poor and working class people there must be special effort. The involvement of the poor and working class in community development and the democratic process is critical if their needs are to be factored into decision-making. What can librarians do?

Librarians, Democracy, and the Implementation of the Poor People's Policy

> The happiness of others is a goal worth pursuing, and the method
> for achieving it, democracy, is a risk worth taking.
>
> *—Earl Shorris*[46]

Participation in the democratic process requires a perception that one is a member of the community and that one can have an effect on the community. The May 2000 issue of *American Libraries* focused on isolating aspects of poverty, including homelessness, imprisonment, rural lack of connectivity, and lack of access to the ideas of the humanities.[47] Providing a way to learn the ideas of the humanities as the way for poor people to break free of poverty is one of the points that Earl Shorris makes in his book *Riches for the Poor,* in which he lays out the argument that in the United States the poor have been excluded from the circle of power.[48] One way to ameliorate this is to provide an entrance to reflection and the political life through the humanities.[49] Shorris' case for the humanities as a "radical antidote to long-term poverty rests finally on the question of who is born human and to what extent a person is capable of enjoying his or her humanity."[50] Shorris makes the point, like Jonathan Kozol in his book *Ordinary Resurrections,* that poor people in our society are seen as people who work to survive but are not given the opportunity for reflection.[51]

What better service can librarians provide to poor people than to develop support for them at the beginning of a journey to full participation in democracy? The first step in this journey is, of course, literacy. ALA has a long history of supporting literacy initiatives, as do state library agencies and libraries at the local level.[52] This support continues with renewed emphasis today. "Literacy in Libraries Across America" is a current three-year national initiative in partnership with the Lila Wallace-Reader's Digest Fund designed to strengthen library-based adult literacy programs. Its purpose is to support selected public libraries in their efforts to provide educational services to adult learners. Public libraries in four states are receiving a total of $2.7 million to improve the curriculum and instruction available to adult students. In addition, the libraries are expanding their use of computer technology and developing better methods to measure and document the gains made by learners. The fund has made a related grant of $1.3 million to ALA to coordinate technical assistance to participating libraries, organize a series of conferences for participants, develop a telecommunications network, create a Web site for library literacy, and implement other strategies to strengthen the field of library-based literacy programs.[53]

Individuals make their own journeys toward participation in democracy. The structure librarians can provide for adult literacy is a basic way to help poor people. Another way is to activate opportunities for new readers to gain access to the ideas of the humanities by supporting reading and discussion programs such as National Connections or Prime Time Literacy, reading and discussion programs for new readers funded by the National Endowment for the Humanities.[54]

With the integration of electronic technology in all aspects of United States life and work, librarians have made a concerted effort to provide equitable access to digital resources. This effort has had a national focus in the successful work to move from LSCA to the Library Services and Technology Act (LSTA) achieved in 1996. Administered through the Institute of Museum and Library Services, LSTA continues to make money available to local libraries through state agencies. Its priorities include electronic networking and targeting the unserved.[55] There are specific provisions for developing services to help people whose incomes are below the poverty threshold. Additional technology support for libraries serving communities with residents in poverty has come from the Gates Library Foundation, which has partnered with libraries to provide access to the Internet.

Another strong emphasis for librarians is to help create an information literate society as exemplified by Nancy Kranich's Committee on Information Literacy Community Partnerships, which is intended to bring together librarians and community members and organizations. Through this initiative librarians will "help the public learn how to identify and evaluate information that is essential to making decisions that affect the way they live, work, learn and govern . . . . These are the critical-thinking skills so essential to lifelong learning, so necessary for effective participation in our democracy."[56] One pertinent example of the kind of information literacy analysis that examines the use of technology for social activism demonstrates the need for information literacy to teach both paper-based and digital sources to support democratic citizen action.[57]

Literacy, reflection on the ideas of the humanities, and the ability to find and evaluate information in an information society are among the needs of poor people. The involvement of librarians in these initiatives to work with poor people has come about because librarians have a history of collective action. The fifteen policy objectives of ALA's poor people's policy, as librarians work to achieve them, may all be seen as contributing to building a greater capacity for poor people to participate in the democratic process. But we still have much work to do.

Democracy: The Only Way out of Poverty

> To be prevented from participation in the political life of the community cannot but be a major deprivation.
>
> —*Amartya Sen*[58]

In his January 2000 presentation for the Wingspread Conference on "The New Information Commons," Harry C. Boyte characterized civic professionalism as a public craft that does not deny the importance of scientific knowledge, disciplined effort, or assiduously learned skills, but rather integrates such things into far more contextualized and interactive practice—work "with" people rather than simply "for" them. Professions practiced as public crafts add public judgment or wisdom to knowledge. Boyte goes on to state that forms of civic work influenced many professional traditions through most of the twentieth century, including librarians, who saw themselves as citizens first.[59] Ronald B. McCabe explores these ideas in his book, *Civic Librarianship: Renewing the Social Mission of the Public Library,* which reaffirms the traditional public library mission of providing education for a democratic society.[60]

The social mission of the public library can only be activated through librarian participation in the life of the various communities served. For this reason, some librarians participated in Dialogue on Poverty 2000: Leading America to Community Action, the democracy project of the national network of community action agencies. The project goal was to re-engage Americans, especially poor people, with each other and the process of developing public policy to address the dilemma of poverty in the midst of plenty.[61] The heart of working with the community to build capacity for participating in democracy and making changes for a better quality of life is to be there as its residents identify the direction they want to take.[62]

The responsibility of librarians extends beyond the local community to considerations of what they can do to ameliorate information inequity in a global context. These are the concerns of the International Federation of Library Associations' (IFLA) Social Responsibilities Discussion Group and are identified in a composite paper edited by Alfred Kagan, "The Growing Gap between the Information Rich and the Information Poor, Both within and between Countries."[63] As librarians deliberate their role in supporting democracy among all people in the United States and among all people in the world, they can support the idea of a "pragmatic solidarity," as optimistically described by Heena Patel in *Dying for Growth.*[64] During Jubilee 2000 librarians can work with international organizations to provide information about relief for highly indebted poor countries.[65] As they work with people, librarians will practice their profession as a public craft, recognizing with Amartya Sen, Nobel winner in economics, that democracy is the only way out of poverty.[66]

Notes

1. American Library Association, *ALA Handbook of Organization 1999–2000* (Chicago: ALA, 1999), policy 61.
2. Because many poor people may be undocumented or working in the United States without legal status, the more inclusive term *residents* is used throughout this paper rather than *citizens,* except in quotations.
3. Jane Robbins, *Citizen Participation and Public Library Policy* (Metuchen, N.J.: Scarecrow Pr., 1975). This provides a thoughtful analysis of citizen participation that makes valid points of continuing value.

4. Christopher T. Gates and Drew O'Connor, "Toward a Healthy Democracy," *National Civic Review* 89 (summer 2000): 167.

5. Jesse H. Shera, *Foundations of the Public Library: The Origins of the Public Library Movement in New England 1629–1855,* reprint (Hamden, Conn.: Shoestring Pr., 1974), vi.

6. Ibid.

7. See for instance, Michael H. Harris, "State, Class and Cultural Reproduction: Toward a Theory of Library Service in the United States," in *Advances in Librarianship,* Wesley Simonton, ed. (New York: Academic Pr., 1986), 211–52.

8. Shera, *Foundations of the Public Library,* 221–22.

9. Sidney H. Ditzion, *Arsenals of a Democratic Culture: A Social History of the American Public Library Movement in New England and the Middle States from 1850–1900* (Chicago: ALA, 1947), 74.

10. Carlton B. Joeckel and Amy Winslow, *A National Plan for Public Library Service* (Chicago: ALA, 1948), 16.

11. Douglas Raber, *Librarianship and Legitimacy: The Ideology of the Public Library Inquiry* (Westport, Conn.: Greenwood Pr., 1997), 3.

12. Kathleen de la Peña McCook, "Stimulation," in *The Service Imperative for Libraries: Essays in Honor of Margaret E. Monroe,* Gail A. Schlachter, ed. (Littleton, Colo.: Libraries Unlimited, 1982), 127.

13. Robert D. Leigh, *The Public Library in the United States* (New York: Columbia Univ. Pr., 1950), 19.

14. The Public Library Inquiry consisted of seven volumes all published by Columbia University Press: Bernard Berelson, *The Library's Public* (1949); Alice I. Bryan, *The Public Librarian* (1952); Oliver Garceau, *The Public Library in the Political Process* (1949); Leigh, *The Public Library in the United States* (1950); James L. McCamy, *Government Publications for the Citizen* (1949); William Miller, *The Book Industry* (1949); and Gloria Waldren, *The Information Film* (1949). Supplementary reports were issued on library finance, public use of the library, effects of the mass media, music materials, and work measurement. For complete list see Raber, *Librarianship and Legitimacy,* 82.

15. Public Library Association, Public Library Principles Task Force, "The Public Library: Democracy's Resource, A Statement of Principles," *Public Libraries* 21 (1982): 92.

16. Jean B. Wellisch et al., *The Public Library and Federal Policy.* Sponsored by the System Development Corporation under a Grant from the United States Office of Education (Westport, Conn.: Greenwood Pr., 1974), 161.

17. American Library Association, Committee on Economic Opportunity Programs, *Library Service to the Disadvantaged: A Study Based on Responses to Questionnaires from Public Libraries Serving Populations over 15,000* (Chicago: ALA, 1969); Margaret E. Monroe, "Reader Services to the Disadvantaged in Inner Cities," in *Advances in Librarianship,* Melvin J. Voight, ed. (New York: Seminar Pr., 1971),

253–74; Kathleen Weibel, *The Evolution of Library Outreach, 1960–1975 and Its Effects on Reader Services: Some Considerations*, University of Illinois, Occasional Paper, No. 16 (Urbana, Ill.: Graduate School of Library and Information Science, 1982), ERIC ED 231376; Helen Huguenor Lyman, *Literacy and the Nation's Libraries* (Chicago: ALA, 1977); Clara S. Jones, *Public Library Information and Referral Service* (Syracuse, N.Y.: Gaylord Professional Publ., 1978).

18. American Library Association, Coordinating Committee on Revision of Public Library Standards, *Public Library Service: A Guide to Evaluation, with Minimum Standards* (Chicago: ALA, 1956); American Library Association, Public Library Association, Standards Committee, *Minimum Standards for Public Library Systems, 1966* (Chicago: ALA, 1967).

19. States, however, did continue to develop standards. It should be noted that actions of the Public Library Association and the American Library Association, which tend to be the narrative thread that is followed in this discussion, are by no means the entire story of the development of public library mission and direction. State library agencies, through their own long-range planning; state library associations; federal entities such as the Department of Education's Office of Library Programs, the National Commission on Libraries and Information Science, and today the Institute of Museums and Library Services; private foundations; multi-type library consortia; library systems; and local libraries and their boards are all participants in the constant process of deliberating on the directions of public library service.

20. Verna L. Pungitore, *Innovation and the Library: The Adoption of New Ideas in Public Libraries* (Westport, Conn.: Greenwood Pr., 1995), xi.

21. McCook, "Stimulation," 134.

22. Vernon E. Palmour, Martin C. Belassai, and Nancy V. DeWath, *A Planning Process for Public Libraries* (Chicago: ALA, 1980); Douglas L. Zweizig and Eleanor Jo Rodger, *Output Measures for Public Libraries: A Manual of Standardized Procedures* (Chicago: ALA, 1982).

23. Public Library Association, Goals, Guidelines and Standards Committee, *The Public Library Mission Statement and Its Imperatives for Service* (Chicago: ALA, 1979). Public Library Association, Public Library Principles Task Force, "The Public Library: Democracy's Resource."

24. Pungitore, *Innovation and the Library*, 94.

25. Michael Harrington, *The Other America: Poverty in the United States* (New York: Macmillan, 1962). While libraries do not figure in the works of Harrington, readers might be interested to note that, as a student at St. Louis University High School, Edward M. Harrington was a member of the Library Association. See Maurice Isserman, *The Other American: The Life of Michael Harrington* (New York: Public Affairs, 2000), photo following p. 178.

26. Public Library Association, Public Library Principles Task Force, "The Public Library: Democracy's Resource."

27. Public Library Association, Public Library Data Service, *Statistical Report* (annual, 1992–present) (Chicago: Public Library Association), continues *Public Library Data Service Statistical Report* (Chicago: Public Library Association, 1988–91); Nancy Van House et al., *Output Measures for Public Libraries: A Manual of Standardized Procedures* (Chicago: ALA, 1987); Charles R. McClure et al., *Planning and Role Setting for Public Libraries: A Manual of Options and Procedures* (Chicago: ALA, 1987); Peggy O'Donnell, *Public Library Development Program: Manual for Trainers* (Chicago: ALA, 1988); Virginia A. Walter, *Output Measures for Public Library Service to Children: A Manual of Standardized Procedures* (Chicago: Association for Library Service to Children, Public Library Association, American Library Association, 1992); and Virginia A. Walter, *Output Measures and More: Planning and Evaluating Public Library Services for Young Adults* (Chicago: Young Adult Library Services Association, Public Library Association, American Library Association, 1995). The committee, association, and consultant collaboration that resulted in the PLDP projects are explained with clarity by Pungitore in "PLDP: The Modified Innovation," 107–19.

28. Debra Wilcox Johnson, "An Evaluation of the Public Library Development Program," for the Public Library Association, 1995.

29. Ethel Himmel and William James Wilson with the ReVision Committee of the Public Library Association, *Planning for Results: A Public Library Transformation Process* (Chicago: ALA, 1998).

30. Kathleen de la Peña McCook, *A Place at the Table: Participating in Community Building* (Chicago: ALA, 2000), 29.

31. Nancy Kranich, "Libraries: The Cornerstone of Democracy," *American Libraries* 31 (Aug. 2000): 5.

32. Arthur W. Hafner and Jennifer Sterling-Folker, "Democratic Ideals and the American Public Library," in *Democracy and the Public Library: Essays on Fundamental Issues* (Westport, Conn.: Greenwood Pr., 1994), 9–43.

33. "12 Ways Libraries Are Good for the Country," *American Libraries* 26 (Dec. 1995): 1113–19. Also on the *American Libraries* Web site at www.ala.org/alonline/news/12ways.html.

34. American Library Association, *ALA Handbook of Organization 1999–2000* (Chicago: ALA, 1999), 45.

35. "Librarianship and Information Service: A Statement on Core Values." Accessed Oct. 24, 2000, www.ala.org/congress/corevalues/draft5.html. Though these values were not adopted, the dialogue is illustrative of current discourse on broad mission and principles.

36. "NCLIS Adopts Principles for Public Library Service," www.nclis.gov/news/pr99.html, accessed Oct. 24, 2000.

37. Saul Alinsky, "Statement of Purpose of the Industrial Areas Foundation," as quoted in Sanford D. Horwitt, *Let Them Call Me Rebel: Saul Alinsky, His Life and Legacy* (New York: Vintage, 1992), 105.

38. Oscar Romero, *The Violence of Love,* comp. and trans. by James R. Brockman, S. J. (Farmington, Penn.: Plough Publishing, 1998), 162.

39. Gordon M. Fisher, "The Development and History of the Poverty Thresholds," *Social Security Bulletin* 55 (winter 1992): 3–14.

40. "Revising the Poverty Measure," *Focus* 19 (spring 1998). This is the newsletter of the Institute for Research on Poverty, University of Wisconsin–Madison. This issue reports on the project "Implementing New Measures of American Poverty," funded by the Annie E. Casey Foundation.

41. Linda Barrington, *Does a Rising Tide Lift All Boats? America's Full-Time Working Poor Reap Limited Gains in the New Economy* (New York: Conference Board, 2000), 5.

42. Center on Budget and Policy Priorities, "Poverty Rate Hits Lowest Level since 1979 As Unemployment Reaches a 30-Year Low," news release, Oct. 10, 2000. Accessed Oct. 22, 2000, www.cbpp.org/9-26-00pov.htm.

43. National Center for Children in Poverty, "Young Child Poverty Fact Sheet," July 2000. Accessed Oct. 22, 2000, http://cpmcnet.columbia.edu/dept/nccp/ycpf.html.

44. Lawrence Mishel et al., *The State of Working America 2000–2001* (Ithaca, N.Y.: Cornell Univ. Pr., 2001).

45. Theda Skocpol, *The Missing Middle: Working Families and the Future of American Social Policy* (New York: W. W. Norton, 2000).

46. Earl Shorris, *Riches for the Poor: The Clemente Course in the Humanities* (New York: W. W. Norton, 2000), 256.

47. Kathleen de la Peña McCook, "Ending the Isolation of Poor People," *American Libraries* 31 (May 2000): 45.

48. Shorris, *Riches for the Poor,* 256.

49. Ibid., 100.

50. Ibid., 115.

51. Jonathan Kozol, *Ordinary Resurrections: Children in the Years of Hope* (New York: Crown Publ., 2000).

52. Gary O. Rolstad, "Literacy Services in Public Libraries," in *Adult Services: An Enduring Focus for Public Libraries,* K. M. Heim and Danny P. Wallace, eds. (Chicago: ALA, 1990), 245–65.

53. ALA, Office for Literacy and Outreach Services, "Literacy in Libraries across America." Accessed Oct. 24, 2000, www.ala.org/literacy.

54. McCook, *A Place at the Table,* 63 (For background on National Connections, visit Prime Time Reading Program, www.ala.org/publicprograms/primetim/guidelines.html).

55. Gwen Gregory, "From Construction to Technology: An Update on Federal Funding," *American Libraries* 30 (June/July 1999): 22–23. See also Institute of Museums and Library Services, www.imls.gov.

56. Nancy Kranich, "Building Partnerships for 21st Century Literacy," *American Libraries* 31 (Sept. 2000): 7.

57. Dorothy A. Warner and John Buschman, "The Internet and Social Activism: *Savage Inequalities* Revisited," *Progressive Librarian* 17 (summer 2000): 44–53.

58. Amartya Sen, "Democracy: The Only Way out of Poverty," *New Perspectives Quarterly* 17 (winter 2000): 29.

59. Conference on the New Information Commons. Center for Democracy and Citizenship. Accessed Oct. 24, 2000, www.publicwork.org/case/nic2000.htm.

60. Ronald B. McCabe, *Civic Librarianship: Renewing the Social Mission of the Public Library* (Metuchen, N.J.: Scarecrow Pr., 2001).

61. Dialogue on Poverty 2000: Leading America to Community Action, "National Data Report, Preliminary Findings." Accessed Oct. 24, 2000, www.nacaa.org/d2.htm.

62. Kathleen de la Peña McCook, "Librarians and Comprehensive Community Initiatives," *Reference and User Services Quarterly* 40 (fall 2000): 20–22.

63. Alfred Kagan, ed., "The Growing Gap between the Information Rich and the Information Poor, Both within Countries and between Countries," *IFLA Social Responsibilities Discussion Group in Alternative Library Literature, 1998/1999,* Sanford Berman and James P. Danky, eds. (Jefferson, N.C.: McFarland, 2000), 293–300. See also the IFLA Web site for revision of recommendations, www.ifla.org/VII/dg/srdg/index.html#1.

64. Heena Patel et al., "Pragmatic Solidarity," in *Dying for Growth: Global Inequality and the Health of the Poor* (Monroe, Maine: Common Courage Pr., 2000), 392.

65. Robert W. Edgar, "Jubilee 2000: Paying *Our* Debts," *Nation* 271 (Apr. 24, 2000): 20–21.

66. Sen, "Democracy," 29.

II. Libraries and Civil Society

Libraries and Civil Society

Joan C. Durrance
Karen Pettigrew
Michael Jourdan
Karen Scheuerer

Public libraries are unique providers of civic and government information in the community. No other organization or agency has responsibility to provide access to the broad spectrum of community information (CI). In recent years, building on the success of earlier decades in providing access to CI, librarians have made great strides in using the Internet to greatly increase access to the information that people need to function as citizens.[1]

This article identifies some of the "best practices" identified through two research projects funded by the Institute of Museum and Library Services (IMLS), both of which are featured on the following project Web site: www.si.umich.edu/helpseek. The first grant, "Help-Seeking in an Electronic World: The Impact of Electronic Access to Community Information on Citizens' Information Behavior and Public Libraries," was designed to gain a better understanding of how public libraries are poised to provide CI in the next decade and to develop the tools they will need to effectively evaluate their work. "Help-seeking," funded by IMLS in 1998, is a multi-stage research project that includes a two-stage national survey, active collection of best-practice data from a number of Web sites, and site visits to three communities with public-library-sponsored community networks. Librarians in our study have identified scores of ways that citizens, community organizations, and government agencies have benefited from library provision of CI. They sent us many examples, both of agencies that rely on library CI in the course of providing service and of parents, students, job seekers, and others who have benefited from library CI. The second study, "How Libraries and Librarians Help," based on extensive field research, instrument development, and testing, will result (by the end of 2002) in a suite of context-based evaluation tools that are easily implemented, capture richness, and show patterns that reflect how digital community services affect people's lives.

The best practice examples, drawn from this federally funded research, have been grouped into the five categories below to give readers an indication of a much larger body of research we have brought together in the project Web site.

The Community Information File: The Foundation of Library CI

A lasting legacy of public library information and referral services is the community information database. Our national survey of CI librarians showed that the CI file continues to play a prominent role in any community information service.[2] CI files, we were told, have undergone several iterations in the past twenty years, from paper to database to OPAC, in some cases. As software has improved, the current iterations of the many CI files are database-driven with Web accessibility. Below are two of many examples of CI files in our Best Practices site.

Community Resource Database (www.crdli.org). Funded and managed by a coalition of public agencies, private foundations, and businesses, the Community Resource Database (CRD) of Long Island features more than eight thousand listings for community resources and services. The Middle Country Public Library (MCPL) is the central manager for the database, which is available via public access terminals at libraries and on a subscription basis elsewhere. What makes CRD different from many other community information initiatives is the way in which it looks to the private sector as a source of ideas and funding. The staff at MCPL has turned to a variety of private firms—such as banks and local corporations—for financial sponsorship of CRD. This, in turn, has given the library credibility with the private sector while also addressing issues such as long-term sustainability and potential overlap with services provided by other agency databases. For more information about CRD, see our profile at www.si.umich.edu/helpseek/Profiles/CRD.html.

Community Connection (http://sfpl.lib.ca.us:8000/SOCSER). The San Francisco Public Library's Community Connection provides comprehensive searchable listings of social service agencies, government offices, neighborhood groups, and nonprofit organizations. The database is available online at all member libraries, via dial-in access, and by telephone. The library also offers the AIDS Foundation Database, a separate resource with information on HIV service providers. According to Julie Beach of the Children's Council of San Francisco, "the San Francisco Community Connection is an example of the smart use of the technology that's particularly valuable to nonprofit organizations."

Increasing Access to Relevant Local Content, Including Civic, Government, and Job Information

The library Web site is the most effective tool that librarians have at their disposal to increase access to civic and government information. Even though community information has been available within library walls for decades, most citizens have no idea that it is available. Web sites, on the other hand, bring information to people twenty-four hours a day, seven days a week, and can be accessed wherever people are—in their homes, at school or work, at a community technology center, or on a friend's computer. Library Web site hits far exceed the more traditional measures of in-house use and circulation. The messages from Web sites help people understand the library's role in the community and potentially provide a vehicle for civic discourse.

Well-designed library CI Web pages enable citizens to find out what boards and commissions will meet this week and where, what business the city council will address next Tuesday, what the local schools are planning to do about student test scores, and what millage increases will be requested in the upcoming school election. Citizens who aren't able to get to these meetings can send messages to decision makers. In addition, residents can find out about where and when to catch the bus or how to get a dog license or a building permit. In fact, they may even be able to transact the purchase online starting with the local library's Web site. Below are examples of how public libraries provide access to government and job information.

Government Information

West Bloomfield Public Library (www.wblib.org/commgov.html). The West Bloomfield Public Library offers an impressive Web site of well-organized government information. This extensive collection places an emphasis on community information pages and then extends to global resources. The site lists community organization contact information alongside content on transit routes, voter precincts, and school board representatives. The library's CI is not limited to local information, however. A thorough, annotated listing of federal and state agencies' Web links is also provided. In addition, the library features information from some of the better known international organizations.

Onondaga County Public Library (www.ocpl.lib.ny.us). Equally extensive in scope is the government information on New York State's Onondaga County Public Library Web site. In addition to state and federal government information, the library gives users access to Web-linked legal resources. Visitors can find out how their local congressperson voted in the last election by accessing United States voting records. The site also features links to sites on political campaigns and bills in the state legislature, as well as answers to frequently asked questions about New York State.

These and many other "best practice" sites by public libraries avoid burying local information deep within the Web site. Public libraries that put an emphasis on how to get and use local information epitomize the role that libraries can play in citizenship education and civic engagement. The message to citizens is clear: the library is the place to get vital information not only about what's going on in the community, but also about how to participate as a citizen.

Job Information

One of the most sought after types of CI is business and employment information. The citizens we interviewed for our IMLS project repeatedly told us that they regularly sought job information through library CI.

New Haven Free Library (www.nhfpl.lib.ct.us). Job information is featured prominently on the New Haven Free Library Web site. Local recreation, entertainment, education, health, and history pages are also highlighted. The site provides annotated links in these subject areas in addition to library-compiled data on topics ranging from crime to population, education to economics. Moreover, in keeping with public library commitment to information access, the New Haven Free Library provides a Spanish-language version of its Web site.

ChicagoJobs (www.chicagojobs.org). Maintained by a staff member at the Skokie Public Library, ChicagoJobs seems to be the definitive Chicago-area job and career guide. This site not only points to classified ads and Web pages that match employers to job seekers, but it also directs visitors to career counselors and provides links to training resources, résumé tips, and salary guides.

CascadeLink Jobs (www.cascadelink.org/jobs/index.html). CascadeLink offers extensive job listings, especially for government positions, as well as information on job training and employment agencies. When we conducted a survey of the users of Multnomah County Public Library's CascadeLink, we discovered that a large number of respondents rely on the site's extensive job resources. Users were effusive in their praise. For example, a recruiter for the city of Portland noted that she often refers people to CascadeLink for job information because "it cuts through all of the garbage often found on the Internet, and gets straight to the heart of the matter" with its thorough and easy-to-navigate links. Another respondent told us that she, her husband, and her son had all turned to CascadeLink for assistance in job searches because it is a time saver: "CascadeLink is really the best place to go because everything is right there. It saves a lot of time to go to this one stop rather than having to go to each employer individually."

Designing Services to Help
Immigrants and Cultural Minorities

Ever since the major waves of immigration in the late nineteenth century, libraries have served immigrants by offering safe havens and equal access to learning. In the last hundred years, libraries in major coastal cities have shown an ongoing commitment to immigrants. Through the decades librarians have developed incredible expertise in helping hundreds of thousands of new arrivals better understand life in North America. Today's immigrant lives not only close to a border, but all across the United States. This means that more American public libraries have the opportunity to provide essential lessons in citizenship to the foreign born in their communities.

Queens Borough Public Library, N.Y. (www.queenslibrary.org). "Nearly one in ten Americans is foreign born! The U.S. Census Bureau says that between 1990 and 1998, the growth in the foreign-born population was nearly four times that of the native population. What do these figures mean for community information providers?" asks Angela Napili in an article on the Community Connector Web site at www.si.umich.edu/Community.

This fine article is an excellent profile of the way one public library, Queens Borough Public Library (QBPL) in New York, has developed services designed to reach immigrants. New York City has long been a port of entry for immigrants from all over the world. Often, these new residents settle down in one of the outlying, more affordable boroughs. In Queens, for example, one in three residents is foreign born. QBPL has responded to the needs of its diverse constituency by designing reference and collection policies that cater to newcomers to the United States. The Queens Directory of Immigrant-Serving Agencies, www.queenslibrary.org/webcontact/contactsearch.htm, is a centerpiece of the library's Web site, and stands as a reflection of the library's deliberate efforts to serve their diverse clientele. Librarians compiled this massive searchable database of organizations offering services in more than fifty languages to immigrants. Organizations in the database provide everything from academic counseling to substance abuse counseling to information on transportation for the disabled. The directory is available in print as well, and it is a wonderful example of how, with some database knowledge and the right connections with the community, a library can manage to publish an entire reference work.

Austin (Tex.) Public Library (www.ci.austin.tx.us/library/default.htm). The Austin Public Library features its New Immigrants Project, www.ci.austin.tx.us/library/newip.htm, on the library's home page. However, this resource does not exist solely in cyberspace. In an effort to serve Austin's "new, primarily non-English speaking, immigrant population," three of Austin's library branches have incorporated New Immigrants Project Centers into their building space. Visitors to the centers can learn English, study for the U.S. citizenship exam, identify community resources, attend classes, and check out books and magazines in their mother tongues. Librarians also guide immigrants to legal resources, local cultural organizations, or immigration services. In addition, immigrants are given advice on navigating bureaucratic agencies so they can fill out tax forms and apply for driver's licenses and social security cards.

San Jose (Calif.) Public Library (www.sjpl.lib.ca.us/Outreach/cultures/multicult.htm). The San Jose Public Library has compiled pages on its Web site catering to many multicultural groups in the area, including people with disabilities, gays and lesbians, ethnic minorities, seniors, and at-risk youth. On the Immigration Resources page, visitors will find articles pertaining to immigration and naturalization regulations in both English and Spanish. Among the handy features on this site is a zip code identifier that people can use to locate the closest social security administration office or download an INS form. Also available on the site is a bibliography of books, periodicals, and videos pertaining to American immigrants and refugees.

Fostering Interaction with Community Information: Building Information Communities through Community Networking

Community networks have been around in one form or another since the mid-1980s. Public library involvement can be traced back in most cases to the early and mid-nineties. Public library Community Network (CN) initiatives focus primarily on community information but may also include opportunities for dialog.

Library CNs provide a variety of ways to help citizens better understand the community, foster civic participation, make it easier to volunteer, and engage in activities that result in information and resource sharing by community organizations.

The Community Connector (www.si.umich.edu/Community). The Community Connector, the University of Michigan's comprehensive Web resource for communities, has developed a definition often used to describe this phenomenon: "A community network is a locally based, locally driven communication and information system designed to enhance community and enrich lives" (www.si.umich.edu/Community/faq/What.html).

When libraries take action to foster interaction with community information, they help to assure increased citizen involvement in the local community. This is a step beyond that of informing citizens, which we have discussed in the sections above. One result of our IMLS research has been an analysis of various community network models. Below are brief descriptions of several library-sponsored community networks. Considerably more detail can be found on our project Web site, www.si.umich.edu/helpseek. Follow the links to profiles and best practices.

Tallahassee Freenet (www.tfn.net). The Tallahassee Freenet (TFN), Florida's first community network and one of the nation's first library-community network partnerships, was started in 1993 by faculty from Florida State University. Early on, the LeRoy Collins Leon County Public Library joined as an operating partner. Over time partners have changed, but the public library has continued to be a primary stakeholder. TFN has ties to county government, state government, universities, a newspaper, hospitals, and hundreds of community organizations. It seeks to serve as "a catalyst for the educational, social, and economic growth of Tallahassee, Leon County and Florida through online community networking." The network does this by involving community businesses and individuals as supporters, partners, and volunteers who serve in a variety of capacities, including acting as editors of content Web pages.

Darien (Conn.) Community Information Network (http://darien.lib.ct.us). The Darien Community Information Network is a notable example of the role that a library can play in the creation of a small town's information infrastructure. The library hosts the Web sites for town-related organizations, such as the town hall, schools, library, and nonprofit organizations. Louise Berry, director of the Darien Public Library, notes that "the library has received increased financial and political support as a result of taking the leadership role in technology for the town."

Three Rivers Free-Net (http://trfn.clpgh.org). The Carnegie Library of Pittsburgh (http://trfn.clpgh.org) has designed a unique approach to building community using the Internet through their community network, the Three Rivers Free-Net (TRFN). TRFN, a fixture of Pittsburgh since 1995, interacts with

Pittsburgh-area nonprofit organizations and local governments. TRFN's mission is to facilitate "the collection, organization and dissemination of Pittsburgh regional information in a public space." The TRFN Web site, built with a librarian's eye for organization, is divided into twenty carefully considered subject areas, ranging from Cultural Activities to Employment to Social Services. Organizations are often placed in several categories. TRFN uses electronic space to bring together organizations by using an easy to navigate directory and template design on the Web site. Its guidelines encourage community nonprofits to identify and link to organizations that do similar work, thus strengthening community ties. Not only does this make it easier for TRFN users to find what they are looking for, it also helps unify Pittsburgh's nonprofit community. In addition, agencies that have yet to build a presence on the Internet can look to TRFN's subject pages for inspiration. For more information, please refer to the online profile at www.si.umich.edu/helpseek/Profiles/TRFN_profile.html.

NorthStarNet (www.nsn.org). A partnership between the North Suburban Library System and the Suburban Library System, NorthStarNet (NSN) community network is designed to help bring Chicago's widely dispersed suburban communities together in virtual space. By linking together 124 communities, NSN makes life in Chicago's suburbs more cohesive. While the various member libraries all share in NSN's mission of using the Internet to build community, the specifics of how each goes about accomplishing this goal varies considerably. This level of autonomy is a hallmark of NSN. It pays off because this freedom means that each individual library has greater flexibility to reflect its community online. One result of library autonomy is that NSN comes across not as one large site but rather as a gateway to a collection of smaller community sites, referred to as Communities on the Web. Under the NSN umbrella, you'll find links to sites like LaGrange Community (www.lagrangeil.com), NorthStarNet Arlington Heights (http://ahkhome.northstarnet.org), Park Ridge Community Network (www.park-ridge.il.us), and SkokieNet (www.skokienet.org). All of these sites are housed on the NSN server and coordinated by library staff at member libraries, and yet each has its own domain name, its own look and feel, and, to a certain extent, its own policies and procedures. For more information, see the profile on the Helpseek Project Web site, www.si.umich.edu/helpseek/Profiles/NSN_profile.html.

Fostering Civic Engagement among Today's Youth

A number of observers have realized that young people have the potential for taking leadership in revitalizing American democracy. We have long known that values developed early have a way of following an individual through adulthood. By providing kids with opportunities to find out more about their communities and to become involved and make a difference in their communities, there is a chance that a new civic generation will emerge. Robert Putnam found that "much of the decline in civic engagement in America during the last third of the twentieth century is attributable to the replacement of an unusually civic generation by several generations (their children and grandchildren) that are less embedded in community life."[3] Wendy Lesko observes that youth constitute 26 percent of the population and have the potential for making enormous contributions to their communities.[4] Her project, Activism 2000, encourages teens to transform their ideas into pragmatic proposals and participate in the policy-making arena.[5]

Public librarians can play a valuable role in helping young children and teens better understand, become involved in, and make a contribution to their community. Programs that foster civic engagement among youth are making an investment in future citizen activism and possibly a revitalization of democracy. A number of initiatives focus on involving youth in gaining the skills they need to become involved in and influence change in their communities.

Youth ACCESS. Youth ACCESS is an after-school program developed by selected libraries in conjunction with Libraries for the Future (www.lff.org). The program has been adapted by libraries in New York City's Harlem; Newark, New Jersey; Oakland, California; and Detroit, Michigan. Youth ACCESS, like other emerging youth-empowerment programs in public libraries, is designed to enhance the educational, literacy, and employment skills opportunities of young people ages eight to eighteen. Librarians who run programs such as Youth ACCESS structure the experience to help kids learn to work together, learn about their community, engage in problems and issues of importance to them, and communicate with the larger world by means of Internet-based media.

Eastside Cybrary Connection of the Riverside (Calif.) Public Library (www.cybraryconnect.org).[6] The mission of this project is to ensure the opportunity for lifelong learning by providing free computer training, information literacy, and access to electronic information resources to an at-risk population—Riverside's Eastside youth (ages 10 to 14) and their families. Students gain skills in the following skill areas: computer training, information literacy, after-school homework assistance, and Internet access. The goal is to give the youth who go through the program lifelong learning skills to close the digital divide gap by gaining computer and Web-searching skills. This project is framed more broadly than civic engagement. However, these skills (as we see below in the Flint project) can be used for civic engagement.

Flint (Mich.) Public Library (www.flint.lib.mi.us/fpl.html). The Flint Public Library (FPL) has a solid history of developing services designed to strengthen its community. FPL's youth programs reach out to at-risk youth. Recent programs, some of which have been collaboratively developed with the University of Michigan School of Information, include features found in such programs as Youth ACCESS. In the early days of the Internet (1996), FPL staff worked with Flint teens to develop Weblinks, a program designed to help at-risk youth learn about organizations in Flint that are designed to assist youth by having these young people develop Web sites for the organizations. In the process, the teenagers gained skill in interviewing, learned about the services of the agencies, and—along the way—gained the technical skills they needed to create a Web site. Over the years, programs like this have been modified, but always with the aim of providing teens the technology skills they can use to make positive contributions to their community.

What We've Learned

There are a number of exciting models that show leadership and creativity by librarians in increasing access to community information, which will in turn strengthen civil society. Most of our findings are on the IMLS-funded project Web site at www.si.umich.edu/helpseek. They are displayed so that they can be approached from a number of perspectives. The project Web site provides a great deal of detail and many more examples. This article has only scratched the surface. We have chosen examples from five areas that contribute toward a more viable democracy.

Our data show that at present librarians are unable to determine the impact of their community information services. We are now in the process of developing the indicators of impact for these and other digital community information services from the perspective of the people who use them. The services we have described in this article suggest that librarians are making strong contributions toward giving citizens the tools they need to build a more viable democracy.

Notes

1. Joan C. Durrance and Karen E. Pettigrew, "Community Information: The Technological Touch," *Library Journal* 125, no. 2 (Feb. 1, 2000): 44–46.

2. Ibid.
3. Robert D. Putnam, *Bowling Alone: The Collapse and Revival of American Community* (New York: Simon & Schuster, 2000), 275.
4. Wendy Schaetzel Lesko and Emanuel Tsourounis II, *Youth! The 26% Solution* (Kensington, Md.: Activism 2000 Project, 1998).
5. Ibid.
6. Carolyn A. K. Denny, "Redefining Librarianship: The Case of the Eastside Cybrary Connection." *Public Libraries* (July/Aug. 2000): 208–13.

Additional References

Barber, Benjamin. *A Passion for Democracy*. Princeton, N.J.: Princeton Univ. Pr., 1998.

Children's Partnership. *Online Content for Low-Income and Underserved Americans: The Digital Divide's New Frontier*. Santa Monica, Calif.: The Children's Partnership, 2000.

Durrance, Joan C. *Armed for Action: Library Response to Citizen Information Needs*. New York: Neal-Schuman, 1984.

———. "Community Information Services: An Innovation at the Beginning of Its Second Decade." *Advances in Librarianship* 13 (1984): 100–28.

———. "Spanning the Local Government Information Gap." *RQ* 25 (fall 1985): 101–9.

Durrance, Joan C., and Karen E. Pettigrew. "Community Information: The Technological Touch." *Library Journal* 125, no. 2 (Feb. 1, 2000): 44–46.

Firestone, Charles M., and Jorge Reina Schement, eds. *Toward an Information Bill of Rights and Responsibilities*. Washington, D.C.: Aspen Institute, 1995.

Molz, Redmond Kathleen, and Phyllis Dain. *Civic Space/Cyberspace, The American Public Library in the Information Age*. Cambridge, Mass.: MIT Press, 1999.

Putnam, Robert D. *Bowling Alone: The Collapse and Revival of American Community*. New York: Simon & Schuster, 2000.

Civic
Librarianship

Ronald B. McCabe

Jesse Shera once made the following assessment of the usefulness of studying library history:

> If future generations can learn anything from an examination of library history, it is that the objectives of the public library are directly dependent upon the objectives of society itself. The true frame of reference for the library is to be found in its coeval culture. No librarian can see clearly the ends which he should seek when his country is confused about the direction in which it is moving. When people are certain of the goals toward which they strive, the function of the public library can be precisely defined.[1]

The bad news for public libraries has been that Americans have been confused and deeply divided since the social conflict of the 1960s, a time that E. J. Dionne Jr. has described as America's "cultural civil war."[2] The good news is that, after decades of cultural warfare and political gridlock, America is beginning to find its balance, thanks to a major cultural shift toward strengthening communities and other endangered social structures. This new community movement is an intellectual as well as a social phenomenon. It reaffirms traditional ideas concerning democracy and education while developing powerful new strategies for reforming contemporary social life. Civic librarianship is an effort to apply community movement ideas and strategies to the public library.

To understand the potential contribution of the community movement to public library development, it is necessary to understand the problems raised by the cultural civil war and the community movement's proposed solutions to

---

A version of this chapter appears in the author's book, *Civic Librarianship: Renewing the Social Mission of the Public Library* (Metuchen, N.J.: Scarecrow Pr., 2001).

these problems. It is also necessary to understand the specific impact of the cultural civil war on public libraries. After a discussion of these important background issues, civic librarianship will be described.

America's Cultural Civil War

America's cultural civil war can best be viewed as an explosive interplay between the three major strands of American culture identified by Robert Bellah and his co-authors in their influential 1985 book, *Habits of the Heart: Individualism and Commitment in American Life.* Bellah describes these strands as "biblical, republican, and modern individualist." He notes two types of modern individualism, "utilitarian individualism" and "expressive individualism."[3] The biblical strand is, of course, the moral perspective of America's dominant religions. The republican strand is the civic tradition of American democracy that grew out of the philosophical ideas of the eighteenth-century Enlightenment. Utilitarian individualism refers to the tradition of personal economic freedom that has been the driving force behind American capitalism. Expressive individualism, which refers to a tradition that advocates freedom from social constraints limiting personal expression, was popularized by American writers who were influenced by Romanticism in the nineteenth century and by the cultural successors of Romanticism in the twentieth century. The religious and civic traditions of social morality have been interacting with both types of individualism throughout our nation's history. The recent cultural warfare is one of the most explosive of these interactions.

America's cultural civil war was ignited by a tremendous surge in the popularity of expressive individualism that resulted from the emergence of the counterculture and its political wing, the New Left. The counterculture rebelled against a dominant culture that was perceived to be narrowly rational and biased against the subjective reality of the individual. This dominance was thought to be especially unfair to women, ethnic minorities, and the poor. At its best the counterculture was, like the work of Martin Luther King Jr., a search for a beloved community that would include and support all Americans. The counterculture clearly hastened long-needed reform in areas such as women's rights, minority rights, and environmental protection. It has become increasingly obvious, however, that the counterculture's contribution to our present culture has been marred not only by lifestyle excesses related to drug use and sexuality, but by erroneous assumptions borrowed from the expressive individualism of Romanticism.

The inability of Americans to understand the influence of Romanticism on the political Left and on the culture as a whole is an important reason why the cultural war is so difficult to resolve. Romanticism was a reaction to what Isaiah Berlin described as the "closed, perfect pattern of life" of the eighteenth-century Enlightenment.[4] Berlin explains that the Romantics believed in:

> will, the fact that there is no structure to things, that you can mould things as you will—they come into being only as a result of your moulding activity—and therefore opposed any view that tried to represent reality as having some kind of form that could be studied, written down, learned, communicated to others, and in other respects treated in a scientific manner.[5]

The Romantics did not believe in the ability of people to develop a commonly shared knowledge of the world and the human condition. This was not only a break with the Enlightenment, but with the entire tradition of Western thought. Both the moral perspective of biblical religion and the civic tradition of American democracy depend on a shared sense of social reality that can be communicated through education to form the basis for law and social order. The Romantics and their cultural successors advocated an extreme individualism that challenges social authority over the individual by denying the existence of a shared reality. They have fought society on behalf of the individual by promoting a moral relativism that denies social norms or, in some cases, by adopting a "counter morality" that supports values opposite to those of traditional morality.

The counterculture took this perspective, which for over one hundred fifty years had been at the fringe of the culture, to the center of the cultural stage. Ideas that were viewed by the proponents of the biblical and republican traditions to be dangerous but weak in influence were now popular enough to be a real threat to social order. Proponents of religious and civic morality were particularly concerned when they saw increasing crime rates, divorce rates, and other measures of social disorder as well as a sharp decline in civic participation.

Although the counterculture's utopian world of complete individual freedom did not materialize, the counterculture succeeded to a great extent in challenging social authorities and purposes as enemies of individual freedom. The result was a libertarian consensus based on an alliance of the expressive individualism of the Left and the utilitarian individualism of the Right. E. J. Dionne Jr. explains how the counterculture's New Left contributed to the extreme antigovernment sentiment of the Reagan years of the 1980s.

Far from being inconsistent with the antiauthoritarian thrust of the 1960s, much of what passed for conservative politics in the 1980s was really *libertarian*. Many young voters who had been drawn to the New Left and the counterculture because they attacked authority were drawn to conservatism because it attacked the state. Thus did the New Left wage war against the paternalistic liberal state and defeat it. The right picked up the pieces.[6]

Sociologist Francis Fukuyama describes the post-counterculture convergence of the interests of the Left and Right as mutual support of

> a very powerful cultural theme: that of the liberation of the individual from unnecessary and stifling social constraints. Both the Left and Right participated in this effort to free the individual from restrictive rules, but their points of emphasis tended to be different. To put it simply, the Left worried about lifestyles, and the Right worried about money. . . . As people soon discovered, there were serious problems with a culture of unbridled individualism, where the breaking of rules becomes, in a sense, the only remaining rule.[7]

This new coalition for individual freedom pushed both the traditional liberals on the Left (the republican tradition) and the social conservatives on the Right (the biblical tradition) to the margins of the culture. The strong challenges to social and governmental authorities and purposes raised by the New Left were successful. The marketplace and its service to individuals (utilitarian individualism) filled the resulting vacuum.

The Community Movement

The movement toward increased individualism and away from the biblical and republican traditions of social morality began to lose momentum in the 1990s. America is now moving toward social reintegration. In his book *The Great Disruption: Human Nature and the Reconstitution of Social Order*, Fukuyama notes that, "Evidence is growing that the Great Disruption has run its course and that the process of renorming has already begun. Rates of increase in crime, divorce, illegitimacy, and distrust have slowed substantially and even reversed in the 1990s."[8]

These trends in the larger culture are mirrored and refined by some of America's most accomplished intellectuals. In addition to Fukuyama, Amitai Etzioni, Robert Bellah, Robert Putnam, Benjamin Barber, Stephen Carter, E. J.

Dionne Jr., and a host of other writers have contributed to the ideas of the growing community movement. Topics have included the following:

- renewing a social morality that balances rights and responsibilities;
- discovering social and political common ground;
- replacing argument with civility and dialogue;
- collaborating to solve social problems;
- strengthening the institutions of civil society;
- stressing character development and civic education in public schools;
- integrating law enforcement into neighborhood life through community policing;
- restoring the democratic purpose of the press through civic journalism; and
- reexamining zoning laws and community planning to enhance civic life.

Community movement ideas and concerns dominated the social and political agenda of both Clinton-Gore administrations in the 1990s and began to influence the rhetoric of the Republican Party and George W. Bush in the 2000 election campaign.

Etzioni and other community movement writers who describe themselves as *communitarians* have articulated a forceful response to the libertarian consensus of the 1980s. Unlike the libertarian position, Etzioni's communitarianism does not attempt to be a consistent proponent or opponent of either the individual or society, but proposes that the relationship between the individual and society be brought into balance.[9] As social morality and individual liberty are both found to be necessary facets of American culture, neither the biblical and republican traditions nor utilitarian and expressive individualism are rejected. The result is a powerful synthesis of these cultural strands that acknowledges the importance of each strand while rejecting the excesses of those who advocate one or two of these cultural traditions at the expense of the others.

Communitarians seek a balance between individual liberty and social order, between rights and responsibilities.[10] Unlike the expressive individualists of the Left, communitarians understand that democracy is not the unlimited pursuit of individual freedom, but an ongoing effort to balance the needs of individuals and society as a whole. Like the Founding Fathers, the originators of the republican tradition, communitarians believe that an informed and productive citizenry fully engaged in the life of the community is the basic requirement for democracy. Society needs to protect individual freedom; individuals need to fulfill the responsibilities of citizenship.

Etzioni has described the community movement as an "environmental movement" to save America's endangered social environment.[11] It is clear to communitarians that the moral infrastructure of social authority and purposes must be rebuilt to provide a foundation for America's efforts to strengthen such social structures as families, neighborhoods, churches, civic groups, and communities. The moral infrastructure concerning rights and responsibilities must be developed, whenever possible, through the consensus-building efforts of education and dialogue rather than through coercion. The communitarian approach is not as reliant upon government solutions as the traditional Left because of its belief that solving social problems requires comprehensive community support as well as the responsibility of individuals to help themselves. The communitarian approach differs from the political Right in that it finds that government does have an important role to play in solving social problems.

The Libertarian Public Library

Although it benefited from many reforms supported by the New Left, the public library, like other social institutions, has been seriously damaged by the extreme individualism of the counterculture that challenged all social authority and purposes. In the decades since the 1960s, the public library has been moving away from the library's traditional mission of education for a democratic society to a new mission of access to information for individuals. To demonstrate this change of mission, it is helpful to discuss the 1852 report of the trustees of the Boston Public Library, which requested tax support for the nation's first major public library; the view of the public library movement held by revisionist historians such as Michael Harris in the 1970s; and *A Planning Process for Public Libraries* published by the Public Library Association in 1980.

In their report, the Boston trustees viewed the public library as important both to the growth of individuals and to the political, economic, and social advancement of the community:

> And yet there can be no doubt that such reading ought to be furnished to all, as a matter of public policy and duty, on the same principle that we furnish free education, and in fact, as a part, and a most important part, of the education of all. For it has been rightly judged that,—under political, social and religious institutions like ours,—it is of paramount importance that the means of general information should be so diffused that the largest possible number of persons should be induced to read and understand questions going down to the very foundations of

social order, which are constantly presenting themselves, and which we, as a people, are constantly required to decide, and do decide, either ignorantly or wisely.[12]

This view of the public library's mission grows directly out of the republican tradition of American democracy and is clearly linked to the concern that self-governance requires that a society educate its citizens.

In the 1970s, revisionist historians such as Harris attacked the founders of Boston Public Library and the traditional public library in general. Harris found that the public library movement did not stem from "a passion of liberal and humanitarian zeal," but from an effort to control rebellious Irish immigrants that was characterized by "authoritarianism and elitism."[13] This challenge reflects the expressive individualist view that social leadership and education violate the rights of individuals and specific interest groups. The result of such attacks was a withdrawal from the public library's traditional mission of providing education for a democratic society.

E. J. Dionne Jr.'s assessment of the general culture offers an apt description of the post-counterculture change in the public library: "Thus did the New Left wage war against the paternalistic liberal state and defeat it. The Right picked up the pieces."[14] With the loss of the public library's historical mission, the values and developmental strategies of the private sector's utilitarian individualism filled the vacuum. The new libertarian view of the public library combined hostility toward social purposes and social authority with a shift toward the values and methods of the marketplace.

The 1980 Public Library Association manual *A Planning Process for Public Libraries* offers a blueprint for the libertarian public library. To avoid any sense of authoritarianism or elitism, the authors of the planning manual are careful not to prescribe a public library mission. "It is not the library that is making decisions about what it will do for its community so much as the community which is deciding what it wants its library to be."[15] As public librarians and trustees are encouraged not to lead, they are also encouraged not to educate. The authors shift the focus of public library service from education to information. "The ultimate purpose of any library is to meet the information needs of its community."[16] Offering bits of content without any particular educational intent is clearly preferred to acting in the potentially controversial role of educational authorities. In keeping with this reluctance to exercise social authority, the manual leans heavily toward demand in the traditional debate between *quality* and *demand* in materials selection.

The private sector developmental methods of utilitarian individualism are evident throughout the manual. It is clear that the goal is to serve individual "customers" belonging to selected market segments. The focus on individual service rather than service to groups or the community as a whole is evident when the authors insist that, "Communities don't have information needs; individuals do."[17] In its recommended process of selecting service roles, the manual clearly mimics the private sector strategy of developing specialized market niches.

Civic Librarianship

The following working definition of civic librarianship is offered to begin a dialogue among librarians and trustees concerning the use of community movement ideas in developing public libraries. *Civic librarianship seeks to strengthen communities through developmental strategies that renew the public library's mission of education for a democratic society.* Unlike the libertarian public library, civic librarianship honors the historic mission of education for a democratic society and uses developmental techniques appropriate to a governmental agency. Public librarians and trustees can benefit from the community movement's support for social purposes and social authority, its stress on the importance of public education and civic participation, and its powerful new strategies for community development.

Civic librarianship holds that public libraries are community development and problem-solving agencies, not mere distributors of materials and services. Public librarians use their knowledge of materials and services and their knowledge of community needs to obtain a positive result for both individuals and the community. The demand-oriented libertarian public library reduces the importance of the librarian's judgment regarding materials and services and community needs and, in doing so, disregards the importance of the outcome or results of the service provided. Such an amoral distribution of service reduces public librarianship to a technical, mechanical function that is no longer worthy of professional status.

Several major tasks need to be accomplished by those interested in civic librarianship. These tasks include reestablishing the philosophical framework of public librarianship as well as developing strategies for action. Potential reforms include the following:

- restoring the confidence of public librarians and trustees in exercising social authority;
- renewing the public library's historical mission of education for a democratic society;
- developing the public library as a center of the community;

- developing strategies to build communities through public library service (such strategies might include promoting community identity, dialogue, collaboration, and evaluation);
- using services and collections to meet social as well as individual needs; and
- strengthening the political efforts of public librarians and trustees.

Until recently the only community movement strategy to gain much attention among librarians and trustees has been the strategy of community collaboration. Other community movement ideas and the underlying philosophy of the community movement have received little or no attention. Thanks to the 1999–2000 American Library Association theme, Libraries Build Community, chosen by Sarah Ann Long, and the 2000–2001 theme, Libraries are the Cornerstone of Democracy, chosen by Nancy Kranich, a much broader discussion of the social mission of America's libraries is now underway. The social mission of education for a democratic society is emerging from the shadows after decades of serving as a rhetorical backdrop for an institution increasingly preoccupied with serving individual preferences.

Library literature is taking up this discussion in books such as *Civic Space/Cyberspace: The American Public Library in the Information Age* by Redmond Kathleen Molz and Phyllis Dain, *A Place at the Table: Participating in Community Building* by Kathleen de la Peña McCook, and my book, *Civic Librarianship: Renewing the Social Mission of the Public Library*.[18] The organization Libraries for the Future has helped sponsor community building projects in public libraries. Libraries throughout the nation are experimenting with new ways in which to balance library service to groups and communities with the service provided to individuals.

Conclusion

A major cultural shift toward social reintegration is beginning to solve the problems of decades of extreme individualism. This cultural shift has renewed support for America's great civic tradition of democracy. This is extraordinarily good news for America's public libraries, as the public library was founded to support this civic tradition by providing education for a democratic society. The importance of public education and civic participation in the original framework for American democracy gives the public library a powerful role to play in the life of the nation. As antisocial and antigovernmental feelings wane, the changing national mood offers a great opportunity for public library development. Using community movement ideas and strategies, librarians and trustees can lead the public library into a powerful new era of service to America's communities.

Notes

1. Jesse H. Shera, *Foundations of the Public Library: Origins of the Public Library Movement in New England 1629–1855* (Chicago: Univ. of Chicago Pr., 1949), 248.

2. E. J. Dionne Jr., *Why Americans Hate Politics* (New York: Simon and Schuster, 1991), 11.

3. Robert N. Bellah et al., *Habits of the Heart: Individualism and Commitment in American Life*, updated ed. with new intro. (Berkeley: Univ. of California Pr., 1996), 27–28.

4. Isaiah Berlin, *The Roots of Romanticism* (Princeton, N.J.: Princeton Univ. Pr., 1999), 105.

5. Berlin, *The Roots of Romanticism,* 127.

6. Dionne, *Why Americans Hate Politics,* 54.

7. Francis Fukuyama, *The Great Disruption: Human Nature and the Reconstitution of Social Order* (New York: Free Press, 1999), 13–14.

8. Fukuyama, *The Great Disruption,* 271.

9. Amitai Etzioni, *The Spirit of Community: The Reinvention of American Society* (New York: Simon and Schuster, 1993), 9–10.

10. Ibid., 9–10.

11. Ibid., 2.

12. Shera, *Foundations of the Public Library,* 281.

13. Michael Harris, "The Purpose of the American Public Library," *Library Journal* 98, no. 16 (Sept. 15, 1973): 2509, 2511.

14. Dionne, *Why Americans Hate Politics,* 54.

15. Vernon E. Palmour, Marcia C. Bellassai, and Nancy V. De Wath, *A Planning Process for Public Libraries* (Chicago: ALA, 1980), 7.

16. Ibid., 41.

17. Ibid., 8.

18. Redmond Kathleen Molz and Phyllis Dain, *Civic Space/Cyberspace: The American Public Library in the Information Age* (Cambridge, Mass.: MIT Pr., 1999); Kathleen de la Peña McCook, *A Place at the Table: Participating in Community Building* (Chicago: ALA, 2000); Ron McCabe, *Civic Librarianship: Renewing the Social Mission of the Public Library* (Metuchen, N.J.: Scarecrow Pr., 2001).

Information Literacy for the Twenty-First-Century Citizen

Elizabeth L. (Betty) Marcoux

Rapid changes in information technology and the overwhelming glut of information sources make being an information-literate citizen more critical. Information literacy is one way to be successful in meeting the challenges of the twenty-first century. Information literacy cuts across all community settings and all aspects of society, including the corporate, professional, and public sectors. Access and integration of technological and information-seeking skills will define the abilities of future individuals to attain a viable citizenship—one that productively contributes to society.

Twenty-First-Century Concerns for Information Literacy

The premise of E-learning is to link innovations of the New Economy with building the knowledge base and skill levels of people. The predicted outcome is people able to benefit directly from the best education opportunities available throughout the world, thus improving their educational opportunities to participate in the New Economy. However, sociological concerns related to technology and its uses are ever present. The U.S. Department of Commerce recently reported in *Falling through the Net* (2000) that there is an increase in urban minority access to technology for information (from 11.2 percent in 1998 to 23.5 percent in 2000).[1] However, there is a continued lag in information access for these citizens when compared to urban majority citizens at 46 percent access. While this may seem like major progress, these individuals are only half as likely to have access compared to the urban population as a whole. This same report also indicates that rural households are consistently less likely to have Internet access than urban households at all income levels. Thirty percent of urban school-age youth live at or below the poverty level, indicating a potentially serious lack of access to information sources in the home.[2]

Equity issues have historically made a difference in how effective a citizen can be and constitute ongoing civic and economic concerns for society. Current data now extrapolate the widening of this difference unless the needs of all citizens to be active participants are addressed. Economically, the question of interfacing nontechnological goals with technological means for citizens looms as an issue, for the concerns of economic lifeskills now include the abilities of information access and use from a technological viewpoint. The information-literate community is, and will be, an information-smart and economically successful community. Technology and information skills are not separable; rather, they are like a homogeneous alloy. With electronic connectivity there is more technological efficiency in providing access to resources.

Many projects are underway in the United States that are aimed at providing connectivity and opportunity to underserved populations. Initiatives have begun to move this agenda forward as more rural and lower socio-economic populations are being considered in the information conversation. Through its Gates Library Program for public libraries, the Gates Foundation is supporting technology access in the United States and Canada with a $200 million commitment. The foundation believes that libraries are the ideal place to offer public technology access. In September 2000, approximately 120 locations on the Navajo, Hopi, and Havasupai reservations were supplied with high-speed Internet services.[3] Northern Arizona University recently wired the Navajo Tribal Chapter Houses to provide Internet access to educational opportunities for this rural minority population.[4] Loriene Roy is the project director of "If I Can Read, I Can Do Anything," a reading incentive project at schools on tribal reservations.[5] Its mission is to assist libraries serving Native American children to improve their reading skills while preserving Native identity through a family literacy program. The Urban Libraries Council has partnered with the Wallace Reader's Digest Funds Initiative to help public libraries develop programs and activities that support educational and career development of young people during nonschool hours. All of these initiatives and many others are working toward creating better technical and skill access to information for populations not usually served by traditional information services and programs, thus opening access to more equitable information use and the opportunity to participate more actively in today's society.

What Is an Information-Literate Citizen?

A citizen, by definition, is a person entitled to the rights and privileges of a free person, but who owes allegiance to a government that is charged with that free person's protection.[6] In order to capitalize on these rights and privileges and to give allegiance, the information-literate citizen of the twenty-first century will need the capacity to find, understand, and appropriately use information as a participant in a viable citizenry. Information literacy, for the purposes of this essay, is defined as the ability to find and use information. *Information Power: Building Partnerships for Learning* may have said it best when it defines how to have effective use of ideas and information.[7] *Information Power* lists three ways to accomplish this:

- provide intellectual and physical access to materials in all formats;
- provide instruction to foster competence and stimulate interest in reading, viewing, and using information and ideas; and
- work with others to design learning strategies to meet the needs of individuals.

The Association of College and Research Libraries (ACRL) has similarly defined information literacy as a "set of abilities requiring individuals to 'recognize when information is needed and have the ability to locate, evaluate, and use effectively the needed information.'"[8] ACRL emphasizes the commitment to assessment—of measuring the effect of information literacy on learners by identifying performance indicators and outcomes that demonstrate the achievements of the learner. In the twenty-first century this measurement can determine direction and focus on information literacy as it relates to a viable citizenry.

How Can One Become an Information-Literate Citizen of the Twenty-First Century?

Creating an information-literate citizen of the twenty-first century is complex and often difficult to achieve equitably. Nancy Kranich, in "Libraries: The Cornerstone of Democracy," states that an "informed public constitutes the very foundation of a democracy" and that such democracies create the opportunity to have discussion and discourse, ensuring the preservation of its record with free and open—equitable—access to that information.[9] The dilemma is not only with the haves and have-nots, but the cans and cannots as well as the wills and will-nots—those that are or aren't information literate for any reason, including being technologically astute. The learning community of the information-literate citizen will be limited by personal abilities to access, evaluate, and then effectively use information. Approximately 95 percent of schools in the United

States are now connected to the Internet, but teacher use of the Internet for authentic learning and teaching remains very low, often limiting the student's abilities to learn information literacy skills.[10] The recognition and use of modern information technology to improve everyday life is a necessity, both economically and socially. This issue will most likely divide future viable citizenry.

What is necessary for a citizen to be information literate in the twenty-first century? Required are not only the abilities to access, evaluate, and effectively use information, but also the abilities to cope with the concerns of information overload to individuals and the social responsibility for information in life and society. The Web is changing everything—it is unpredictable but relentless in pushing society to define its needs and actions. The Web provides a political weapon for personal use and power while providing unprecedented access to information. It offers a forum to publish opinions and, therefore, has attracted uses that are antithetical to its basic intent and nature. Concerns of misinformation loom even larger on the Web than in print.

Providing services needed by society for all to participate in an equitable manner will require higher civic and economic participation rates of underserved populations. Participation will include not only the abilities of these populations to be discriminating users of the Web, but also assurance that appropriate services are available to such populations. Potential for inclusion of such populations makes technology and its changes to information access potent allies of information literacy. Cultural preservation and maintenance, while improving the information literacy skills of these populations, are possible with new technologies. The digital divide for the informationally disenfranchised can be narrowed, and information literacy skills can offer ways for communities to improve their economic situations, health choices, and other life goals. Throughout, the ability to access, evaluate, and effectively use information is paramount—regardless of the format and medium.

An Information-Literate Citizen Accesses, Evaluates, and Uses Information Effectively and Efficiently

An information-literate citizen of the twenty-first century will access information effectively and efficiently. Leading to access is the recognition that information is central to meeting the needs and challenges of daily living. Recognition is followed by the ability to effectively seek out appropriate information and then to evaluate the information for its accuracy and usefulness. Knowing the question, understanding how to structure the search for information, and then pursuing the correct information allow the information-literate citizen to move more thoughtfully and critically toward the access of appropriate and valuable information.

"Valuable" Information

The term "valuable information" is worrisome. It can connote that information has equitable value to all. The value of information, like the value of knowledge, is determined by its usefulness to the individual for personal purposes. Information is not value-neutral—it is determined by perception. What is considered an information-poor environment to one culture or community can be an information-rich environment to another. Evaluation of information for personal use and need determines its value. A constant for most communities and cultures is that the better informed a person, the better judgment that can be expected, which idealistically leads to a more responsible and civic-minded citizen. It is difficult to have a discussion about information literacy without running into values, for information literacy itself is a value-linked concept. For example, does an information-literate person have to be a reader? If knowing more potentially creates a broader horizon, does the information-literate person better recognize that there is or could be a question or discourse that is a result of being information literate? Carl Rogers believed that if independence was valued and the conformity of knowledge, values, and attitudes was disturbing, it was important to set up conditions of learning that make for uniqueness, for self-direction, and for self-initiated learning.[11] Information literacy facilitates that individuality while providing a mechanism for inclusive citizen participation.

Information Delivery and Acceptance

How information is delivered and accepted also determines value, for information can facilitate meaning and conversation. In many cultures, the elders of the community are respected for their abilities to teach and practice local life in culturally appropriate ways—a context. Walt Crawford believes that libraries are about "stories" and not just about information.[12] It is the context of these stories that allow for information application to an individual's life. When information is viewed as contextual or in a story, it can open possibilities for a more valuable approach to information literacy to those whose cultures use stories as their learning base. The use of oral tradition is known as the original transfer of information and knowledge. Crawford goes on to suggest that narration provides context—another value-added characteristic of information—suggesting that it "facilitates communication."[13] Narration establishes an information organization system that is often culturally determined. The more that is known about this organization system, the greater the potential for understanding the culture. Wayne Wiegand believes that people look for stories to read for inspiration and identity reinforcement, and he cautions against underestimating the value of the story as an information delivery mechanism.[14] Learning may more readily happen through the context of stories than through information bits, and may allow minorities closer to the perceptions of the majority's perceptions of information as well as vice versa. It will also allow for more minority participation in viable citizenry when seen as an important tool for learning and being information literate. An information "story" often will provide a context that assists in recognizing and validating aspects of knowledge, which in turn contribute to being information literate.

New Ways of Knowing and Sharing Information

Recently there has been a dramatic shift from information and knowledge generated by the expert to that of a model based on the information needs of the individual person who uses it to create personal knowledge.[15] Information-literate citizens develop their own systems of constructing information needs and questions, finding pertinent information, evaluating it to determine its usefulness, and then applying it to resolve the concern or answer the question. The research strategy can be customized to the learning style and needs of the individual. The use of technology to facilitate personal learning strategies has enabled interoperable systems to be more successful educationally with a variety of communities and cultures, allowing for individual learning styles and schedules to participate diversely yet synchronously in a learning situation.

The successful application of information to a solution by the information-literate citizen ultimately defines the personal value of that information. In using information, the user's success is determined not only by the accuracy and appropriateness of the information, but also by the creative application of information to generate knowledge. Rather than suggesting that the information-literate citizen simply use what information is found in its original form, emphasis is placed on the thinking process—drawing conclusions and developing new understandings. Information is managed skillfully with an effective outcome in a variety of contexts. Diverse purposes are determined individually and then applied to a range of audiences and a variety of formats. Focus of the information use is brought about through the individual thinking and application process. Information is used to draw conclusions and develop new understandings or knowledge, which are used in the ways the individual deems most appropriate.

An Information-Literate Citizen Is an Independent Learner

An information-literate citizen of the twenty-first century is an independent learner able to pursue information interests related to personal needs and interests. When applying the practices of information access, evaluation, and use, the information-literate citizen will determine which information enriches his or her personal life and knowledge, as well as how the information fits into the greater scheme of society's knowledge map. The appreciation of the value of information is part of the personality of the information-literate citizen and facilitates the ability to use information in meaningful ways that define societal contributions. However, the appreciation of the value of information is also measured by the translation of information into knowledge and solutions or in generating new information for others to use in their information quest. New technologies and information, while opening up the potential for much greater equity, also require a greater watch on inclusion of diverse and minority populations as they translate that information into useful knowledge for themselves. An information-literate citizen will be one who has the ability to evaluate information, determine its usefulness on a personal level, and critically and analytically reconstruct information into personal knowledge packages to meet personal needs. Yet an information-literate citizen will also be mindful of the larger societal information map or picture. Concepts of information and their translation into knowledge will be affected by the sense of identity the user possesses and by the sense of citizen participation believed in by that individual.

An Information-Literate Citizen of the Twenty-First Century Is Socially Responsible

An information-literate citizen of the twenty-first century will be a socially responsible citizen by constructively contributing to the overall learning community. A community can be defined four ways: a geographic community, a demographic community, a cultural community, or an interest community. A learning community can bridge all four. Libraries often are perceived as bridging regional and intellectual communities by providing information that connects these communities, regardless of intellectual abilities and social acceptance. As Kranich's statement in "Libraries: The Cornerstone of Democracy" says, a citizen must have the "resources to develop the information literacy skills necessary to participate in the democratic process" of "dialogue" and "freedom of expression."[16] An important aspect of the "dialogue" is the information-literate citizen's ability to contribute positively to the discourse by being knowledgeable and recognizing the importance of contributing to a democratic information society. This discourse can be diverse in viewpoint, traditions, and especially in cultural perspectives, yet remain inclusive as it contributes to a democratic society.

Ethical and Equitable Behavior

The concerns of ethical and equitable behaviors are paramount to the practice of being an information-literate citizen in the twenty-first century. They extend to the practices of technological as well as nontechnological uses and practices of information. While access to information has shrunk the world environment, it has also brought about serious discussions regarding rights and ownership concerns. Unrestricted sharing of cultural information is not appropriate to everyone and relates to issues of information access and use. Contributing positively and equitably to the learning community means being culturally and ethically responsible—respecting the principles of intellectual freedom and intellectual property and responsibly using technology. There are many economic, legal, and social implications of information that fall within the realm of ethical information and culturally responsible behaviors. Communicating information can also determine that the dynamics of interaction—face to face or not—be structured with the same responsibility that allows for full participation in the information dialogue. This includes exercising critical judgment and cultural sensitivity about information authenticity and appropriate information use. An information-literate citizen will seek to share information and ideas across perspectives and cultures, acknowledging the insights and contributions of a variety of societies and cultures. Generation of solutions will be personally creative and meaningful, yet inclusive of all involved in the conversation.

Economic Necessity of Being Information Literate

Information literacy is, and will increasingly be, an economic necessity. Information speed, the selectivity of information and its use, as well as access to appropriate and timely information will define the success of information literacy as an economic concern. The new economy has brought about new partners in the information environment, expanding business scopes and opportunities, affecting all aspects of society. There are few absolutes in defining what will constitute an information-literate citizen of the twenty-first century. Those who will meet the definition will be those who know how to seek, find, evaluate, and constructively use information that allows access to and use of the human record as deemed useful both personally and to society. The combination of these skills allows the information-literate citizen not only to know what to look for and how to look for it, but also why to look for it and how to use it. Information literacy as a lifelong learning habit supports the belief that, through learning, information becomes knowledge and gives meaning and understanding to that particular individual, who, in turn, shares it with others and finds effective uses for it. In measuring the impact of information literacy on the learner and on society, there will need to be a continual focus on outcomes, the ability for flexibility and change, and the embracing of extended cultural values and meanings. The economic viability of information will be one such outcome measure.

Conclusion

Information needs are defined by individuals and by their society. Information that is pragmatic and easy to apply gives a level of certainty to the person whom it helps get through the day. But it is the quality and value of the information that will afford the individual a chance to be a citizen participant. Knowledge worth understanding will be that which is enduring, at the heart of the individual need, worth uncovering or rethinking, and potentially engaging. The ability to become and continue to be a viable citizen in the twenty-first century remains the focus of being information literate. Changes in how this is done—like the progressive integration of technology with information—will still require abilities to think critically and use information effectively. The mission of the information-literate citizen remains the same as before—to have effective use of ideas and information in society. The goal is to always have enough information to satisfy the need, and to share it in a meaningful manner. The information-literate citizen of the twenty-first century will be aware of the need for information and will pursue it with productive results. Information, however, will never displace wisdom or thoughtfulness. As Kuhlthau states, "the major challenge . . . is to educate children for living and learning in an information-rich environment."[17] The goal will be to equip students and citizens with a sufficiently complete foundation to allow them to continue to learn whatever else they will need in the future and to then make constructive use of that learning. Good habits of mind are still needed with any information and its use.

Notes

1.   U.S. Department of Commerce, "Americans in the Information Age: Falling through the Net," www.ntia.doc.gov/niahome/digitaldivide.

2.   Urban Libraries Council, "Public Libraries as Partners in Youth Development," www.urbanlibraries.org/youth.html.

3.   M. Sink, "Indian Tribes Take Technological Jump," *New York Times*, Sept. 21, 2000, G11.

4.   J. Sanchez, M. Stuckey, and R. Morris, "Distance Learning in Indian Country: Becoming the Spider on the Web," *Journal of American Indian Education* 37, no. 3 (1998): 1–17.

5.   Loriene Roy, "If I Can Read, I Can Do Anything Reading Incentive Project," www.gslis.utexas.edu/~ifican/mission.html.

6.   Merriam-Webster Online, www.eb.com:180/cgi-bin/dictionary.

7.   The American Association of School Librarians and the Association of Educational Communications and Technology, *Information Power: Building Partnerships for Learning* (Chicago: ALA, 1998).

8.   Association of College and Research Libraries, *Information Literacy Competency Standards for Higher Education* (Chicago: ALA, 2000).

9.   Nancy Kranich, "Libraries: The Cornerstone of Democracy," www.ala.org/kranich/democracy.html.

10. K. Cooper, "Internet at School Is Changing Work of Students and Teachers," *The Washington Post*, Sept. 5, 2000, A2.

11. C. Rogers, *On Becoming a Person: A Therapist's View of Psychotherapy* (Boston: Houghton Mifflin, 1995).

12. W. Crawford, "From Petroglyphs to CD-ROMs: A Story about Information," *American Libraries* 31, no. 1 (2000): 72–74.

13. Ibid., 74.

14. W. Wiegand, "Librarians Ignore the Value of Stories," *The Chronicle of Higher Education*, Oct. 27, 2000, http://chronicle.com/weekly/v47/i09/09b2001.htm.

15. K. Smith and E. Berman, "Advancing Student Learning through Outcomes Assessment," www.ic.arizona.edu/~assess1.

16. Kranich, "Libraries: The Cornerstone of Democracy."

17. C. Kuhlthau, *The Virtual School Library: Gateway to the Information Superhighway* (Englewood, Colo.: Libraries Unlimited, 1996), 95.

Additional Reading

Cushman, K. "Information, Literacy, and the Essential School Library." *Horace* 12, no. 1 (1995): 1–8.

National Academy of Sciences. "FITness Report—Fluency in Information Technology." http://books.nap.edu/html/beingfluent.

Revenaugh, M. "Toward a 24/7 Learning Community." *Educational Leadership* 58, no. 2 (Oct. 2000): 25–28.

Stoffle, C., J. Fore, and B. Allen. "Advancing Learning through Assessment: The Instructional Librarian, the Library and Instructional Space" (proceedings from LOEX Conference, May 20, 2000).

U.S. Department of Commerce, Office of Technology Policy. "The Digital Work Force: Building Infotech Skills at the Speed of Innovation." www.nyia.doc.gov/ntiahome/fttn99/execsummary.html.

III. Libraries, Technology, and Democracy

Libraries, the Internet, and Democracy

Nancy C. Kranich

Democracies need libraries. Since their inception, libraries have served as pivotal community institutions upholding, strengthening, and realizing some of the most fundamental democratic ideals of our society. Libraries are the only American institutions that make knowledge, ideas, and information freely available to all citizens. They are where people can find differing opinions on controversial questions and dissent from current orthodoxy. They serve as the source for the pursuit of independent thought, critical attitudes, and in-depth information. And in so doing, they guard against the tyranny of ignorance, the Achilles heel of every democracy.

An informed public constitutes the very foundation of a democracy—after all, democracies are about discourse, discourse among the people. Consequently, the pursuit of knowledge and self-enlightenment lies at the heart of this democracy. That is, if a free society is to survive, it must ensure the preservation and provision of accessible knowledge for all its citizens. Note that libraries in a free society perform the fundamental function of keeping the public well informed. Libraries are the cornerstone of democracy in our communities because they assist the public in locating a diversity of resources and in developing the information literacy skills necessary to become responsible, informed citizens and to participate in our democracy. As James Madison eloquently stated: "Knowledge will forever govern ignorance and a people who mean to be their own governors must arm themselves with the power knowledge gives. A popular government without popular information or means of acquiring it is but a prologue to a farce or tragedy or perhaps both."

An earlier version of this article appeared in *Managing the Internet Controversy*, edited by Mark Smith (New York: Neal-Schuman, 2001), 1–21.

Libraries ensure the freedom of speech, the freedom to read, the freedom to view. A truly democratic institution, libraries are for everyone, everywhere—no one should be excluded. They provide safe spaces for public dialogue. They provide the resources needed for the public to inform itself in order to participate in every aspect of our information society. They disseminate information so the public can participate in self-governance. They provide access to government information so that the public can monitor the work of its elected officials and benefit from the data collected and disseminated by public policy makers. In America, libraries were "invented" and exist in order to give all people equal access to learning and self-determination. Libraries are uniquely democratic.

Libraries and Civil Society

As libraries serve to prepare citizens for a lifetime of civic participation, they also encourage the development of civil society. They provide the information and the opportunities for dialogue that the public needs to make decisions about common concerns. As community forums, they encourage active citizenship and renew communities. When people are better informed, they are more likely to participate in policy discussions in which they can communicate their ideas and concerns freely. Most important, citizens need civic spaces where they can speak freely, share similar interests and concerns, and pursue what they believe is in their interest.

Effective citizen action is possible when citizens develop the skills to gain access to information of all kinds and to put such information to effective use. Librarians teach the public how to identify and evaluate information that is essential to making decisions that affect the way they live, work, learn, and govern themselves. Beyond the individual, libraries also provide the real and virtual spaces for members of the community to exchange ideas—ideas fundamental to democratic participation and civil society. Ultimately, discourse among informed citizens assures civil society; and civil society provides the social capital necessary to achieve sovereignty of the people, by the people, and for the people.[1]

The Information Rich and the Information Poor

No city in the world enjoys such rich cultural and information resources as my hometown—New York. And no city contains so many rich residents. At the same time, New York also harbors some of the poorest people in America, impoverished not just by their incomes, but also by their lack of access to the wealth of information and other cultural resources that surround them. While the digital age promises the potential of closing this gap between rich and poor, the haves and have-nots will likely grow further apart in the race to dominate commerce in the digital age. Electronic entrepreneurs become millionaires overnight and science and knowledge advance at breakneck speed. Nevertheless, this new age of abundance, now stripping away the ravages of scarcity, has yet to benefit many of those left behind and has yet to close the gap between the information rich and information poor.

While e-commerce creates a new class of information rich, many of New York's children suffer from poor reading abilities. School libraries lack both books and professional staff to improve reading scores even though studies have proven that good school media programs increase learning. Twenty percent of American adults do not read well enough to earn a living wage. Public libraries in New York lose one-quarter of their staff each year because of low salaries and, thus, barely supplement the poor services offered to children in the schools.

By contrast, New York boasts a magnificent new science and industry library with access to electronic databases that many of the Fortune 500 companies lack and a refurbished humanities center that is the envy of all America. The public libraries have worked hard to supplement their diverse collections and services by providing Internet and electronic database access in branches located in virtually every neighborhood in the city. But demand for unfettered access dramatically outstrips supply; and, regrettably, too much of this demand results from New York's poor-quality school libraries, which are forced to filter the Internet, severely limiting access to the most basic resources.

Indeed, college students at private universities in the city wallow in lush, extensive library collections supplemented by thousands of licensed electronic tools, while students at public universities have barely the books or electronic databases to complete their class assignments, let alone advance scholarship. As compensation, libraries should offer the equal opportunities Americans seek to succeed in the information society; yet libraries are stressed to the limit in their abilities to deliver on this covenant.

This is a hard story to tell, but there is reason for optimism. The Internet promises to bridge the gap between the information haves and have-nots in New York and elsewhere. No longer hindered by geographic, linguistic, or economic barriers, electronic information can span boundaries and reach into any neighborhood with just the click of a mouse. Truly, the dream of an equitable information society offers new hope for rekindling the democratic principles put forth by our founding fathers in the Constitution. Even if a household cannot afford or chooses not to connect to the Internet, families have the option of logging on at a library or school. Under the universal service provisions of the Telecommunications Act of 1996, nearly every community will soon be connected, thus ensuring an on-ramp to the information superhighway providing an opportunity for everyone to participate in their communities' economic, educational, social, political, and leisure activities.

The Clinton administration has drawn the nation's attention to the "digital divide" and the gap between the information rich and poor in America.[2] Recent research indicates that, despite a significant increase in computer ownership and overall usage, many low income, minority, disabled, rural, and inner city groups are falling behind in their ownership of computers and access to telecommunications networks. And, beyond the purchase of hardware and connectivity to the Internet, librarians have stepped into this gap to ensure public access to a broad array of information resources, promoting twenty-first century literacy and reducing barriers to intellectual freedom and fair use.

The Digital Content Divide

Into the milieu of this new century comes the Internet with affordable and accessible content, content that was previously unavailable to many communities, both in the United States and abroad. However, access to an abundance of information does not necessarily mean access to a diversity of sources. Cyberspace is sparse when it comes to local information, particularly for rural communities and for those living at or near the poverty level. The vast majority of Internet sites are designed for people with average or advanced literacy levels. For the more than 20 percent of Americans whose reading levels limit them to poverty wages and for the 30 million Americans speaking a language other than English, few Web sites are readily comprehended.[3] Furthermore, ethnic and racial minorities are unlikely to find content about the uniqueness of their cultures. A recent report by the Children's Partnership estimated that at least 50 million Americans—roughly 20 percent—faced a content-related barrier that stood between them and the benefits of the Internet. For example, in March 2000 only three Web sites could be found for institutions operating in Harlem. The Children's Partnership study also indicates that adults want practical information focusing on local community, information at a basic literacy level, content for non-English speakers, and racial and ethnic cultural information. It also found that Internet use among low-income Americans was for self-improvement, whether for online courses, job searches, or other information. In short, the poor and marginalized individuals seek information that helps them with their day-to-day problems and enables them to participate as members of their democratic community.

Libraries are well positioned to meet these needs. Targeting Web sites and digital library development toward special populations is crucial if we are to ensure widespread participation in the information society. We must ensure that sites are easy to navigate, translated into languages spoken by residents, and responsive to local needs. Information equity must become a priority for the entire community. We must purchase licensed materials and convert older items that contain content of interest to those at the margins of our communities. Libraries must join forces with community groups and institutions to bridge the digital content divide.

Information Literacy in a Highly Mediated World

Copyright registrations now exceed 560,000 per year. The number of new book titles published annually in the United States has jumped more than 30 percent over the last decade. More than 100,000 federal and 10,000 United Nations documents enter circulation annually, along with untold numbers of state and local documents.

Even more astounding is the exponential growth of the Web. A February 1999 study reported in *Nature* concluded there were about 800 million publicly available Web pages, with about 15 trillion bytes of textual information and 180 million images weighing in at about 3 trillion bytes of data. The rapid growth of the Web is estimated to be slightly more than doubled in size every year, though some sources estimate that it doubles every six months.[4] As of April 2000, the Censorware home page reported that the Internet included 1,820,000,000 Web pages and 409,000,000 images; and that the lifespan of a Web page is about 44 days, which means that 41,300,000 pages and 9,300,000 images change daily. In just the last 24 hours, the Web has added 3,690,000 new pages and 831,000 new images.[5]

Yet as many librarians know too well, much of the information available over the Internet is either erroneous or tailors its information to advocate a position; there is no validation like peer review to guide users. Much of the "good" information is licensed and restricted to those who have invested and contracted for access. Not surprisingly, the complexity of finding, evaluating, and using information in the electronic age has become a major challenge for the 60 percent of the workforce that engages in some information-related activity. Librarians are needed more than ever to ensure that the public has the information literacy skills it needs to live, work, learn, and govern in the digital age.

Americans need sophisticated information literacy skills to succeed in the twenty-first century. Even those already proficient at finding, evaluating, and applying information to solve daily problems can be overwhelmed by the proliferation of information and the difficulty of sorting through it. To cope successfully, citizens must be able to identify, evaluate, and apply information and communicate it efficiently and effectively. Americans will have to become information literate to flourish in the workplace as well as to carry out the day-to-day activities of citizens in a developed, democratic society. Libraries of all types must work together to develop a process to engage community groups in identifying information needs, initiate a dialogue aimed at encouraging a more information-literate populace, and facilitate the development of skills to use information strategically. Granted, the need for information literacy skills has been around for generations; nevertheless, the dawning of the information society forces us to develop broader information skills if we are to separate the wheat from the chaff, the true from the untrue, the rumor from the real.

In the contemporary environment of rapid technological change and proliferating information resources, communities face diverse, abundant information choices. The uncertain quality and expanding quantity of information pose large challenges for society. The sheer abundance of information will not in itself create a more informed citizenry without a complementary cluster of abilities necessary to use information effectively.

Community Networks

Comparable to libraries, community networks such as freenets create channels of communication for public dialogue. The movement toward community networks reflects the desire for a democratic institution capable of recognizing the centrality of information access and communication to modern life. Here too, libraries have led. Working closely with a broad array of community partners, the conceptualization of these networks derives directly from the model of the public library. Community networks offer many of the services provided by libraries, including training, e-mail, Web page development, and small business assistance. They also focus users on local assets and services, pulling together essential information and communication resources that might otherwise be difficult to identify or locate. Of special interest here, they offer opportunities for libraries to collaborate and build partnerships in support of local history projects, civic education programs, and community enterprises—such as information and referral services—that might be overlooked by the commercial sector. Significantly, librarians bring added value to this movement by offering skills and expertise to those who sustain these ventures. Especially for public libraries, community networks offer an exceptional opportunity for them to forge new roles in their communities.[6]

Government Information

Over the last decade, the persistent voice of librarians and the promise of new technologies have improved access to government information. The result has been the promotion of the public's right to know along with the advancement of citizens' involvement in governance. A fifteen-year struggle to promote equal, ready, and equitable access to government information culminated in passage of the GPO Access Act, the Electronic Freedom of Information Act, and other policies endeavoring to strengthen public access in the digital age. Still the victory has been incomplete. While the public benefits from ever more direct access to government records and documents (witness the speed with which the unedited version of Kenneth Starr's report reached citizens' hands), more and more data were slipping into private hands, getting classified under the guise of national security, or exempted from release under the Freedom of Information Act. In 1999 a proposal to ensure permanent public access to electronic government documents was forwarded by the library community to Congress and promptly ignored. At that very moment, links to important documents disappeared unnoticed, and a court of appeals allowed federal agencies to destroy electronic documents resident in word-processing or e-mail systems once a copy was made for record keeping. So while public access to government information produced at taxpayer expense is more freely available than ever before, the threat to public access persists. Yet even more vulnerable, state and local electronic information rarely falls under depository and other open-access statutes. We should savor our victories while recognizing that we must remain vigilant and continue the struggle for truly open access.

Copyright and Fair Use

Against the promise of easy access to networked electronic information loom new technological protection measures. The ubiquity of digital information, the widespread use of networks, and the proliferation of the Web create new tensions in the intellectual property arena. The ease with which data may be copied impels information producers to seek ways of protecting their investments. Their intentions are perfectly understandable. Unfortunately, measures proposed to protect creators endanger users' fair-use rights to view, reproduce, and quote limited amounts of copyrighted materials. This high-stakes policy debate might well result in a pay-per-view or—even more chilling—a pay-per-slice digital information economy, in which only those willing and able to pay can access electronic information. With librarians in the vanguard, the delicate balance between creators' and users' rights to information has been carefully negotiated for print materials over the past century. However, as we enter the information age, the balance has begun to tilt toward intellectual property owners. Should this imbalance persist, it will endanger free speech, the promotion of learning, and the rekindling of civil society.

The Digital Millennium Copyright Act of 1998 was the first measure to criminalize illegal use of digital materials and places additional limits on the rights of electronic information users. As a consequence, the widespread deployment of pay-per-view systems could effectively reduce libraries from repositories of valuable knowledge to mere marketing platforms for content distributors. Fair use was only negotiated into the bill after librarians and public interest activists threatened to defeat it. Subsequently, fair use barely survived as new restrictions were imposed on unauthorized access to technologically restricted work. The act prohibits the circumvention of any effective technological protection measure (TPM) used by a copyright holder to restrict access to its material unless adverse affects on the fair use of any class of work can be demonstrated. Thus, the burden of proof rests with those of us seeking open access and the free flow of information.

A second copyright-related bill, the Collections of Information Antipiracy Act, will protect investment rather than creativity for database companies and overturn more than 200 years of information policy that has consistently supported unfettered access to factual information. This bill draws its support from a small but powerful group of database publishers, including Lexis-Nexis (owned by Reed-Elsevier), the New York Stock Exchange, and the National Association of Realtors, and will allow a producer or publisher unprecedented control over the uses of information, including factual information as well as government works. Even though the Supreme Court had held that constitutional copyright principles prohibit ownership of facts or works of the federal government and current copyright law already protects database companies, some corporations continue to press hard for this overly broad protectionist legislation. Should they succeed, they will accomplish a radical departure from the current intellectual property framework that protects expression—not investment—and thereby endanger the doctrine of fair use. If these special interests prevail, we will wind up with a pay-per-view digital economy where the free flow of ideas is limited to the obsolescent world of print and photocopy machines.[7]

Universal Service and Filtering

Since the early decades of the twentieth century, Americans have held the belief that maximum access to public information sources and channels of communication is necessary for political, economic, and social participation in a vigorous democracy. Everyone must have access to information communication networks in order to participate in our democratic way of life. Under the universal service provisions of the Telecommunications Act of 1996, the Federal Communications Commission has authorized a program to ensure equitable access to telecommunications technologies by offering schools and libraries discounted rates that were once reserved for only the largest corporate customers. In this way, schools and libraries may be connected as a first step toward widespread public access. Known as the E-Rate, more than $2 billion in discounts and grants is now earmarked annually for distribution from fees collected by long distance phone carriers. In addition, the E-Rate helps bridge the digital divide by expanding access and connectivity to needy communities.[8] Still, it took some horse trading to gain acceptance for the E-Rate. Telecommunications companies agreed to this amendment to the 1996 Telecommunications Act in return for deregulation of their markets. Even so, several of the major carriers who benefited most from deregulation have tried to sabotage this program through court challenges and by highlighting the universal service charge on consumer bills without explanation, thereby inciting their enormous customer base.

Where corporate attempts to stop the flow of subsidies to schools and libraries ended, Congress has added its own twists. New laws that require local communities to install filters to protect children from obscenity and child pornography in order to receive E-Rate and other subsidies threaten the feasibility of the funds. Attempts to tie federal funding to content restrictions raise serious constitutional questions similar to those brought forward in *Reno v. American Civil Liberties Union* (1997), which challenged the constitutionality of the Communications Decency Act. These laws will impose federal regulations over local community control of information access. First Amendment protections must extend to the digital sphere if we are to ensure open dialogue across the full spectrum of opinion in the information age.

Many states have proposed or passed similar laws to restrict Internet access in schools and libraries by mandating a filtering requirement in order for these institutions to receive state and local funding. Unfortunately, filters do more harm than good; they sweep too broadly, blocking only some of the sites with indecent materials while restricting access to legal and useful resources. In those libraries that currently employ filters, users complain that they block such home pages as Super Bowl XXX, the Mars Exploration site (MARSEXPL), a site on swan migration in Alma, Wisc. (swANALma), Mother Jones magazine, the National Rifle Association, and millions of other sites of legitimate interest. Filtering systems have trouble distinguishing between users who are six and sixteen years old and apply the common denominator of the youngest users at the expense of all others.

Furthermore, filters are not effective in blocking much material that some consider undesirable for children; they give parents a false sense of security, leading them to believe that their children are protected from harm. Most importantly, filters do not take the place of preferred routes that include the development of community-based Internet Access Policies, user education programs, links to great sites, and safety guidelines. The extraordinary benefits of Internet access are too often overshadowed by controversies fueled by groups who stoke imagined fears about the power of images and words in an effort to control access to information. According to a recent study by the National Coalition against Censorship, "the evidence of harm from Internet access at public institutions is at best equivocal, and the blunt-edged approach advocated by pro-censorship advocates ignores the individualized need of children and their parents. Fortunately, most libraries have found ways of balancing the interests of all parties effectively, without censorship. . . ."[9]

The Tide of the Information Age

Over the last twenty years, with the emergence of personal computers and telecommunications technologies, we have seen a transformation of the information creation, transport, and dissemination industries from independent operators mostly involved with infrastructure to a highly integrated, multinational sphere of megacompanies looking to optimize profits and dominate access to home and business. In the United States, a period of deregulation and privatization has shifted the information policymaking arena to the private sector, where questions of the public interest are harder to raise.

What is at stake is not only the availability and affordability of information essential to the public interest, but also the very basis upon which local libraries serve the public's information needs. As communications and media industry giants stake their claims in cyberspace, the public interest must not be overlooked. The new information infrastructure must ensure public spaces that are filled by educational and research institutions, libraries, nonprofits, and governmental organizations charged with promoting and fulfilling public policy goals. They must constitute a public sphere of free speech and open intellectual discourse, which enhances democracy.

If the public's right to know is to be protected within a free-market national information infrastructure, the library community must work together with public groups, who must stand up and speak out for the public interest. Librarians are well positioned to lead the charge because we are committed to ensuring the free flow of information in our society and we understand what is at stake. Librarians have already staked a claim in the newly emerging national information infrastructure. After all, we are the information professionals who represent more than half of the country's adults, as well as three-quarters of its children, who use libraries. Librarians excel at identifying, acquiring, organizing, housing, preserving, archiving, and assisting in the use of information. We have extensive experience working with community groups in providing essential local information and promoting the public's right to know. Furthermore, local libraries serve as the community's historic, cultural, political, and social record and are identified as a center for reflection and stimulation by area residents. We inform citizens about the activities of their local, state, and federal governments through depository and other government information dissemination programs.

What the library community brings to the information infrastructure issue is the perspective of cooperative, not competitive, information professionals serving the public interest. Politically neutral institutions, libraries are charged with strengthening democracy by facilitating public access to information in all its forms. The library mission includes providing such access regardless of a person's economic status, education level, or information-seeking skills. In an electronic age, this mission requires equal, ready, and equitable access to the nation's telecommunications infrastructure, access that will be even more crucial in the future. Without technologically sophisticated libraries available in every community, the evolving information infrastructure can only intensify the gulf between the information rich and the information poor.

Librarians Leading the Charge for Public Access

Librarians must act quickly and decisively to affect the ever-growing policy issues that will change the means by which information is produced and distributed. Neutrality will not work; the stakes are very high—namely, our democratic way of life, which depends upon an informed electorate. We must recognize why these issues are so important. We must be informed about the issues and the players on all sides. However, we cannot be effective on our own. We must work together with others to make a difference. We must enter the struggle adequately armed. We must make every effort to balance the influence of a well-organized corporate community. We must build coalitions to promote public access, to increase our strength and influence, and to galvanize grassroots action.

The promises of the twenty-first-century information society must not be placed in peril by those intent on restricting public access to information and the free flow of ideas. A high-tech society must not become a highly controlled society. The vigilance and activism of those concerned with protecting free expression is more important than ever if the American ideals embedded in the First Amendment of the Constitution are to remain the beacon of our way of life in the new millennium. We must speak up and fight for information equity for all. Otherwise, we will endanger our most precious right in a democratic society—the right of free speech and inquiry.

Notes

1. In recent years, the essential processes of democracy have undergone serious rethinking led by Robert Putnam's analysis of social capital and its relationship to civic participation cum civil society. See, for example, "Bowling Alone: America's Declining Social Capital," *Journal of Democracy* 6, no. 1 (Jan. 1995): 65–78, and *Bowling Alone: The Collapse and Revival of American Community* (New York: Simon & Schuster, 2000).

2. For a more detailed view of the "digital divide," see *Falling through the Net: Defining the Digital Divide*, Washington, D.C.: U.S. Department of Commerce, National Telecommunications and Information Administration, vols. 1–3, 1995, 1998, 1999, 2000, www.ntia.doc.gov/ntiahom/fttn99; *What's Going On, Losing*

Ground Bit by Bit: Low-Income Communities in the Information Age, Washington, D.C.: Benton Foundation, 1998, www.benton.org/Library/Low-Income; and Thomas P. Novak and Donna L. Hoffman, "Bridging the Digital Divide: The Impact of Race on Computer Access and Internet Use," Nashville, Tenn., Vanderbilt University e-lab manuscripts, Feb. 2, 1998, www2000.ogsm.vanderbilt.edu/papers/race/science.html.

3. The Children's Partnership, *Online Content for Low-Income and Underserved Americans: The Digital Divide's New Frontier—A Strategic Audit of Activities and Opportunities* (Washington, D.C.: Children's Partnership, 2000).

4. See Steve Lawrence and C. Lee Giles, "Searching the World Wide Web," *Science* 280 (Apr. 3, 1998): 98–100, and "Accessibility of Information on the Web," *Nature* 400 (July 8, 1999): 107–9.

5. The Censorware Project home page provides a daily count on Web size at www.censorware.org/web_size.

6. For more information about community networks, see Joan Durrance and Karen Pettigrew, "Community Information: The Technological Touch," *Library Journal* 125, no. 2 (Feb. 1, 2000): 44–46; Douglas Schuler, "Let's Partner as Patriots: The Future of Democracy May Lie in Linking Libraries with Community Networks," *American Libraries* 28, no. 8 (Sept. 1997): 60–62; and Douglas Schuler, *New Community Networks: Wired for Change* (Reading, Mass.: Addison-Wesley, 1996).

7. Up-to-date information about copyright issues is available from the American Library Association's Washington Office Web site at www.ala.org/washoff/copyright.html, which links to numerous other sites concerned with protecting fair use in the digital age.

8. For more information about the E-Rate, see the American Library Association's Washington Office Web site, www.ala.org/washoff/e-rate.html.

9. See the National Coalition against Censorship, *The Cyber-Library: Legal and Policy Issues Facing Public Libraries in the High-Tech Era* (New York: NCAC, 1999), 8, www.ncac.org/cyberlibrary.html; the American Library Association, Office of Intellectual Freedom Web site www.ala.org/oif.html; and the Freedom to Read Foundation Web site at www.ftrf.org/index.html. Up-to-date information about congressional bills that require filtering is available on the ALA Washington Office Web site on E-Rate issues, www.ala.org/washoff/e-rate.html.

The Library Internet Access Controversy and Democracy

Susan B. Kretchmer

[Citizens] must always remain free to inquire, to study and evaluate, to gain new maturity and understanding . . . [to] explore the unknown, and discover areas of interest and thought . . . [for] access to ideas makes it possible for citizens generally to exercise their rights of free speech and press in a meaningful manner. . . . [The] library is the principal locus of such freedom.

—*Board of Education v. Pico* (1982)

It is no exaggeration to conclude that the content of the Internet is as diverse as human thought. . . . [a] new marketplace of ideas . . . The Web is thus comparable, from the readers' viewpoint, to . . . a vast library including millions of readily available and indexed publications . . . The interest in encouraging freedom of expression in a democratic society outweighs any theoretical but unproven benefit of censorship.

—*Reno v. American Civil Liberties Union* (1997)

The analogy that the Supreme Court suggests about the library and the Internet as fundamental institutions in a democracy is particularly appropriate given the challenges and opportunities presented to both by rapidly changing contemporary American society. In an increasingly digital environment that is transforming the world and human relations, both the library and the Internet must negotiate their place in this new milieu, individually and in the public sphere that joins them at their nexus in public library Internet access.

It should come as no surprise that controversy has developed at the intersection of one of the oldest embodiments of democracy and one of the newest. When considered in a historical context, it is clear that the current debate parallels the legal turmoil and societal upheaval created by the introduction of every major innovation in communication technology—writing, the printing press, the telegraph, the telephone, radio, and television. Perhaps more importantly, because libraries are the cornerstone of democracy, they will always be the site of cultural struggle, tests of democracy and democratic ideals, and a crucible for a society that is constantly moving toward a more perfect union.

This essay explores the current library Internet access controversy in the context of American democracy. Specifically, we consider the democratic values implicated in library Internet access, briefly review the nature of the controversy, and examine the often paradoxical considerations raised in the resulting debate.

Democratic Values

Rather than simply a pragmatic choice to regulate the operation of civilized society, democracy is based on and augments characteristics of individual and social existence valued by the citizenry. As Masaryk notes, "Democracy is not only a form of government, it is not only what is written in constitutions. Democracy is a view of life, it rests on the faith in men, in humanity, and in human nature."[1] Democracy, for example, calls for a broad electorate with universal suffrage; refuses to admit privilege derived from birth, wealth, race, or creed; safeguards against the oppression of individuals by government and the right of citizens to oppose their government in a peaceful manner; and demands the right of freedom of speech, freedom of the press, and freedom of religion. In so doing, at the same time, democracy recognizes the inner dignity of all people, honors their equality, values the protection and success of every individual, and affirms that the lives of all the people are enriched by the promotion of individual accomplishments.

Our ideals are entrusted to and manifest in the institutions of our democracy, such as libraries. From equal access to the free flow of information, libraries epitomize democracy and the values shared by American citizens. As one participant in a recent study explained:

> I think as we are seeing the population . . . stratifying along class lines in a huge way . . . the library is one of those symbolic things that is left, that is a cornerstone of "we all do this for everyone" so that everyone can use it.[2]

Indeed, as Oprah Winfrey observed, libraries are inseparable from our democracy: "Getting my library card was like citizenship; it was like American citizenship."[3] Similarly, the management of library resources is carried out in a manner that aspires to mirror the dignity and fairness that is key to democracy. For instance, acceptable use policies (AUPs) specify the conduct required of the patron in exchange for acquiring the benefits of library use and the penalty for violation of the established rules. AUPs, however, like the democratic system of laws and justice, do not involve the intervention of the library to constrain individual freedom until after a transgression is committed.[4]

While the democratic values represented by libraries may be clear, the values we invest in our technology may not be as evident. In 1986, Langdon Winner suggested that technologies are a "form of life."[5] As we have seen with democracy, technologies shape their users and the way those users view the world. Feenberg's notion of a "technical code" illuminates the unexamined underlying social and cultural assumptions, values, and norms that are literally designed and built into our technological artifacts.[6] The choices manifest in technologies have a profound, and often unanticipated, impact. On a broad scale, consider that cars created the suburbs and television made the world smaller. As a discrete example, consider the New York City-to-Long Island parkway overpasses that were built too low to allow clearance for city buses and, thereby, enforced social class bias by preventing lower-income individuals from reaching Long Island.

As such, the Internet conveys meaning well beyond the information it transmits. The recognition of that capacity is part of the reason that so many see the Internet as the fulfillment of democratic promise. In the United States, as a recent study has shown, two-thirds of users and nearly half of nonusers believe that the Internet is making the world a better place.[7] On the Internet we find the empowering combination of low barriers to entry; worldwide public communication available to both speakers and receivers; and a genuine marketplace of ideas exemplified by a multiplicity of human thought, an unlimited storehouse of knowledge and energy, and a space in which truth can challenge falsehood and cultivate enlightenment. In essence, the Internet is the locus of citizenship and individual success in modern civil society.

Yet, in addition to this utopian vision and its frequently cited distopian counterpart, the information technology we create imparts and embeds equally profound, but more nuanced, values into our lives as well. From issues of privacy to corporate power structures:

> given the importance and omnipresence of technology today, technical design decisions are increasingly substituted for what were once issues of public debate and politics. That's why we have an emerging and increasingly urgent "politics of design," politics with no candidates, campaigns or slogans, but politics with serious consequences.[8]

For instance, a major concern at present involves the collection of personal information from Web site visitors without their knowledge or consent, and its subsequent sale to third parties. This raises a value choice that pits economic gain against personal freedom and free will.

Thus, as individuals and as a nation, we are in the process of negotiating the place of the Internet within our democratic value frame. That is a central, but not at all clear, task. The disconnection—social, cultural, political, economic, intellectual, emotional, moral, ethical, legal—wrought by the Internet arouses the same sort of passion, tension, and strife as previous technological innovations. But, this struggle is exacerbated by the unprecedented rapidity of the diffusion of the technology; while it took nearly fifty years for electricity, nearly forty years for the telephone, and seventeen years for television to reach one-third of American homes, the Internet has achieved that level of penetration in only seven years.

The Controversy

In this context, a major controversy has erupted across the nation as public libraries have made the Internet widely accessible to patrons. Those libraries now face a complex dilemma as well as new and challenging legal difficulties.

Since the Supreme Court overturned the Communications Decency Act (CDA) in June 1997, there has been public outrage about the availability of sexually explicit, "harmful," and otherwise "adult" or objectionable content on the Internet. In response, a coast-to-coast crusade has developed to mandate that public libraries install stand-alone blocking software designed for the home market, such as CyberPatrol, on Internet-connected computers designated for use by both children and adults. However, this insufficiently fine-tuned software can block or fail to block sites inappropriately. While some view blocking software as a tool for protecting children, others see it as "censorware," unconstitutional when imposed in publicly funded libraries, government institutions bound by the First Amendment.

In addition to the arena of public debate, this increasingly passionate nationwide controversy has been unfolding in legal and political forums as well. Two legal cases were argued in federal district court in 1998 and 1999. In *Mainstream Loudoun et al. v. Board of Trustees of the Loudoun County Library* (24 F.Supp. 2d 552 [E.D. Va. 1998]), the judge ruled that mandatory library blocking software unconstitutionally infringed on free speech rights, and *Kathleen R. v. City of Livermore, et al.* (Cal. Super. Ct., Alameda Co., Case No. V-015266-4 [1998]) is pending on appeal.

As of 2000, Kentucky, South Dakota, and Arizona had passed filtering legislation, and other states may follow. Michigan passed a law requiring that children be shielded from sexually explicit material online. Holland, Michigan, installed filters to comply, even though the voters had rejected that policy in a previous ballot initiative. On the federal level, on December 15, 2000, both houses of Congress passed a Labor, Health and Human Services, and Education Appropriations Bill (HR 4577) with a filtering rider, the Children's Internet Protection Act (S. 97). This legislation, signed into law by President Clinton, mandates that schools and libraries install and maintain filtering software on their Internet-connected computers or lose their essential E-Rate federal funding. As of this writing, the ACLU has promised to challenge the constitutionality of this regulation.

Democratic Values and Library Internet Access

The central issue in the library Internet access controversy has far less to do with the democratic values we ascribe to the Internet and far more to do with determining the values implicated by filtering software and its place within our democratic way of life. In fact, the Supreme Court, which concluded that the Internet deserved the highest order of First Amendment protection, seems somewhat unsure about the nature of blocking software. In *Reno v. ACLU* (117 S.Ct. 2329 [1997]), the Court noted that the software might be a reasonably effective, less restrictive alternative to CDA. Yet, they affirmed this only in the context of individual parental choice, observing, for example, that it is a "method by which parents can prevent their own children from accessing material which the parents believe is inappropriate" for their own children. In addition, the Court indicated that the software was in the infancy of its development and not in wide or standardized use. Thus, it appears unlikely that the software could pass constitutional muster in the publicly funded governmental institution of the library.

Nevertheless, at present, public opinion is for the most part working at odds with legal precedent, and it is not surprising that legislators have intervened on a politically popular topic.[9] The very notion of limiting or controlling the power of the new technology of the Internet through filters plays into the basic tension within a democracy toward constraining freedom in the face of fear over potential harm. As Pool explains:

> The characteristics of media shape what is done with them, so one might anticipate that these technologies of freedom will overwhelm all attempts to control them. . . . Technology . . . shapes the structure of the battle, but not every outcome. While the printing press was without doubt the foundation of modern democracy, the response to the flood of publishing that it brought forth has been censorship as often as press freedom . . . the easy access, low cost, and distributed intelligence

of modern means of communication are a prime reason for hope. The democratic impulse to regulate evils, as Tocqueville warned, is ironically a reason for worry.[10]

Thus, as our culture and democratic institutions strive to adapt to the Internet, filtering software has emerged as a possible "protection." Although much discussion has been devoted to what the software can and cannot *do,* and there is general agreement that it is appropriate within one's home, if one so chooses, and for employees at places of business, little attention has been paid to the more important issue of what the software *means* within our democratic society; what remains to be negotiated is the propriety and significance implicated in the employment of the software in civic forums such as public libraries. The struggle to resolve this issue has highlighted some particularly poignant paradoxical considerations in our democratic values.

Protecting Children

Perhaps the most hotly contested aspect of the library Internet access controversy is the attempt to determine the best way to safeguard the well-being of children as they explore the wonders of the information superhighway. Because of the heightened level of concern that surrounds children's issues, the incongruities that arise in this aspect of the filtering debate are quite stark.

For example, according to recent surveys, 84 percent of Americans worry about the availability of pornography to children, and 78 percent of parents are "strongly" or "somewhat" concerned that their children might view sexually explicit material.[11] In addition, 92 percent of Americans believe that school computers should block pornography and 79 percent think they should bar hate speech.[12] Antithetically, it has repeatedly been documented that, of the children who go online at home, 58 percent are not supervised by adults and only a third of parents use blocking software.[13] Further, the percentage of children who have actually accessed pornography on the Internet is relatively small; only 15 percent of children age 10–13 with computers at home have seen a pornographic Web site.[14] In fact, it has been estimated that only 1.5 percent of the pages on the Web contain pornography, so the possibility of accidentally viewing it is statistically very small.[15] Also, all major Web sites targeted to children employ their own filters in the chat areas they provide so that inappropriate material cannot be posted.

Another inconsistency emerges as we consider the values about the protection of children from sexual exploitation that are being applied in the library Internet access controversy. For instance, in the United States there are

103,845 confirmed cases of sexual abuse of children by parents and caretakers per year.[16] In contrast, there are fewer than 800 cases, confirmed or under investigation, of Internet-related child sexual victimization.[17] Similarly, $90 million per year is being spent to purchase Internet filtering and blocking software by 2001.[18] In comparison, the combined budgets of all Children's Trust Funds, state agencies that work with legislatures and seek out private funds to combat child abuse, are severely limited.

There are additional issues at stake that go to the heart of our democracy beyond "this incredible conflict [that] . . . [p]eople trust their kids with the Internet, but they don't trust the Internet with their kids."[19] For example, large majorities of Americans feel that children learn and benefit from using the Internet. Also, according to Papert, computers allow children to master knowledge that was previously inaccessibly difficult, and foster an unprecedented diversity of learning styles and self-directed work.[20] Thus, the Internet furthers our shared desire to teach independence, freedom of thought, good judgment, and responsibility to our children. We, in turn, however, may limit our children's ability to develop these democratic values by imposing filters on this resource. Further, by requiring children to find an alternative means to access the information they are denied through a filtered computer, we may well be unintentionally instructing them to defy authority.

Civic Engagement

Active citizenship is the basis of a democratic society and, therefore, making the modern tools of citizenship universally available is essential. Yet, that can be a major problem given the limitations of filtering software. Numerous studies have shown that valuable civic information is erroneously blocked, including a substantial number of the Web sites of political candidates in the 2000 election.[21] Moreover, material of great national import has been made inaccessible by the software; for instance, Kenneth Starr's report on President Clinton and the Lewinsky affair, which Congress posted on the Internet as crucial civic reading, was blocked from view in public libraries that employ the software.

In addition, while we hold certain basic principles of citizenship as central to democracy, the use of filtering software may negatively affect our ability to operationalize them. For example, in respect for individual dignity, democracy dictates that citizens be exposed to all viewpoints, even those that are offensive. In opposition, the paternalistic attitude embodied in library Internet filtering disrespects that dignity by eliminating individual decision making to "protect" patrons from what others consider to be "dangerous." Further, use of the software may cultivate a climate that socializes and conditions the uncritical acceptance of restrictions on debate in public forums, which is the foundation of democratic deliberation. As Jeffrey Pollack, a conservative congressional candidate from Oregon in 2000 who had advocated mandatory filters in schools and libraries until his own Web site was blocked by CyberPatrol, explains:

> I found out how much power over our free speech we're giving the people at, say CyberPatrol, to make these God-like decisions over what gets blocked and what doesn't. . . . parents should step up to the plate and accept responsibility.[22]

Likewise, "government by the people" demands a citizenry well-informed on political and social issues. This full participation in democracy may be thwarted, though, by the intrusive control of filters, as much random as organized, on information. Moreover, as John Stuart Mill argued, in a free marketplace of ideas, truth and justified belief triumph through the citizens' opportunity to seek out, test, and rationally consider all the competing facts and arguments on an issue.[23] Therefore, library filtering software may be antagonistic to democracy, which relies upon the competence of citizens to function as their own filters. In fact, the software essentially strips the responsibility for making decisions and choosing values away from not only the individual, but from the local community as well, and invests that authority instead in unelected corporate entities.

Another paradoxical value choice that arises in the Internet access controversy involves our desire to include all citizens in our shared future by bridging the digital divide. The government has limited funds with which to provide assistance to disadvantaged libraries in low-income, racially diverse, and rural areas. The legislation requiring filtering, however, diverts these scarce resources away from the democratic ideal of expanding access by refusing to provide funds to libraries unless they install software that can cost $8,000 initially and $3,000 per year to maintain.[24] Also, the notion that privileged citizens who have Internet access without the use of public facilities can choose whether or not to use filters, while those dependent on government-funded access have no choice, is inimical to the nature of democracy.

Analogies

Finally, it is instructive to consider the disparate analogies that are invoked as we try to ascertain the meaning of this new technology in our democracy. For example, although the Internet in general has been heralded as the incarnation of democratic values, it has been suggested that, when placed in the library, its purpose is to supply pornography easily and effortlessly to children. In addition, this risk of exposure to harmful content has been advanced as a force that is driving countless citizens away from the medium. In a democracy, however, as the Supreme Court notes in *Reno v. ACLU* (117 S.Ct. 2329 [1997]):

> [that] argument [is] singularly unpersuasive. The dramatic expansion of this new marketplace of ideas contradicts the factual basis of this contention. . . . governmental regulation of the content of speech is more likely to interfere with the free exchange of ideas than to encourage it.

Further, there are dichotomous conceptions of the impact of Internet filtering software in the library. One view maintains that blocking Internet content is analogous to removing a book from the library shelf; the Internet is a single integrated system similar to a set of encyclopedias and, therefore, blocking software expunges particular disfavored content. Conversely, the other perspective asserts that blocking Internet content is equivalent to the decision not to purchase a book; the Internet is a vast interlibrary loan system and, as a result, blocking software is like a standard decision to selectively acquire certain materials. One of the difficulties with the latter position, in a democracy, is that it fails to account for the freedom of individuals. When patrons enter the library, they can bring with them any material they choose and read it in the library. If citizens are not limited by the library's collection in the physical world, our democratic values tell us that neither should they be blocked from bringing material into the library via the electronic world.

Conclusion

> All culture belongs to all people. Books and ideas make a boundless world. . . . To keep that world indivisible is our most urgent difficult task.
> —*Daniel J. Boorstin*[25]

Although in 1985 Boorstin was speaking of books and the profound charge with which libraries are entrusted in a democracy, his call to rise to the task is equally applicable today as libraries strive to realize that ideal through the addition of the Internet to their repository of knowledge. To determine how best to fulfill this duty in the midst of the library Internet access controversy, it is instructive to consider what filtering technology *means* within our democratic way of life, not only what mechanical function it does or does not perform. While evaluation through other value frames may lead to different conclusions, when viewed through the prism of democracy, we see that filtering and blocking software is incompatible with the imperative of a publicly funded government institution such as the library.

It is not unusual to blame our technology for all our societal ills. Yet, technology itself cannot solve the nontechnical problems that it raises.[26] As Nika Herford of Net Nanny Software International Inc. explains, "legislation is well-meaning, but may not necessarily have the outcome the people who wrote it hoped it would have."[27] It has often been noted that balancing conflicting values is central to life in a culture with democratic institutions. The specific harms feared from the Internet must be addressed, but we must also be vigilant to safeguard against broader harms to our democratic society.

In the present controversy, the greatest challenge may well be what values we look to for guidance in regulating our access to information in the age of digital technology. Nearly 90 percent of Americans consider public libraries as valuable as, or more valuable than, other tax-supported services, and consistently express high levels of trust, esteem, satisfaction, and even love for them as cherished institutions that embody community culture, values, and identity.[28] In contrast, public confidence in the performance and trustworthiness of politicians, parties, and the other basic institutions of government is at or near an all-time low.[29] As Hirschkop observes, democracy depends:

> upon a fight, and upon social forces with the interests, will, and intelligence to struggle for it. Technology will doubtless have a role in this struggle, but it offers no shortcuts: one cannot buy democracy off a shelf, or download it from a Website. It demands courage, fortitude, and political organization, and . . . software [has yet to be designed] that can deliver these.[30]

Indeed, in the current library Internet access controversy, we will not find democracy in legislated filtering technology, but rather in turning to the democratic values and wisdom that Americans have historically invested in the public library as the cornerstone of democracy.

Notes

1. Karel Capek, *Masaryk on Thought and Life: Conversations with Karel Capek* (New York: Macmillan, 1938).

2. "Buildings, Books, and Bytes: Libraries and Communities in the Digital Age," *Library Trends* 46 (summer 1997): 178–224.

3. American Library Association, "Quotable Quotes about Libraries," Mar. 16, 2000, www.ala.org/advocacy/libraryquotes.html.

4. Susan B. Kretchmer and Rod Carveth, "Meeting the Challenge," in *The Boundaries of Freedom of Expression and Order in American Democracy*, Thomas R. Hensley, ed. (Kent, Ohio: Kent State Univ. Pr., 2000).

5. Langdon Winner, *The Whale and the Reactor: A Search for Limits in an Age of High Technology* (Chicago: Univ. of Chicago Pr., 1986), 11–12.

6. Andrew Feenberg, *Alternative Modernity: The Technical Turn in Philosophy and Social Theory* (Berkeley: Univ. of California Pr., 1995); Andrew Feeney, "Subversive Rationalization: Technology, Power, and Democracy," in *Technology and the Politics of Knowledge*, Andrew Feenberg and Alastair Hannay, eds. (Bloomington: Indiana Univ. Pr., 1995).

7. Paul Van Slambrouck, "Internet Becomes the New Family Hearth," Oct. 26, 2000, www.csmonitor.com/durable/2000/10/26/fp2s1-csm.shtml.

8. Gary Chapman, "Seeing the Value in the Social Impact of Design," *Los Angeles Times*, Sept. 18, 2000, www.latimes.com/business/columns/dnation/20000918/t000088138.html.

9. Susan B. Kretchmer and Rod Carveth, "Challenging Boundaries for a Boundless Medium: Information Access, Libraries, and Freedom of Expression in a Democratic Society," in *The Boundaries of Freedom of Expression and Order in American Democracy*, Thomas R. Hensley, ed. (Kent, Ohio: Kent State Univ. Pr., 2001).

10. Ithiel de Sola Pool, *Technologies of Freedom* (Cambridge: The Belknap Press/Harvard Univ. Pr., 1983), 251.

11. National Public Radio, "Survey Shows Widespread Enthusiasm for High Technology," www.npr.org/programs/specials/poll/technology/index.html; Joseph Turow, *The Internet and the Family: The View from Parent, the View from Press* (Philadelphia and Washington, D.C.: Annenberg Public Policy Center of the Univ. of Pennsylvania, 1999).

12. Rebecca S. Weiner, "Survey Finds Support for School Filters," *New York Times*, Oct. 18, 2000, www.nytimes.com/2000/10/18/technology/18EDUCATION.html.

13. National Consumers League (NCL). 2000. Online Americans more concerned about privacy than health care, crime, and taxes, new survey reveals; NCL forms new partnership with Dell to educate consumers about privacy, security, and children's safety online. Press release, 4 October. Washington, D.C.: National Consumers League; Turow, *The Internet and the Family*; Dow Jones and Co., "Web Not Personally Disrupting" (study, Oct. 25, 2000).

14. National Public Radio, "Survey Shows Widespread Enthusiasm."

15. Steve Lawrence and C. Lee Giles, "Accessibility of Information on the Web," *Nature* (July 8, 1999): 107–9.

16. U.S. Department of Health and Human Services, *Child Maltreatment 1998: Reports from the States to the National Child Abuse and Neglect Data System* (Washington, D.C.: Government Printing Office, 2000).

17. David Finkelhor, Kimberly J. Mitchell, and Janis Wolak, "Online Victimization: A Report on the Nation's Youth. National Center for Missing and Exploited Children," www.missingkids.org/download/InternetSurvey.pdf.

18. John Schwartz, "Protest over Web Filtering Business," *New York Times*, Dec. 21, 2000, www.nytimes.com/2000/12/21/technology/21FILT.html.

19. Ted Bridis, "Net Survey Shows Parents Have Mixed Feelings," *Buffalo News*, May 11, 1999, 9D.

20. Seymour Papert, *The Children's Machine: Rethinking School in the Age of the Computer* (New York: BasicBooks, 1993).

21. Bennett Haselton and Jamie McCarthy, "Blind Ballots: Web Sites of U.S. Political Candidates Censored by Censorware," http://peacefire.org/blind-ballots.

22. Alexandra Marks, "A Clash over Filters to Block Internet Smut," Dec. 7, 2000, www.csmonitor.com/durable/2000/12/07/p2s1.htm.

23. John Stuart Mill, "Of the Liberty of Thought and Discussion," in *On Liberty*, reprint (New York: Penguin Books, 1974).

24. American Civil Liberties Union, "Censorship in a Box: Why Blocking Software Is Wrong for Public Libraries," ACLU white paper, www.aclu.org/issues/cyber/box.html.

25. Daniel J. Boorstin, address at general conference of the International Federation of Library Associations, Chicago, Aug. 19, 1985.

26. Dow Jones & Company, Inc., "Scientists: Tax Net to Put Needy Online (report, Oct. 5, 2000).

27. Lisa M. Bowman, "Congress Ignites Net Filter Fight," *ZDNet News*, Dec. 19, 2000, http://dailynews.yahoo.com/h/zd/20001219/tc/congress_ignites_net_filter_fight_1.html.

28. "Off to the Library," *The Economist* 348 (Sept. 12, 1998): 30; "Buildings, Books, and Bytes."

29. Susan J. Pharr and Robert D. Putnam, *Disaffected Democracies: What's Troubling the Trilateral Countries?* (Princeton, N.J.: Princeton Univ. Pr., 2000).

30. Ken Hirschkop, "Democracy and the New Technologies," in *Capitalism and the Information Age*, Robert W. McChesney, Ellen Meiksins Wood, and John Bellamy Foster, eds. (New York: Monthly Review Pr., 1998), 217.

Libraries, the New Media, and the Political Process

Nancy C. Kranich

In March of the first year of the twenty-first century, Arizona's Democratic Party pioneered a new frontier in America's oldest ritual. Over four days, members of the party cast ballots for their party's presidential candidate, many of them doing so electronically through the medium of the Internet. Total voter turnout increased from 13,000 in the primary of 1996 to this year's 89,000, where 40 percent cast Internet ballots. And, while many experienced the novelty of voting from their own homes, a significant number used one of America's oldest institutions, the public library. One final note, Arizona's primary becomes even more historic when one recognizes that the huge increase in voting took place during a primary with only one candidate, because Bill Bradley had already withdrawn from the race.

No doubt we can look forward to Internet voting as a feature of future elections. Yet as we do, we will need to remind ourselves that the pursuit of knowledge and self-enlightenment lies at the heart of our democracy. Effective citizen action is possible when citizens know how to gain access to information of all kinds and have the skills to become responsible, informed participants in our democracy. Over the past three decades, we have seen a decline in voter turnout and less attendance at political rallies, fewer people engaging in politics and government, and a reduced involvement with civic organizations. As countries throughout Eastern Europe and elsewhere seek to establish democratic institutions, we appear to be experiencing a deepening cynicism about public affairs in the United States. Concern about civic disengagement has sparked a renewed interest in reinvigorating American democracy. So, perhaps the Arizona experience bodes well for the twenty-first century.

This article originally appeared in *iMP: Information Impacts Magazine,* May 2000 (www.cisp.org/imp/may_2000/05_00kranich.htm).

How, then, can we meet the challenge of maintaining a vigorous democracy? Surely, technology is not enough. A good part of the answer lies at our doorstep. One institution well equipped to face the challenge to strengthen citizen action and civil society in our communities is the library. Citizens need civic spaces where they can speak freely, share similar interests and concerns, and pursue what they believe is in the public's and their own interest. Libraries not only serve as those civic spaces, but they also offer new possibilities to revitalize civic discourse by using new technologies to deliberate on issues and the challenges facing their communities. After all, libraries promote the kind of discourse that makes democracy possible.

Libraries uphold, strengthen, and realize some of the most fundamental ideals of our democratic society. They are dedicated to providing access to knowledge, ideas, and information available to all citizens—a place where people can find differing opinions on controversial questions and dissent from current orthodoxy. As such, they are the only institution in American society whose sole function is to provide this information to guard against the twin tyrannies of ignorance and prejudice.

America's libraries, at the heart of every community, stand in defense of freedom. Benjamin Franklin founded the first lending subscription library even before he helped found the new republic. Franklin, James Madison, and Thomas Jefferson were among the nation's founders who believed that a free society must ensure the preservation and provision of accessible knowledge for all its citizens. When they turned their attention to designing a government capable of preserving freedom for the citizenry, they looked to an institution with the potential for realizing their ideal. For if an informed public is the very foundation of American democracy, then America's libraries are the cornerstone of that democracy. As Madison eloquently stated, "Knowledge will forever govern ignorance and that people who mean to be their own governors must arm themselves with the power that knowledge gives. A popular government without popular information or means of acquiring it is but a prologue to a farce or tragedy or perhaps both."

Benjamin Franklin's novel idea of sharing information resources was a radical one. In the rest of the civilized world, libraries were the property of the ruling classes and religion. American democracy was founded on the principles of freedom of information and the public's right to know. America's libraries ensure the freedom of speech, the freedom to read, the freedom to view. Libraries provide the resources the public needs to be well informed and to participate fully in every aspect of our information society.

Libraries provide the real and virtual spaces in communities for the free and open exchange of ideas fundamental to democratic participation and civil society. As community forums, libraries present thoughtful, engaging, and enlightening programs about problems facing our democratic way of life—programs that have a vast potential to renew communities and encourage active citizenship. From librarians, we can learn how to identify and evaluate information that is essential for making decisions that affect the way we live, work, learn and govern ourselves. America's libraries are ideally suited to play a critical role in rekindling civic spirit by providing not only information, but also the expanded opportunities for dialogue that the public needs to make decisions about common concerns.

Today, libraries continue to operate at the leading edge of citizen participation in the political process. For years, the public has registered to vote and cast election ballots in libraries. Citizens attend forums with candidates in local libraries and learn more about their positions and voting records. They monitor the work of both elected and appointed officials through the reports housed in library depositories of government information, where they also gather data for taking positions on various issues facing their communities. During campaign seasons, citizens find voter guides and other relevant information about elections and referenda in libraries and engage with authors who write about political issues at events held in libraries. They also find information about deadlines for voter registration, locations of polling places—and valuable electronic links to high-quality electoral information in print as well as on the Web.

Libraries use new media to reach out to communities across America. One key way in which they support democratic action and citizen participation is through the development of electronic Web sites that guide users to valid and reliable information that informs their choices about candidates and issues. Publicly accessible sites such as those hosted by the University of Michigan and University of California-Berkeley libraries offer a comprehensive map of the electoral process including links to political history sites, political search engines, candidates' voting records, campaign finance information, past election results and speeches, political statistics, media coverage, advocacy and lobby groups, and political party platforms and conventions. (See www.lib.umich.edu/libhome/Documents.center/psusp.html and www.igs.berkeley.edu:8880/library/agpp.html.)

Libraries also provide information in a variety of media ranging from books and magazines to videos, audio recordings, and electronic resources that inform the public about the political process, resources that can be used either in the library or outside with community groups and school children. They also collaborate with community and nonpartisan groups to promote greater political participation, such as the invaluable League of Women Voters (www.lwv.org) as well as a newer electronic organization—Project Vote Smart (www.vote-smart.org), which offers electronic access to candidate and voting information. The American Library Association has posted an electronic tip sheet guiding libraries to good election sites through its home page at www.ala.org.

Politically neutral institutions, libraries are charged with strengthening democracy by facilitating public access to information in all its forms. The library mission includes providing such access regardless of a person's economic status, education level, or information-seeking skills. In an electronic age, this mission requires equal, ready, and equitable access to the nation's telecommunications infrastructure, access that will be even more crucial in the future. Without technologically sophisticated libraries available in every community, the evolving information infrastructure can only intensify the gulf between information rich and information poor.

Now comes a new challenge for this venerable institution. A meaningful discussion on issues of the day requires access to a broad representation of viewpoints. Only free and open access to a wide range of sources ensures the flow of information necessary for a rich and robust public debate. Here, then, is a major dilemma for the 115,000 school, public, academic, and special libraries concerned with ensuring the public's right—and need—to know in a commercially driven information age. While libraries are more popular than ever, they do not command the public attention or the financial support to counter the heavy influence of marketplace stakeholders. Their limited funds for purchases must now cover very expensive electronic resources, many of which duplicate their print holdings. As a result, libraries, the institutions charged with providing the broadest array of opinion, cannot ensure access to the full array of opinion.

Amidst an information revolution that is changing the way we work, live, and learn, we can no longer assume that the descendants of Franklin's brainchild will offer a safe haven for all the world's ideas and points of view. The forces that are driving media conglomerations are also threatening our information access rights. Access to abundance does not translate into access to diversity. Instead, we now have access to more of the same ideas, with alternatives marginalized by such forces as corporate profiteering, political expediency, and the whimsy of the marketplace. New technologies are not likely to empower everyone if powerful political and economic forces continue their assault on free expression, fair use, information equity, and the freedom of information. Battles to protect free expression are now seriously threatening our basic freedoms and undermining support for libraries and our most cherished democratic rights.

The promises of this twenty-first-century information society must not be eclipsed because we acquiesced to the free market restricting public access to information and the free flow of ideas. A high-tech society must not become a highly controlled society. Librarians are fighting hard for information equity for all. But they need help to counter the heavy influence of commercial corporations in the public policy process. The vigilance and activism of those concerned with protecting free expression is more important than ever if the American ideals embedded in the First Amendment of the Constitution are to remain the beacon of our way of life in the new millennium. The stakes are high. Responsible corporations should work to support libraries and their mission and to guarantee that all Americans enjoy access to the kind of information necessary for full-bodied democratic participation. Activists, too, must join forces to fight for the future of not just a democratic media, but also our most precious free speech institution in America—our libraries.

Future voting efforts will doubtlessly include electronic polling, with libraries key to ensuring broad participation by all citizens. In Arizona, a major concern of the Democratic Party and voting rights advocates was the potential for excluding voters who lacked computer access. To ensure that the maximum number of eligible Democrats could vote, twenty-five Arizona public libraries served as polling places for electronic voting. "We think that there is something wonderfully symbolic about public libraries being used as polling places," said GladysAnn Wells, State Librarian. "Libraries have always been places where everyone in a community can find common ground, so it is logical that libraries would be places where people without computers could come to vote." One Scottsdale resident stated:

> I am excited to be part of the first online election. My wife and I have supported the Scottsdale Public Library for years and libraries linking to on-line voting is a logical role for them to play.

According to Judy Register, Scottsdale City Librarian:

> Libraries are determined to play a leading role in helping people bridge the so-called "digital divide." Now, helping bridge this "electoral divide" is a great use of the technology available in public libraries in Arizona.

Our democratic way of life depends upon an informed electorate. The vigilance and activism of those concerned with protecting democratic values and promoting free expression is more important than ever if the American ideals embedded in the Constitution are to remain strong in the digital age. We who believe in the democratic mission of libraries must speak up and fight for information equity for all. Otherwise, we will endanger our most precious rights in a democratic society—the rights of free speech, inquiry, and self-governance.

Sex, Democracy, and Videotape

Randy Pitman

We can neither endure our vices nor face the remedies needed to cure them." Although these words (once you subtract the eloquence) could just have easily been written by a contemporary handwringer railing against Hollywood's perceived stock in trade—sex and violence—they actually date from the dawn of the Christian era. The author is Livy (c. 59 B.C.–17 A.D.), and the quote can be found in the preface to his great work, *The History of Rome*. A card-carrying member of the going-to-hell-in-a-handcart school of thought long before hell was even a widely acknowledged concept, Livy would die twenty years before the legendary Emperor Caligula—a profligate, sadistic madman who not only proclaimed himself a god, but was rumored to have nearly had his horse appointed as a consul—came to power as the living embodiment of the writer's worst nightmare. Just under four centuries later, the glory that was Rome would be reduced to no-cash-just-carry booty for land pirates who went by the distinctly non-mellifluous name of Visigoths.

While it is literally impossible and figuratively questionable that all roads should, in fact, lead to Rome, we are drawn—human nature being the curious beast that it is—to poke about the entrails of the past for clues that may help us discern our future. Rome is a particularly fertile brooding ground, not only because its excesses are often held up as the blueprint for our own purported cultural malaise, but also because our "republic"—indeed our elected Senate—was consciously modeled on that of the original shining city on a hill.

Whether Roman debauchery did actually lead to what Edward Gibbon, in his beautifully penned doorstop, termed *The Decline and Fall of the Roman Empire,* is open to debate. What cannot be argued, however, is that the fall of the house of Rome ushered in a new era in which the unfortunate marriage of church and state systematically wrested control over humanity's affairs away from the *vox populi* (whose power was, admittedly, more pro forma than actual) and into the hands of theocratic leaders. We call this period, not without reason,

113

the Dark Ages; a time when humankind was more or less content to allow supposed representatives of the Lord (many of whom turned out to be just as
amenable to wholesale corruption as their political counterparts) to dictate both
the personal and social lives of the people. Speculation, invention, and reflection (secular, anyway) were not encouraged, and sometimes harshly punished.

If I may borrow the name of one of Doctor Dolittle's fabulous creatures, the
struggle for liberty has always been a "pushmi-pullyu" business, with the polar
opposites of absolute tyranny and absolute freedom yanking the populace
around like a macrocosmic taffy pull. Too much freedom, cry history's dictators,
censors, and social engineers, leads to licentiousness amongst the people; too
little, say the liberals, intellectual freedom fighters, and followers of Cheech
and Chong, is a repressive bummer, man.

While over the years a strong sense of conviction + sufficient numbers +
elbow grease + (often) some measure of serendipity have won us precious freedoms that even the most free-spirited of toga partygoers would have considered
shocking in ancient times (women in the Senate, for Jove's sake!), we forget—
at our peril—that we are still gathered, as the poet Matthew Arnold once said,
on that "darkling plain" where armies eternally clash. Somewhere in America,
people are arguing over the body count in the latest Hollywood gorefest, various ethnic and gender groups are bristling over objectionable lyrics in a rap
song, and Harry Potter is being denounced as the devil's spawn.

Those who maintain that the battle over tyranny is already won, that
Orwell's nightmare has been driven into the light of day, are engaging in a bit
of mental self-prestidigitation. Orwell's mind-numbingly contradictory slogans,
which make a mockery of truth and sense, are today's Fifth Avenue billboard
fodder; his downtrodden masses, the consumer junkies who belly up to the
sales counter shifting through credit cards in an elaborate shell game of trying
to find the one not yet maxed out. Ten years ago, the prospect of a wrestling star
being elected governor would have seemed laughable; thirty years ago, the
proposition that a Hollywood actor would become president might have been
hooted down. The boundaries of the unthinkable, as the creators of *South Park*
well know, are remarkably elastic.

Of course, the trump card in any discussion of modern humankind's capacity for tyranny is the Holocaust, which did not occur at the dawn of civilization
over 5,000 years past, but a mere 50 years ago; for many of us, within our lifetimes. Media shorthand being what it is, Adolf Hitler has been held up as the
monstrous architect of so much misery, but we must not make the mistake of simply writing this abominable chapter off as the aberrations of a madman. The systematic murder of 6 million people is, by definition, not a solo effort; it cannot

even be accomplished with a small cadre of upper echelon henchmen. It takes a helluva lot more than a village, and to think that it could not happen again is a comforting illusion that we can ill afford.

If we believe, as I do, that an informed populace is the best hedge against those who would usurp power from the people in order to further their own ends, then we must also recognize the miracle of public, school, and academic libraries, those information citadels that aspire to be repositories of the sum of human knowledge. We must further acknowledge the singular achievement of the most democratic institution on earth, the public library, a veritable warehouse of educational, informational, and recreational treasures equally shared across the entire socio-economic spectrum. Finally, on the cusp of the twenty-first century, we can only wonder at the wide variety of media comprising today's cutting edge library: books, periodicals, videocassettes, audiobooks, CD-ROMs, online databases, DVDs, the Web, and eBooks. We've come a long way, Livy, from the days of papyrus scrolls and wax tablets.

How did we get here? The Roman Emperor Tiberius (42 B.C.–37 A.D.) reputedly got his jollies poring over pornographic drawings; today, porn is as prevalent on the Internet as dust mites in the average American house. While many ills may be rightfully laid at pornography's door, the suppression of channels of information certainly isn't one of them. Many good things, besides ourselves, have come from sex, including the acceleration of the widespread acceptance of cable, video, and the Web. Thanks to the strong early videocassette sales of such dubious artistic fare as *Debbie Does Dallas*, we now have a plethora of extraordinary programming available to public libraries—and, by extension, the public—that would have been inaccessible to all but a handful of urban dwellers frequenting art house cinemas, or catch-as-catch-can television viewers, a mere two decades ago. Wonderful foreign films such as *Cinema Paradiso*, *My Life as a Dog*, or *Life Is Beautiful*; exceptional documentaries, such as Ken Burns' *The Civil War*, Michael Moore's *Roger and Me*, or Henry Hampton's *Eyes on the Prize*; and instructional videos (teacher-on-a-tape, if you will) made to assist people in everything from creating macramé rugs to tracing their genealogical roots, now sit in well-balanced library collections from coast to coast.

Librarians, essentially engaged in collecting a single format for eons, understandably view this onslaught of new technologies with mixed feelings. While a handful continue to embrace the widely held (yet erroneous) romantic assumption, championed by social critics such as Neil Postman and Sven Birkerts, that print holds some mystical supremacy over the other media, more and more libraries are building diverse collections that appeal to patrons with all kinds of learning preferences: print, audio, and visual.

Without disparaging print (I'm all for rendering unto Gutenberg what is Gutenberg's), I would suggest that the great social and political revolutions of the recent past owe a great deal to audiovisual media, especially television. Far from being the "vast wasteland" that Newton Minow decried in 1961, television's impact on personal freedoms, political decisions, and world democracy has been profound. Images of African Americans being accosted by German shepherds and no-neck Southern sheriffs, mute body bags spread across a foreign landscape, and the crumbling of the Berlin Wall did more to bring about the passage of civil rights legislation, the end of the Vietnam War, and the fall of Communism than a whole forest's worth of books, magazines, and newspaper articles.

I say this neither to diminish the very real accomplishments of authors and journalists, nor to suggest that TV is the apex of human culture (far from it), but simply to remind us that former attitudes regarding nonprint media (in itself an absurd term) will not do if the public library is to remain a viable and vital component of our democratic system. At the very least, the nonmedia literate librarian runs the risk of embarrassment (tomorrow's taxpayers will quickly grow tired of reference librarians who, when asked for Martin Luther King's "I Have a Dream" speech, direct them towards the print encyclopedias). Much worse, however, is the prospect of exceptional artistic, social, cultural, and political audiovisual works going unseen because that same librarian subscribes to the dangerously false belief that what's good enough for the local Blockbuster or Hollywood Video store is also good enough for the library.

We have a name for this approach to collection development in our profession: "give 'em what they want." In theory, it's not all that different from the ancient Roman strategy of distracting the people with "bread and circuses," the idea being that if you put food in their stomachs and spectacle before their eyes, the masses will be generally happy campers, and the leaders will be able to get on with the business of daily political life, commissioning statues of the emperor at the taxpayer's expense and whatnot. (The library director's aim, of course, is a bit more modest and defensible: more patrons mean more funding and more materials, which, in turn, attract more patrons . . . and so on.)

Ironically, I've never actually seen a "give 'em what they want" collection, even in those libraries that profess to have one. While these so-called popular collections may indeed be well stocked (and rightfully so) with the latest novels by Stephen King, Danielle Steel, or Tom Clancy, they also invariably carry Homer's epics, both Brontë sisters, and the complete works of the Bard, not to mention copies of the Declaration of Independence, U.S. Constitution, and other documents pertinent to the American enterprise. In addition, these libraries—without exception—offer a wealth of local information, magazines devoted to unbiased consumer advice, career libraries for job seekers, and—I almost forgot—*a multitude of resources across the entire Dewey spectrum.*

What's funny (Webster's second definition: "differing from the ordinary in a suspicious, perplexing, quaint, or eccentric way") and unfortunate is that, for a myriad of reasons, this breadth and depth of material is still too often available only in the print format. Like the laws of quantum mechanics, the concept of the "core collection"—a fundamental precept in creating a balanced library collection—mysteriously breaks down when we shift from particles (books) to waves (audio, video). Casting one harried eye at the local video store for guidance, too many overworked librarians simply mix together current blockbusters, the AFI's 100 greatest films, the entire Disney oeuvre, add a dollop of Jane Fonda exercise videos, and serve it to the public, believing that they are "giving 'em what they want."

A quick Funny Thing Happened on the Way to the Library tale: During the mid-1980s, when I was in charge of building my local library's video collection, a video store less than five blocks away offered free nonfiction titles with each paid movie rental. One of those "free" titles was a documentary on Nostradamus that sat day after day on the shelf gathering dust, while at the library that exact same video was on backorder for an *added* copy due to the half dozen reserves backed up on the high circulating original. People's perceptions are shaped by expectations: If you advertise your establishment as an entertainment center, people will come to you looking for fun; if, on the other hand, you tell your patrons that you are here to help serve the community's educational, informational, and recreational needs, they will cross your threshold with very different expectations.

While precious little exists on the subject of core video collections, viewer's advisory, or multimedia ready reference, I'm confident that, as we move into the twenty-first century, libraries will evolve to meet the wider needs of a much more media savvy patron base. A quarter century ago, AV collections in libraries consisted of children's filmstrips, avant-garde 16mm cartoons, and a bin full of classical LPs. Today, we're faced with the proverbial embarrassment of riches from which to choose. It's no accident that several multivolume videocassette series covering the history of the twentieth century appeared in 1999 and 2000; many of the last century's key events were documented on film, video, or audio (the horrific images of the Holocaust playing out soundlessly in stark black and white have a power to move us—and warn future generations—in ways that abstract numbers on a page cannot).

I do believe that dear Livy would have taken one look at our bound for hell handcart and accused us of adding racing wheels and a turbocharged engine. So much sex. So much violence. So much . . . democracy in the world. The lessons of history are neither always conveniently direct nor suitably applicable: the contents of the back corner of a number of America's video stores would make a Roman orgy-goer blush, but far from being a nation morally adrift in a sea of licentiousness, America boasts greater freedoms, a higher standard of living, and a more advanced technological infrastructure than most of her peers.

Still, while the eighteenth-century dictum that "eternal vigilance is the price of liberty" may strike us as a bit old-fashioned and paranoid today (though it sounded like neither as recently as Dec. 7, 1941), we would do well to keep in mind that our greatest asset as a democratic nation is an informed populace with a voice in its own affairs. Libraries cannot guarantee the latter, but we must ensure the former, by providing equal access to the human record in as wide a variety of formats as possible.

IV. Libraries Supporting Democratic Information Policy

In Support of Democracy
The Library Role in Public Access to Government Information

Anne Heanue

Over many months in 2000, librarians and others had to convince the United States Congress to reconsider drastic cuts in the funds available for federal government information distribution during the fiscal year 2001 appropriations process.[1] Although the severe cuts threatened by the U.S. House of Representatives were turned around in the Senate, the Superintendent of Documents in the Government Printing Office (GPO) will have $2 million less in 2001 to administer the Federal Depository Library Program (FDLP), the government's primary and longest-serving information dissemination activity. As a result, the shift to a primarily electronic distribution program will accelerate, bringing new opportunities and challenges to public access to government information.

The transition to a primarily electronic FDLP is the most profound of the important changes that have taken place over the past few years in the way government information is made available to libraries and to the American public.[2] This electronic transition also highlights the critical role of libraries and librarians in providing public access to government information in support of democracy. Librarians have been using computer technology for decades and have advocated electronic dissemination of government information for just as long.

Most who value government information consider public access a basic right of every citizen, and recognize that the American people need government information to empower and govern themselves and to ensure that government can be held accountable. An informed citizenry is the only basis on which democracy can flourish. Indeed, informing the nation has been a fundamental responsibility of the government since its founding. Our fourth president, James Madison, wrote to W. T. Barry in 1822:

> A popular Government, without popular information, or the means of acquiring it, is but a Prologue to a Farce or a Tragedy: or, perhaps both. Knowledge will forever

govern ignorance: And a people who mean to be their own Governors, must arm themselves with the power which knowledge gives.[3]

Libraries in Support of Democracy

Depository Libraries

Libraries have acted as a principal "means of acquiring" the popular government information that Madison spoke of since the earliest years of the nation. The FDLP traces its roots to 1813 when Congress first deposited congressional materials at certain libraries for public inspection. In the mid-nineteenth century members of Congress designated selected libraries as depositories with the purpose of providing wide geographic access to government documents, regardless of a citizen's income, on a no-fee basis. Congressional intent reflected a commitment to broad-based democracy, keeping the general public well informed, not only the wealthy or landed gentry. Participating libraries in the FDLP provide a critically important service to citizens throughout the country, in rural and urban communities, by furnishing timely, equitable, no-fee access to government information.

Today, 1,330 depository libraries located in most congressional districts make available a broad range of government publications in print and electronic formats to the American public and ensure that the information is preserved for use by future generations. This partnership between libraries and the federal government provides an efficient and effective avenue for the dissemination of government information. Public, academic, law school, federal, and state government libraries make up a system of libraries committed to public access to government information.

Information from all three branches of the federal government is distributed by GPO to depositories in various tangible (e.g., paper, CD-ROM, and microfiche) and electronic online formats. Libraries maintain the physical publications and provide expert staff to make available no-fee access to the information in all formats. Last year, GPO distributed millions of copies of some 40,000 titles. Depositories also purchase additional materials to help make government information accessible. Every state is served by one of fifty-three regional libraries that have agreed to permanently retain all government documents provided to them. The requirement that regional libraries retain government documents is the nation's only guarantee of continued free public access to the vast treasure of government information. Nowhere else in statute or practice is permanent, no-fee public access to federal information assured. Some of these libraries have collections of government documents dating from the eighteenth to the twenty-first centuries, a national treasure.

Depository libraries act as a safety net for public access to federal government information. They contribute resources estimated at some four to five times the cost of the information products they receive from GPO. Librarians help millions of Americans every year to locate print and electronic government information for personal, business, education, legal, and research needs. Federal agencies place information about their current operations on the Internet, but this information is not necessarily easily found, nor is it provided retrospectively. Additionally, few agency Web sites provide systems of assistance to users. Librarians provide that assistance.

The U.S. government is the world's largest producer of information. In every field that one can think of, libraries are repositories for information. Government information is essential primary resource material since the government collects, compiles, or produces information on every aspect of society—statistics, demographics, health, law, commerce, agriculture, transportation, environment, and countless more. Federal laws and regulations, congressional bills, and court decisions are just the tip of the iceberg.

To be informed, Americans must have access to information about their government and its policies. Their needs are both current and retrospective. For example, they need to know the voting records and statements of senators like Joe Lieberman of Connecticut and Jesse Helms of North Carolina—yesterday and fifteen or twenty years ago.

In 1996, the Depository Library Council to the Public Printer undertook a project to collect statements from depository library patrons on their use of the program. Excerpts from their letters were published in *Fulfilling Madison's Vision.*[4] The statements in the book illustrate the diversity of both the users and use of federal government information all across America.

The comprehensive range of the material in the program is accounted for by the broad wording of the definition of government publication in the statute governing the FDLP.[5] The program includes all government information products, regardless of format or medium, of public interest or educational value, except for those which are for strictly administrative or operational purposes, classified for reasons of national security, or restricted by privacy considerations. One of the valuable features of government information distributed through the FDLP is that it is public information, not subject to copyright or censorship.

However, not all government information products pass through GPO to be included in the FDLP. If agencies produce publications on their own, they are required to provide copies to the FDLP. However, the requirement is often ignored. Since many "fugitive" publications are not in the FDLP or the *Monthly Catalog of U.S. Government Publications* prepared, published, and distributed by GPO, skilled documents librarians help identify alternative bibliographic tools and sources to find needed information, such as agency publication distribution programs or government sponsored free or fee-based information clearinghouses (e.g., the National Technical Information Service [NTIS], Educational Resources Information Center [ERIC], and the National Criminal Justice Reference Service). This situation is increasing due to the proliferation of government information sites on the Internet.

Nondepository Libraries

Libraries without depository status provide public access to government information by having basic government documents reference collections. Among the services they provide are the names and telephone numbers of government officials, information from the *Statistical Abstract*, or referrals to depositories. Having electronic access to government information enables nondepositories to do an even better job for their publics. Their role in answering government information related questions has been greatly expanded by using electronic databases from the GPO Access System (www.access.gpo.gov), the Library of Congress Thomas Web site (http://thomas.loc.gov), and numerous other federal agencies that have made databases available through the Internet.

Bridging the "Digital Divide"

Increasingly we hear about the digital divide—the gap in computer literacy and accessibility that separates American society along economic, racial, and ethnic lines. Libraries help to bridge the gap for the still considerable number of people who do not have access to a computer by providing public access terminals. And even if users have a computer, they may not have the high-end equipment, software, or printers required to handle some of the databases from which they need data. One need only visit public libraries to observe the extensive use made of library computer terminals. Even if Americans had all the hardware they needed to access every bit of government information they required, many would still need the help of skilled librarians whose job it is to be familiar with multiple systems of access to government information. Most reference librarians are familiar with various possibilities for access and the principal sources for the distribution of government information such as GPO,

NTIS, the Census Bureau, National Library of Medicine, ERIC, and some other agencies and clearinghouses.

Local, State, and International Information

Just as Americans need public access to federal government information, they also need to use information created by local, state, and international governmental bodies. Local and state governments need access to the information from comparable jurisdictions in order to do their work effectively and efficiently.

Frequently the FDLP has served as a model for the organization of local, state, and international information dissemination since it is a more developed program. Many local and state units of government and international organizations have established depository programs to place their information products in libraries for public access and preservation.

Advocates

As mentioned at the beginning of this essay, librarians and users of government information are often the most dedicated advocates for public access to government information. Whether it is promoting sufficient funding for the FDLP and needed changes to its governing law, preventing harmful changes to a statute or the program, testifying in Congress on information policy issues, influencing regulations related to government information, or providing feedback to federal agencies about various information products, librarians have been in the forefront of advocacy. Without libraries as points of public access and service at the local, state, and federal levels, and without librarians monitoring government information policies and programs and speaking up on behalf of the public, there would be significantly less access to less information from the government.

The American Library Association has been active for many years in the advocacy arena, and other library associations have joined in the effort. Within ALA, the Government Documents Round Table (GODORT) has been especially influential since its founding in the early 1970s. The words of one GODORT founder, Bernadine Abbott Hoduski, in 1995, are as important today as they were then:

> Most urgently, every librarian must ask to meet with every member of Congress to show them what they do with the information and to invite them to their library and

to have real discussions between members of Congress and users of government information.[6]

This strategy worked especially well when librarians were in the forefront of securing passage of the GPO Access Act (PL 103-40) in 1993. Patricia Glass Schuman, at the time president of ALA, and Nancy Kranich, then chair of ALA's Ad Hoc Subcommittee on Government Information, led the winning effort on behalf of ALA. The award-winning GPO Access system is now an Internet information service providing free electronic access to information products produced by the federal government and a key component of public access to government information in electronic formats.

FirstGov

Another development on the federal information front requires careful attention. In September 2000, President Clinton launched FirstGov, a centralized Web portal (www.firstgov.gov), to search the government's 27 million Web pages and provide online access to government services. It was suggested that this system would allow people to track their Social Security benefits or download tax forms, among other things. A wealth of government information and services can be located, but there are operational and policy issues that need to be addressed.

On an operational level, FirstGov has been developed separately and independently from the federal information-producing agencies and the major government information-dissemination programs. The portal's search engine was developed and donated by a private charitable organization, the Federal Search Foundation (Fed-Search). Coordination with federal agencies such as GPO needs to occur to ensure that the public has comprehensive access and to clarify the roles and relationships of the various programs. Although this operational issue and others, such as the relevancy of search results and comprehensiveness of the coverage of government information and services, may be corrected over time, policy issues are particularly challenging.

The FirstGov project has been discussed as an integral part of the movement toward electronic government. It is a presidential initiative to make government more accessible and accountable to citizens. However, there is no legislation authorizing the program, which calls into question its long-term sustainability.

Another major issue is who "owns" the indexed database developed by Fed-Search. While the government information on FirstGov is in the public domain, without charge, and publicly accessible, the indexed database is provided by Fed-Search and maintained by a private contractor that provides search engine services. When the responsibility for the search engine is transferred to the federal government within three years, who will have control of the database, the federal government or Fed-Search?

Still another question arises about funding for this program. As of spring 2000 there is no dedicated funding for this project as there must be if fees for its use are to be avoided and the program is to be sustained over time. The government is paying $4.1 million to Fed-Search to maintain the site for two to three years, after which the government can rebid or take over the arrangement. By contrast, the FDLP is authorized by statute, and an appropriation for its operation is made every year.

Preservation of and permanent public access to the information products and services on FirstGov are a major policy issue. How to do this remains unresolved.

Privacy is still another concern. Although FirstGov includes a clear privacy statement and the U.S. Office of Management and Budget directs federal agencies not to track users of government Web sites, many Americans are concerned about potential misuse of personal information if they use government services over the Internet.

Looking to the Future

The future of public access to government information will be increasingly through electronic formats, particularly online. GPO and librarians have worked hard to make this transition a coherent and balanced one over an appropriate time frame. In 1995, Congress directed GPO to conduct a cooperative study to identify measures necessary for a successful transition to a more electronic FDLP. The comprehensive report identifies many policy issues that effect the public, depository libraries, GPO, publishing agencies, the National Archives and Records Administration, and the private sector.[7] Of concern then, and even more so today, is permanent public access to authentic, official government information given the accelerated trend toward electronic dissemination. Federal agencies are responsible for the authenticity, currency, and availability of their electronic information products. Historically, depository libraries have been responsible for retaining tangible government information products for free use directly by the public. In the electronic era, agencies that created the information might store it, or GPO might, or an agreement may be made with third parties (including libraries) to keep the information. Otherwise the electronic databases will be lost.

The responsibilities of depository libraries and the federal government are changing. GPO developed a plan in 1998 to address these critical issues, *Managing the FDLP Electronic Collection: A Policy and Planning Document.*[8] As the FDLP grows increasingly more reliant on online electronic information, more attention must be paid to ensuring the ongoing accessibility of government electronic products. Librarians and the public cannot leave these policy decisions to chance, but must work to influence the outcome.

When Thomas Jefferson wrote to Richard Price in 1789, "Whenever the people are well-informed, they can be trusted with their own government," he foresaw how important government information would be to American democracy.[9] Libraries and librarians support democracy by playing a key role in providing public access to government information. It is the responsibility of all Americans to ensure that this essential resource continues to be available on a no-fee basis in libraries and that it is preserved for the use of our own and future generations.

Notes

1.   The American Library Association Washington Office Newsline, ALAWON, is located at www.ala.org/washoff/alawon. Numerous articles document ALA's urging readers to contact Congress concerning appropriations for the Federal Depository Library Program. See: ALAWON 9, no. 10 (Feb. 11, 2000); no. 40 (May 3, 2000); no. 41 (May 5, 2000); no. 42 (May 9, 2000); no. 44 (May 16, 2000); no. 45 (May 18, 2000); no. 47 (May 19, 2000); no. 48 (May 24, 2000); no. 49 (May 26, 2000); no. 50 (June 1, 2000); no. 55 (June 20, 2000); no. 57 (June 23, 2000); no. 60 (July 19, 2000); no. 65 (July 31, 2000); no. 71 (Sept. 11, 2000); and no. 71 [sic] (Sept. 21, 2000).

2.   Letter from Francis J. Buckley Jr., Superintendent of Documents, to library directors, August 25, 2000 (Washington, D.C.: U.S. Government Printing Office).

3.   James Madison, *Writings* (New York: The Library of America, 1999), 790.

4.   Depository Library Council, *Fulfilling Madison's Vision: The Federal Depository Library Program* (Washington, D.C.: U.S. Government Printing Office, 1996).

5.   44 USC 1901.

6.   John N. Berry III, "Bernadine Hoduski Speaks: The Current Crisis in Government Information," *Library Journal* 120, no. 9 (May 15, 1995): 28–29.

7.   *Study to Identify Measures Necessary for a Successful Transition to a More Electronic Federal Depository Library Program: As Required by Legislative Branch Appropriations Act, 1996, Public Law 104-53: Report to the Congress* (Washington, D.C.: U.S. Government Printing Office, 1996).

8.   *Managing the FDLP Electronic Collection: A Policy and Planning Document* (Washington, D.C.: U.S. Government Printing Office, 1998).

9.   www.monticello.org/resources/interests.

Information Ethics and Government Power

From the White House E-Mail to the Stasi Files

Thomas S. Blanton

At the cornerstone of democracy lies a fundamental code of information ethics. By this, I mean information ethics in the broadest sense, not only the moment-to-moment decisions we all make, the situational ethics of information management and public service and privacy-versus-access and openness-versus-candor and so forth. Perhaps more important are the ethics at the heart of our raison 'd'être, our vocation, the fundamental morality of our calling as librarians and information professionals, one might almost say the spiritual content of work, our work with information.

This article presents two case studies of information ethics and government power as the basis for a larger argument about the democratic role of libraries and librarians. First, this article details the cutting-edge case of the White House e-mail, which brings into sharp focus some fundamental ethical issues of government accountability, archival practice, and personal privacy.

Second, this article describes the even-more-troubling case of the Stasi files, that massive toxic waste dump of surveillance and slander amassed by the East German secret police and tens of thousands of informers over fifty years. Here we find the core issues of ethics, accountability, openness, and privacy taken to a totalitarian extreme.

Third, the issue of the Stasi files leads directly to the primary challenge for any analysis of ethics, morality, and democracy in the twentieth century, and that is the ultimate horror of the concentration camps, not only Hitler's death camps but also Stalin's gulag. What does this have to do with information ethics? It may well be, as the Maine lobsterman said to the tourist, "you cain't get they-uh from hea-uh." But it is precisely by looking deeply into moral extremes that we can find some guideposts for ordinary life, for day-to-day ethics, and for the heart of the work with information that we do every day.

The White House E-Mail

An enlightening place to begin is with the White House e-mail. An obscure agency inside the White House made what it considered to be a routine ethical decision that ultimately broke open the Iran-contra scandal. Here is how it happened, and the landmark litigation that arose thereafter.

Back in November 1986, President Reagan and Attorney General Meese came down to the White House press room to announce they had just fired the president's national security adviser, John Poindexter, and were sending a staffer named Oliver North back to the Marine Corps because the two had conspired to sell arms to Iran and use the profits to support the contras in Nicaragua. The White House Communications Agency (known as WOCKA) could have just done business as usual. That meant every Saturday they backed up the entire White House computer system onto computer tapes, all the e-mail and databases, and every third Saturday they recycled the oldest tapes, overwriting them with the new data.

But that week in November, the WOCKA commander, Lt. Col. Patrick McGovern, stopped the recycling program for the month. Thinking there might be investigations that would need the information, he set aside all the backup tapes for November 1986, and when investigators came calling, they found out the details of what Poindexter and North were up to, and that pretty much everything they had done, they had done on orders from the president.

The White House had started its first e-mail system in 1982 as a prototype that linked various cabinet departments; but a fully operational system— including all the National Security Council staff—began only in April 1985. In 1985 and 1986, e-mail had become North and Poindexter's favorite means of communication, allowing them a back-channel called "Private Blank Check" that avoided the central bureaucracy at the White House. You have to appreciate these government code words, Private Blank Check, that say it all. By the end of the Reagan presidency in January 1989, more than seven million digital e-mail messages resided in the various White House systems.

As two of the most prolific e-mailers in the entire U.S. government, North and Poindexter had a lot to hide. During the weekend before they were fired in November 1986, Oliver North punched the "delete" button, and he had to delete them one at a time. He eliminated 750 out of 758 e-mail messages saved in his "user area" of the White House system memory; and he believed that they were gone for good. John Poindexter knew about the WOCKA backup process, but he thought he was still covered because of the recycling of the tapes. Poindexter, one at a time, deleted 5,012 out of 5,062 e-mail messages in his own user area that weekend, and he believed that even the backup versions would be automatically blipped as well within a few weeks. He was wrong, because WOCKA did the right thing.

The Iran-contra-related e-mail was set aside, sent off to investigators, where it provided the core evidence for the whole scandal. There's no room for those details here, except to say that the whole episode put us on notice. There was gold in them thar hills.

So in January 1989, as President Reagan was about to leave office, his staff were packing all their boxes and shipping their documents off to the archives. One of the National Security Archive researchers, Eddie Becker, got a little curious about how the National Archives was going to preserve all the other White House e-mail. To Eddie's enormous surprise, the National Archives and Records Administration (NARA) told him they did not consider the White House e-mail to qualify as "records" worthy of preservation. They told him the Iran-contra-related e-mail was all set aside for the ongoing legal cases, but the other e-mail tapes and hard drives from the Reagan White House were scheduled for "disposal" on the night before George Bush's inauguration on the orders of the President's national security adviser, a fellow by the name of Colin Powell.

The news set off a frenzy in our offices. The archive's founder and then-director, Scott Armstrong, was a veteran of the Senate Watergate committee staff and *The Washington Post*; and the parallels were not hard for any of the rest of us to grasp, either. Here was a potential "gap," not of eighteen-and-a-half minutes, as on the Nixon tapes, but of years, involving millions of messages. After a fruitless meeting with top NARA officials on Wednesday, January 18, we huddled in the hallway only a couple of flights up from the Declaration of Independence. Fewer than thirty hours were left before the destruction deadline, so desperation measures were called for. We decided to go to court for an injunction.

That night, we pulled together every piece of information ever published about the White House e-mail system, researched the requirements of the federal records preservation laws, drafted legal papers and affidavits and, as our ultimate insurance policy, designed a series of Freedom of Information Act requests for the entire corpus of e-mail tapes—anything that would give us standing to stop the destruction.

The judge on call the next day at U.S. District Court, the late Barrington D. Parker, called our hearing to order at 5:15 P.M. We were expecting some assistant U.S. attorney to represent the government, but to our surprise, in walked the acting attorney general of the United States, John Bolton. We knew we had won when Bolton said the White House staff were just taking the pictures off their walls, and Judge Parker said, "They are not seeking a restraining order against taking pictures off the wall." Bolton could only claim that "[If the plaintiffs prevail] it would be as if the halls of the White House were filled with furniture from the outgoing administration."

For the entire duration of the Bush administration, from January 1989 to January 1993, the government did not come up with a single argument for e-mail destruction beyond the one John Bolton so lamely offered to Judge Parker. No one at the White House ever seemed to notice that departing tenants neither leave their furniture in the halls, nor pile it on the lawn to burn it. But the courts noticed. In January 1993, Judge Charles Richey ruled that e-mail, including the Bush White House tapes as well, had to be treated like all other government records—covered by the laws, appraised by archivists, and preserved for posterity where appropriate.

Apparently, the Bush White House staff panicked at this point. Out of arrogance or disdain, they had made no plans to save the tapes, and they dreaded the idea of the new Clinton staff pawing through the system. So on January 19, Inauguration Eve 1993, they staged a midnight ride to round up the computer tapes and put them beyond the law. On White House orders, a task force of NARA employees hurriedly rented vans, raced to the Old Executive Office Building, hand-scribbled makeshift inventories, and worked through the night to load thousands of computer tapes into cardboard boxes and haul them away. A subsequent memo from this group complained that due to haste and the lack of bubble-wrap, a number of tapes were simply stacked in boxes with no padding. Several of the tapes were damaged irreparably. The whole process violated NARA's own procedures for taking custody of electronic information.

Several weeks later, through discovery, we found out that the midnight ride was a sideshow to the main event: a secret deal between President Bush and the archivist of the United States, Don W. Wilson. Signed in the last few hours before Bill Clinton's inauguration, the agreement purported to give President Bush control over all the computer tapes, ignoring the Presidential Records Act of 1978, which precludes such a claim. Judge Richey's January 1993 ruling already held that Wilson had abdicated his duties as archivist by approving the original decision to destroy the Reagan White House e-mail. Under fire for the secret deal and for management problems during his tenure at NARA,

Wilson then resigned as archivist and accepted a new job as head of the George Bush Presidential Library to be built at Texas A & M University.

The incoming Clinton administration could have opted for openness. Instead, Clinton-appointed officials marched into federal appeals court in the spring of 1993 to support not only the Bush and Reagan arguments for destruction of the e-mail, but also the now-infamous Bush-Wilson agreement. *The Washington Post* paraphrased top Clinton aide George Stephanopolous as saying, "like Bush's White House, the Clinton White House does not want a succeeding, potentially unfriendly administration pawing over its computer memos."[1] In August 1993, a unanimous appeals panel ruled that the White House e-mail qualified as records, was covered by the records laws, and had to be preserved. Faced with an unbroken string of resounding legal defeats, the Clinton administration finally gave up the preservation argument and decided not to appeal to the Supreme Court.

They had other ideas. Two of them worked: The courts allowed them to declare the National Security Council no longer an agency covered by the Freedom of Information Act. Another court allowed NARA to use a general record schedule to allow wholesale destruction of e-mail and electronic records as long as the historically valuable items have been printed out. This is not just silly, but counterproductive, since the electronic links among records are themselves valuable and unique, and future access and searching will require redigitization at great cost.

Why did they all fight so hard, and for so long? There are three levels of answers. The most valid reason really was privacy. The authors of all that e-mail did not believe that any of it would ever see the light of day, and precisely for that reason, the White House e-mail is a historian's dream, filling in for all that is lost over the telephone. Historian's dream and privacy nightmare. When I published the greatest hits of the White House e-mail in my book-and-disk package five years ago, I tried to address such concern by focusing on policy instead of prurience, and even where I found gossip, emphasizing the e-mail messages that illuminated daily life at the office instead of officials' personal lives. I believe that effective privacy protections are both necessary for and complementary to effective open government processes; as plaintiffs, we did not challenge a single one of the government's privacy claims on the e-mail.

For the National Archives, sad to say, I think they just did not have any truly satisfactory answer to the long-term preservation problems posed by electronic records, so they threw up their hands and went along with the White House. Nobody has the answers completely, but that shouldn't keep us from rising to the challenge.

For the White House, it was a matter of power. Presidents Reagan, Bush, and Clinton wanted to control the information generated on their internal computer systems precisely because it was so candid. Too candid for comfort. Fundamentally, power in the public arena derives from control over the debate, the ability to define the terms and frame the parameters and control the information. So I am proud to say that my little public interest archive helped shake that power and open some hidden histories that the powerful would rather not see public.

We had the great advantage of working in a democracy, and the issues get much more difficult when we look at the confrontation with totalitarianism. However frustrated one gets with the U.S. government, waiting nine years for a Freedom of Information Act (FOIA) response, litigating for eight years whether having a printout of a valuable record means you should destroy the electronic version—even with all that, I never had the Stasi bugging my bathroom. I never had to face the choice, under coercion, of whether to inform on friends.

The Stasi Files

In 1989, around the time we stood up in front of the appeals court the first time on the e-mail case, people in Germany were taking pickaxes to the Berlin Wall. And after the Wall fell, East Germans in particular, led by human rights activists and dissidents, stormed the offices of the secret police, the Stasi, stopped the shredding, and seized the files. The first non-Communist government in East Germany vested control of the Stasi files in one of the Stasi's most outspoken critics, the dissident Lutheran pastor Joachim Gauck. And in one of the few remnants of the short-lived, pre-unification, non-Communist East Germany, the new Germany's parliament in December 1991 ratified Gauck's role as commissioner of the files, and gave him a staff and a budget to begin, as he says, "to shed light on all the dark pages of the former system."

The law decreed three core purposes: to organize the documents to allow individuals to see their own files; to examine the files of possible Stasi officers and informers; and to inform the public about the Stasi's structure and its cooperation with the Communist Party. Gauck also implemented a kind of sliding scale for personal privacy, the single most important ethical issue in the Stasi files. Victims, but not third parties, got to see their files with the names of Stasi officers and informants included. This has an interesting parallel here in the United States, in libel law, where public figures have a different and higher standard (malicious disregard for the truth) to meet in order to prove libel.

In East Germany, the Stasi informants lost their privacy, and tragedies did result. Gerhard Riege, a member of Parliament from eastern Germany and long-time Communist, hung himself in February 1992 after Stasi files that were reported in the press indicated he had been a Stasi informer in the 1950s. "I don't have the strength to live and fight," his suicide note read, "I'm afraid of the publicity."[2] Vera Wollenberger, member of Parliament and long-time eastern German human rights activist, spent hours poring over her voluminous Stasi file, only to realize that many intimate details therein could only have come from her husband, whom the files then confirmed was a Stasi informant. "What I have had to go through," she wrote later, "I wouldn't wish on anybody, not even my worst enemy." Wollenberger and her husband have since divorced.

Obscured by these horror stories, however, is a success story, a model process that removed the Stasi files from political control and that has encouraged real debate on the nature of collaboration and of justice. In fact, the Germans have accomplished a shift in power over the secret files that no other former Communist country has yet undertaken, and that many have deliberately refused.

The bedrock of the Stasi Records Law is the independence of what is now known as the "Gauck Authority." Elsewhere in Central Europe and the former Soviet Union, the secret police files remained in the custody of the interior ministries or the successor bureaucracies of the secret police themselves. The result has been systematic disaster as well as individual tragedy: Wholesale politically manipulated leaks of information, arbitrary and capricious accusations and slanders, and government processes shrouded in secrecy and eroding in trust. Even Lech Walesa, the Nobel Prize-winning hero of Solidarity, found himself faced with a leaked "confession" he had signed under pressure in 1970, with his political opponents claiming this meant he had been an informer.[3]

The contrast with the Gauck Authority's approach is instructive. Instead of a flat "yes" or "no" judgment on someone's collaboration with the Stasi, Gauck's staff produces a full report on request from the courts or the government or prospective employers. The reports not only excerpt the files, but also often include the complete texts of documents cited. When *Der Spiegel* asked Gauck whether a certain prominent church official who later became governor of Brandenburg state had been a Stasi informer, Gauck replied:

> Please note that I presented a 61-page research report on this question, to which are appended numerous annexes in the form of documents and explanations. I am not prepared to answer this question for your magazine in a single sentence.[4]

Many former dissidents disagree with the Gauck approach, using the metaphor of the toxic waste dump and advocating the sealing or even the destruction of the secret police files. But the files have already seeped out, through leaks or through formal purging processes in the former Communist countries. Without correction and argument with the files, what is left is the public pronouncement of secret authority, the flat yes or no from the Czech Interior Ministry, for example. Destroying the files shifts power to the new mythmakers, in particular, any demagogue who wants to make up a past, as Vladimir Zhirinovsky has tried to do in Russia and Slobodan Milosevic managed for so long in the former Yugoslavia. Even sealing the files cedes power, giving rein to the demagogues and shutting out the individuals who want or need a coming-to-terms in their own lifetimes. The Czech writer Milan Kundera said it best: "The struggle of the individual against power is the struggle of memory against forgetting."

The Stasi solution is not perfect. Perfection is impossible when balancing such complexities as the individual victim's privacy and compensatory interests together with the societal interests for truth-telling, history, retribution, and deterrent. But the Stasi solution accomplishes some fundamental shifts in power over the files—out of the government's hands, partially into the hands of the victims, and even partially out of the hands of the Stasi agents who created the files, by the avoidance of simple yes and no, by the provision of context and complexity.

The Stasi solution points us toward an answer of sorts for the twentieth century's greatest moral challenge. This is part three of this article.

Totalitarian Crimes

Now, ordinarily one cannot come to grips with the horror of the concentration camps. Usually one does not even try, because it is too difficult to carry around that much evil and still keep functioning. This is a natural and very human response, almost a need to forget. Very few of us are, or can be, Mother Teresa. But not long ago in Poland, I visited Birkenau, the industrial death camp the Nazis built when Auschwitz's murder rate was too slow. It was a warm and sunny day, with blue skies over Birkenau.

I felt compelled to look closely at the experience of the camps to see what lessons they had for us, we who think we live in a completely different world. I read memoirs of survivors and oral histories of the guards and commanders. Along the way I found a wonderful book by the Bulgarian-French writer Tsvetan Todorov called *Facing the Extreme* (New York: Metropolitan/Henry Holt, 1996), that took those memoirs and testimonies and turned them into a moral analysis of our time.

For Todorov, most of the victims were "neither saints nor heroes," and most of the camp guards for Stalin and Hitler were "neither monsters nor beasts." Rather, he found in the camps ordinary virtues and ordinary vices. The ordinary virtues fall into a certain hierarchy, corresponding to the three pronouns, I, you, they. From the subject's point of view, dignity is the primary virtue. From the human community's point of view, the most important virtue is caring. But from a world historical perspective, it is the life of the mind that counts most because the effects of its products are the most lasting: centuries after their deaths we are grateful to Plato and Shakespeare for having left the world more beautiful and more intelligible than they found it. Artistic and intellectual activity is undertaken on everyone's behalf, whereas caring may have only a few beneficiaries and dignity only one, the self.

Ordinary vices are behavioral traits that are equally common to all and that do not necessarily make us exceptional beings, monsters, or beasts. They include the fragmentation of behavior, or the disconnection of conduct from conscience; the depersonalization of beings caught in the chains of instrumentalist thinking; and the enjoyment of power.

Yet these vices are not enough to explain the ultimate evil of the camps. One Nazi commander long ago testified that "there is a limit to the number of people you can kill out of hatred or a lust for slaughter"—so much for fanaticism and sadism—"but there is no limit to the number you can kill in the cold, systematic manner of the military categorical imperative."[5]

In order to explain an evil of this magnitude, we must thus look not to the character of the individual but to that of the society that imposes such categorical imperatives. The answer is a point of departure, not an end point: the societal trait that allows such crimes to be carried out is totalitarianism, the only attribute that Nazi Germany shares with the Soviet Union.

The novelty of totalitarian crimes lies less in the fact that heads of state could conceive of such projects—there have surely been others throughout history who have fantasized about exterminating substantial portions of humanity—than in the fact that these men were able to realize their projects, an accomplishment that required the collaboration of thousands and thousands of individuals acting on the state's behalf and at its behest. And once the totalitarian system is in place, the vast majority of the population—people like you and me—are at risk of becoming accomplices in its crimes; that is all it takes.

People living in democracies are accustomed to ideological pluralism (and also to public access to many different sources of information). That is why in these countries the danger of fanatical indoctrination is smaller, although not altogether nonexistent. As for professionalism and instrumental thinking, we are certainly acquainted with them too, but unlike fanaticism, they are traits we also admire. In democratic societies, fragmentation and depersonalization do not kill, of course, but they threaten our humanity nonetheless.

But this difference in information terms goes to the core of preventing future camps. After all, the proper functioning of concentration camps requires that neither the inmates—or witnesses—nor even the guards have precise knowledge of what is going on. Therefore, the first weapon against them is the collection and diffusion of information. We know how meticulous the Nazis were in guarding the secret of the "final solution" and how systematically they worked to eliminate all traces of their deeds. As for the Communist regimes, their entire existence was predicated on the pervasiveness of state propaganda. It is no accident that Stalin and Hitler waged a war of information alongside their wars of conquest. The distinctive feature of totalitarianism is that it attempts to control the life of society in its totality, to make everything and everyone dependent on the will of those who wield power.

The Cornerstone of Democracy

If the camps are at one end of the spectrum, then what do we find at the other end? For me, at the other end, is the library—the archetypal combination of ordinary virtues, individual dignity, caring, and the life of the mind. This is not a heroic concept, but an ordinary one, one that provides us with ethical guidance for our lives.

I do not include here in the concept of library just any information service, certainly not the inevitable commodification of information that works however well to ensure the production and wide diffusion of knowledge. I do not even include the Internet or the Web, even though they contribute significantly to the decentralization of power and the life of the mind.

If someone were to ask me why people behave morally, I would have to answer in two ways: first, because we feel profound joy in doing so and, second, because in doing so we conform to the very idea of humanity and so take part in the realization of that idea. That is the core of our calling, as librarians, archivists, information professionals, to conduct ourselves with dignity, to care and to share, and to nourish the life of the mind. That is our contribution at the cornerstone of democracy.

Notes

1. George Lardner Jr., "Justice Officials Back Transfer of Bush Records; Clinton White House Said to Favor Protection of Computerized Presidential Memos," *Washington Post,* May 18, 1993, A6.
2. Stephen Kinzer, "Germans Anguish over Police Files," *New York Times,* Feb. 20, 1992, A10.
3. Stephen Engelberg, "The Mood Turns Darker in East Europe's Drama," *New York Times,* June 14, 1992, section 4, 4.
4. "Official Defends Stasi File Use, Procedure," *Der Spiegel,* May 4, 1992, 31–35.
5. Arthur Seyss-Inquart (Nazi governor of Austria and Holland), quoted in Tzvetan Todorov, *Facing the Extreme* (New York: Metropolitan/Henry Holt, 1996), 125.

Libraries

Where the First Amendment Lives

Paul K. McMasters

Why is it that a nation so enamored of the notion of freedom of expression is so unnerved by its reality? Having built a society on the idea that each member of that society has a right to his say, we nevertheless continue to fashion arguments for silencing certain voices. The attacks are constant and bruising. These days, no form of expression is safe from the savaging, whether art, literature, music, television, movies, the Internet, or video games. No type of speech is beyond censure, whether sexual, violent, hateful, unpatriotic, coarse—anything, in other words, that upsets, displeases, or offends.

Rationales for these assaults range from civility in public discourse to safety for our children. More often than not, however, the unsuppressed voice of the censor is raised in the service of a majoritarian view of what's proper and acceptable. In the United States, of course, that view is at once an affront and a challenge to First Amendment principles and traditions. Of course, there is nothing new about the all-too-human desire to control what others see, hear, think, and say. But the First Amendment is supposed to provide a caution to such thinking. It hasn't. In fact, the urge to silence speech often seems most virulent in the very institutions where one would expect to find at least modest deference to First Amendment rights and values—Congress, state legislatures, local governments, religious organizations, even academe. The unsurprising exception to this tendency among our major institutions is the library. The library, after all, is a monument to all the best impulses in the human mind and spirit. The library is where people are transformed because knowledge is treasured. The library is a sanctuary for the First Amendment.

Unfortunately, the campaigns to suppress speech are neither far-removed nor abstract for the nation's librarians. They are ever mindful of their charge to protect the material they hold in our name for our benefit. So libraries and librarians have become a primary target for the censors. Policymakers propose and pass laws restricting libraries' ability to fully serve their communities. Citizens launch ballot initiatives to force limits on what libraries may offer patrons. Some of those very patrons go to court to challenge libraries' Internet access policies. Employees file hostile workplace grievances because of what patrons access on the Internet. Well-known talk show hosts excoriate libraries on radio and television, saying they are a haven for indecency and a hangout for perverts. All of these things conspire to interrupt, delay, or halt the libraries' civic and intellectual duty to satisfy the constitutional right of all citizens to maximum access to information.

Among all the shapes and forms expression takes on in the technological era, books remain the library's essential resource. Thus, books remain an object of wrath for would-be censors. Each year, hundreds of challenges are mounted against books ranging from perennial favorites like Mark Twain's *The Adventures of Huckleberry Finn* to contemporary bestsellers like David Guterson's *Snow Falling on Cedars*. Political leaders and ordinary citizens in at least twenty states have tried to get the popular Harry Potter books removed from library shelves as well as from classrooms and bookstores. Books are the love of librarians, and so they shudder as school officials cut and rip pages from texts, as judges jail comic book and magazine vendors, and as law enforcement authorities subpoena bookstore sales records.

But the book battles are not the only test for libraries. More and more, battles over the newest medium—the Internet—and the oldest taboo—sex—preoccupy librarians and their supporters. Today, the champions of decency seem to believe that while sexual material is bad in whatever medium it appears, it assumes a peculiar power on the Internet and a potent force in the library. In their view, Internet porn has the ability to leap unbidden from the bowels of the computer onto the screen, terrorizing children, traumatizing adults, and scandalizing anyone in the immediate vicinity. Thus, librarians face significant external and internal pressures to yield to demands to limit access to the Internet for all patrons.

In a series of rulings over the past few years, the courts have declared that Internet speech requires the same degree of First Amendment protection as written speech. Even so, "Net porn" is such a compelling issue that state and federal lawmakers propose hundreds of laws each year to regulate Internet speech. Government officials are ever mindful of the importance their constituents place on family values, religious righteousness, offended sensibilities, or protecting children from Internet content. So, directly or indirectly, ordinary citizens are the driving force behind the challenges to unrestricted access to Internet content. Good people with grave concerns are drawn to the issue because they care about their children. They charge that much of the Internet content is obscene, indecent, and harmful to children. Indeed, the issue is so emotionally gripping that more often than not legal, logical, and ethical niceties get lost in the debate.

At the local level, for example, those individuals and organizations pressing libraries to install filtering software on computers assert the problem but feel no need to demonstrate it. They seldom bother to discuss the issue with the library staff before declaring the threat exists. To them, the number of complaints by patrons or the amount and type of pornography allegedly accessible is immaterial. Quite often, it is enough for the would-be censors that they know someone who knows someone who has said the Internet is filled with smut and something must be done about it.

They are not too careful in defining the material they consider pornographic, either. They apparently believe that material as varied as lingerie ads, images of starlets in bikinis, and information about medical matters and alternative lifestyles is as noxious as hardcore content. They ignore the legal requirements involved in determining whether material is obscene or harmful to minors, instead insisting that librarians, patrons, parents, or citizen groups can make such determinations on their own.

No wonder that the people who work in, make policy for, or support the libraries are caught by surprise and, at any rate, are woefully unprepared to defend themselves when the Internet filtering campaign raises its divisive head. Invariably, the attack is swift, across-the-board, well organized, and well financed. The proponents tell tales of sexual horror rending the moral fabric of the community and endangering the children. By the time community leaders and library supporters muster a response, the problem is publicized, the solution determined, and the public mind fairly well made up.

A lot is on the line in these local struggles. If a library wavers, folds, or suffers defeat anywhere, the fallout reverberates across the nation. National political leaders are emboldened and encouraged to propose even more policies and laws regulating freedom of expression. These community campaigns have their origins in humankind's origins. From the time we could communicate we have worked to control that communication. That is why censorship is so persistent and pervasive, even today, even in a free and open society like our own.

The censors have been among us from the beginning, exhorting us to cower like brutes in caves, snorting and stamping in fear at the wondrous things dancing outside in the sunlight. They urged us to take the torch to books in the Dark Ages. Now, they taunt us into taking a filter to the Internet in the information age. Speech is forever vulnerable because the censor dwells deep within each of us. Sometimes it doesn't take much to fan into flames those book-burning desires smoldering in our breasts. It isn't that most people consider themselves censors; it is just that they seldom protest too loudly or at all when the real censors go to work.

Censors are threatened by the power of words. It is an impressive power. Words cannot be directed nor their impact predicted. They go where they will. They do what they will. Words not only facilitate but validate the human struggle to discern and distill life's goodness and worth. In the process, knowledge is acquired, wisdom formed, and passion inflamed. Those who intrude on that process damage truth and ruin reason. Those who dare to strangle words have their hands on the throat of all speakers; left to their work, they will snuff out that which may be beyond our grasp but is gladly embraced by our imaginings.

For their part, the censors believe they can predict the effect of words on the minds of others. They believe they, and only they, should determine what is acceptable speech and what is not. They believe they, and only they, can wield the dull blade of their own fears and prejudices to lop off the branches of intellectual freedom with no harm to the intellect or to the freedom. That turns out to be an illusion, of course. To prune one branch of this particular tree is to occasion a withering of all branches and the onset of cultural debilitation.

The prospect of such happenings, even on a local level, should galvanize those who temporize in their opposition to the censors. Too few Americans have the resources, the stamina, or the outrage it takes to keep the censor at bay. The fact is that there is much we can to do to reassert the primacy of First Amendment rights and values in our libraries. We can start by being a little less generous in "seeing the censors' point." Anything of consequence in the care of libraries offends someone somewhere. We must make it plain to our political, educational, and moral leaders that to remove or restrict access to controversial material is to invite the ultimate suppression of all material.

We must remember that—as much as they are the principles we have learned to live by—negotiation, compromise, and tolerance seldom work well when it comes to censorship. Censors are hard-eyed and single-minded. They are never satisfied. Rather than being mollified, they are encouraged by tolerance and understanding. When we feel their pain, we feed their fervor.

Finally, we must be prepared to defend bad words for good principles. As perverse, as disruptive, as upsetting as the arrangement of some words and images can be, we must rise to their defense with as much passion and conviction as we do for more acceptable expression. When we have the intellectual courage to allow the good with the bad, we can see that good is more real, more desirable, and more attainable for our having had the opportunity to compare one with the other. As surely as misanthropic expression attracts the weakened mind and repels the fearful mind, it quickens the civilized mind.

One of the main reasons that efforts to stop the censors are ineffective is that those who oppose censorship rely on good hearts and common sense to work such things out. They fail to recognize the depth of guilt felt by parents who yearn for technology to help them guide and protect their children from an overwhelming and threatening world. They fail to measure the scope of Internet illiteracy in the general populace. They fail to understand the power and the passion generated by the fear of sexual and other offensive speech.

Further, there is the inevitable leadership vacuum in such matters. Elected officials want to be on the right side of this issue, meaning the side of values, decency, and simple solutions. Community leaders are slow to get involved and quick to compromise. Religious leaders don't want to be seen as soft on porn. This, in turn, allows the community to avoid the larger issues behind the campaign to regulate Internet content in the public library, for example.

These campaigns are not just about sexual speech. They also are about hate speech, violence, feminism, New Age religion, alternative lifestyles, and other kinds of expression some find offensive or inimical to their view of the world. Such campaigns are not just about the Internet. They also are about the library's video offerings, its magazines and journals, and the books it makes available. These campaigns aren't just about the library, either. They also are about schools, museums, and other institutions. They are about who sets and controls the intellectual, cultural, and moral agenda for the community. They are not about protecting the children as much as they are about limiting access to all in the name of the children.

The welfare of the children, of course, raises the painful question: "What are we doing to our children in the name of protecting them?" The answer is as painful as the question. We are teaching them to do whatever is necessary to win. We are teaching them that librarians are evil people and libraries are dangerous places. We are teaching them that what we can't accomplish by reason and persuasion we should accomplish by coercion. We are teaching them that we have so little faith in our own parenting that we'll let computer software define and enforce our standards for us. We are teaching them that it is all right to deny others the free speech we value for ourselves.

What we need to teach our children—and example is the best teacher—is that all of us must be wary when passionate appeals are made to our worst instincts, our deepest fears, and our meanest motives in an effort to scuttle fundamental democratic principles. What we need to teach ourselves is that we betray our values when we try to force them on everyone else.

The First Amendment stands firmly against the censor's arrogance. It guarantees that the majority will not dictate the speech, thought, or taste of the individual. It warns that the democratic ideal fails its magnificent promise unless we recognize that fear and ignorance are never a match for courage and confidence—and, yes, confrontation—in the defense of free expression.

It is not enough to teach the First Amendment. Or to defend it when it seems convenient. We must model the First Amendment, also. Not just for the kids or our colleagues. But for the censors, too.

Censorship is always imposed for the best of reasons with the worst of results. No matter what technologies we may concoct to communicate our speech, or what new era we may find ourselves in, the nature of speech itself never changes. It must be free to be meaningful.

The First Amendment, Libraries, and Democracy

Susan B. Kretchmer

Scarcely any question arises in the United States which does not become, sooner or later, a subject of judicial debate . . .
—*Alexis de Tocqueville*[1]

The Constitution of the United States, together with the federal laws and treaties passed in accordance with its provisions, is the supreme law of the land. Since it was ratified in 1788, however, the scope and application of the words of the Constitution have changed. This evolution has occurred in several ways. The ten constitutional amendments that comprise the Bill of Rights, guaranteeing American citizens all the privileges and protections believed due the people of a democratic nation, are usually considered to be the most important additions. Also, federal laws enacted by Congress have worked out the details of the broad framework of government promulgated by the Constitution and furthered its meaning. In addition, court decisions, especially those of the final arbiter, the Supreme Court, have provided clarification and extended the words of the Constitution to new situations.

Nevertheless, laws and courts do not exist in a vacuum. Indeed, the greatest impetus for widening the sweep of the Constitution has frequently been the altered customs and usage that have accompanied the movement toward social and political reform. Many of the early settlers who came to the United States hoped to forge a republic based upon the rights of the individual. During and immediately after colonial days, various democratic institutions were established, including public libraries, but much remained to be done. For example, men were allowed to own slaves, voting rights depended on property ownership, and women were not permitted to vote. Reform in state and national laws began as soon as America was established as a nation. Subsequently, after the Civil War, slavery was abolished; by 1890, property requirements for voting had been removed; and in 1920, women won the right to vote. Similarly, social and political movements have brought many reforms since 1920, including workmen's compensation and minimum wage laws; child labor limitations; pensions for old-age, widows, and orphans; and prohibition in 1920 as well as its repeal in 1933.

Stating simply that "Congress shall make no law respecting an establishment of religion, or prohibiting the free exercise thereof; or abridging the freedom of speech, or of the press; or the right of the people peaceably to assemble, and to petition the Government for a redress of grievances," the First Amendment signifies the very foundation of our democratic process and the mandate for libraries as the cornerstone of democracy. Originally applicable only to the federal government, these First Amendment guarantees were extended by the Fourteenth Amendment, added to the Constitution in 1868, to protect citizens from oppression by state governments or any other agencies. Although none of the rights guaranteed by the First Amendment can be regarded as absolute, they hold a preferred position in the Constitutional scheme, and few restrictions on them are permitted.

Yet, the evolution of First Amendment rights and their interpretation by the courts, from their adoption as part of the Bill of Rights in 1791 to the present, has been inextricably bound to the major social and political issues that have been part of the growth and development of our nation. This essay considers five landmark court cases involving freedom of expression in libraries. More than that, through the interaction with the changing fabric of American society, these cases demonstrate the centrality of the library to all our ideas about the heart of a democracy.

Brown v. Louisiana

In *Brown, et al. v. Louisiana* (383 U.S. 131 [1966]), the civil rights struggles that rocked 1960s America intersected with First Amendment rights and the notion of the public library as a public forum. This case came to the U.S. Supreme Court as the fourth suspect conviction in little more than four years under Louisiana's breach of the peace statute; the prior cases that required judicial review involved sit-ins by African Americans at lunch counters catering only to whites (*Garner v. Louisiana*, 368 U.S. 157 [1961]); a sit-in in a "whites only" waiting room at a bus depot (*Taylor v. Louisiana*, 370 U.S. 154 [1962]); and a demonstration by African Americans on public streets near a courthouse and jail (*Cox v. Louisiana*, 379 U.S. 536 [1965]). The civil rights context shifted to the public library on March 7, 1964, in Clinton, Louisiana, when five African American men entered the tiny adult reading and service room of the Audubon Regional Library, which was operated on a segregated basis.

Brown requested a book from the library assistant on duty. After checking the card catalogue and finding that the library did not own the book, the assistant advised Brown that she was requesting the book from the State Library and that when it arrived he would be notified so that he could either pick it up from the bookmobile that served "Negros" or have it mailed to him. She then asked the men to leave the library. Displaying no disruptive conduct, Brown sat down while his four companions stood near him. When they did not leave after they were also asked by the regional librarian and the sheriff, the men were arrested and subsequently convicted of violating the Louisiana breach of peace statute for congregating in the public library and refusing to leave when ordered to do so.

In a 5-4 decision, the Supreme Court reversed the convictions and declared that the Louisiana statute unconstitutionally contravened the African American men's First and Fourteenth Amendment rights of freedom of speech and assembly to peacefully protest the library's infringement of civil rights and to petition for redress of grievances. The Court opinion written by Justice Fortas explains that:

> It is an unhappy circumstance that the locus of these events was a public library—a place dedicated to quiet, to knowledge, and to beauty. It is sad commentary that this hallowed place . . . bore the ugly stamp of racism. It is sad, too, that it was a public library which, reasonably enough in the circumstances, was the stage for a confrontation between those discriminated against and the representatives of the offending parishes. . . . A State or its instrumentality may, of course, regulate the use of its libraries or other public facilities. But it must do so in a reasonable and nondiscriminatory manner, equally applicable to all and administered with equality to all. It may not do so as to some and not as to all. It may not provide certain facilities for whites and others for Negroes. And it may not invoke regulations as to use—whether they are ad hoc or general—as a pretext for pursuing those engaged in lawful, constitutionally protected exercise of their fundamental rights.

Thus, amidst the turbulent social change generated by the struggle for equal treatment in public facilities, *Brown v. Louisiana* affirmed the right of access to the public library in the context of the First Amendment guarantees of freedom of speech, assembly, and petition.

Board of Education v. Pico

In *Board of Education, Island Trees Union Free School District No. 26, et al. v. Pico, et al.* (457 U.S. 853 [1982]), First Amendment guarantees were tested in the perennially controversial social and political atmosphere surrounding children, school libraries, book banning, and the right to receive ideas and information. The case arose in 1976 when a local New York board of education rejected the recommendations of its "Book Review Committee," composed of parents and school staff, and ordered that nine books be removed from its high school and junior high school libraries. The Island Trees Board characterized the books as "anti-American, anti-Christian, anti-Sem[i]tic, and just plain filthy." A group of students then brought this action, contending that their First Amendment rights had been infringed.

In a 5-4 decision, the Supreme Court ruled in favor of the students. The plurality opinion, written by Justice Brennan, asserts that:

> the discretion of the States and local school boards in matters of education must be exercised in a manner that comports with the transcendent imperatives of the First Amendment. . . . In sum, just as access to ideas makes it possible for citizens generally to exercise their rights of free speech and press in a meaningful manner, such access prepares students for active and effective participation in the pluralistic, often contentious society in which they will soon be adult members. . . . [T]he special characteristics of the school *library* make that environment especially appropriate for the recognition of the First Amendment rights of students. . . . [I]n the school library a student can literally explore the unknown, and discover areas of interest and thought not covered by the prescribed curriculum. . . . Th[e] student learns that a library is a place to test or expand upon ideas presented to him, in or out of the classroom. . . . A school library, no less than any other public library, is a place dedicated to quiet, to knowledge, and to beauty. . . . [S]tudents must always remain free to inquire, to study and to evaluate, to gain new maturity and understanding. . . . The school library is the principal locus of such freedom (emphasis in original; internal quotation marks and citations omitted).

Thus, in the complex legal realm of children and schools, *Pico* affirmed the right to receive information through the library guaranteed by the First Amendment. In the process, the Court addressed significant issues related to the basic values of librarianship in a democracy. For example, substantial judicial consideration was given to the unique place of the library within the school environment. The plurality found that, as opposed to compulsory matters of curriculum in the classroom, the school library affords students a venue of entirely free choice for voluntary inquiry and enrichment. The Court also recognized the difference in a library between the studied decision to not acquire a book and the discretionary removal of a book from library shelves. As such,

Pico is a paradigmatic representation of the pivotal role of libraries for children, schools, and citizenship in a democracy rooted in freedom of expression.

American Council of the Blind v. Boorstin

In *American Council of the Blind, et al. v. Daniel J. Boorstin, Librarian of Congress* (644 F. Supp. 811 [1986]), the heated political debate that has continually resurfaced in America about sexuality and culture clashed with First Amendment doctrine about obscene materials, access to information through the library, and content-based restrictions. Courts have determined that *Playboy* magazine cannot be considered obscene material under the obscenity test that the Supreme Court established in *Miller v. California* (413 U.S. 15 [1973]) and, therefore, is constitutionally protected speech. From 1973 to 1985, the Library of Congress, through the National Library Service's Program for the Blind and Physically Handicapped, reproduced and distributed free copies of Braille editions of the textual portions of *Playboy*. In fact, *Playboy* was one of the most popular magazines in the program and had been selected for inclusion based on specific criteria and procedures.

The controversy began in March 1981 and culminated in July 1985 when, after failing to convince the Library of Congress to discontinue the production of braille *Playboy*, a member of the House of Representatives, who thought that the sexual nature of the magazine's content made its inclusion inappropriate, introduced an amendment to reduce the funding for the Library of Congress's Books for the Blind and Physically Handicapped Program by the exact amount of money used to reproduce *Playboy* in Braille. Following the passage of the amendment by Congress, Boorstin announced that the production and distribution of Braille editions of *Playboy* would be discontinued. Although the amendment did not refer to the reproduction of *Playboy* or any other particular material in braille, Boorstin interpreted the Congressional action as a signal to censor *Playboy* due to its content to ensure the continued viability of the Braille magazine program.

The United States District Court for the District of Columbia ruled that Boorstin's viewpoint-based decision violated the First Amendment. Judge Hogan, writing for the court, declared that:

> above all else, the First Amendment means that government has no power to restrict expression because of its message, its ideas, its subject matter or its content. . . . Although individuals have no right to a government subsidy or benefit,

once one is conferred, as it is here through the allocation of funds for the program, the government cannot deny it on a basis that impinges on freedom of speech. . . . Congressional concerns about the nature of *Playboy* may be well-taken, but . . . [t]his dispute is not about the value or merit of *Playboy* but about a viewpoint-based denial of a subsidy, a denial which in a less emotionally charged context Congress and the taxpayers may find less palatable. Censorship whether by Congress or by the Librarian of Congress is equally abhorrent to a society built on the tenets of freedom of speech and expression (internal quotation marks and citations omitted).

Thus, *American Council of the Blind v. Boorstin* affirmed the First Amendment's requirement of content neutral decisions regarding library materials and highlighted the special role libraries play in furthering democratic ideals by serving the information needs of all citizens through access and freedom of choice in selection.

Concerned Women for America, Inc. v. Lafayette County and Oxford Public Library

Concerned Women for America, Inc. and Jolene Cox v. Lafayette County and Oxford Public Library (883 F.2d 32 [1989]) brought the problematic issue of access to public facilities for political and religious group meetings into the library environment. In June 1988, Concerned Women for America (CWA) sought permission to use the auditorium in the Lafayette County Oxford Library for a CWA Prayer Chapter meeting during which CWA members planned to discuss, pray about, and apply Biblical principles to family and political matters. Based on the library's policy of allowing use of the auditorium only for artistic and educational purposes, the CWA's request was denied. CWA then filed suit alleging that the library had violated their constitutional rights of free speech, freedom of assembly, free exercise of religion, and equal protection of the laws.

The United States Court of Appeals for the Fifth Circuit determined that, through practices that frequently extended beyond its policy and permitted diverse groups to use its auditorium, the library had created a public forum from which it could not restrict access based on the political or religious content of a group's meeting. The court's opinion, authored by Circuit Judge Jolly, states:

It is an elementary rule that the government may not exclude speech on the basis of its content from either a traditional public forum or a forum created by government designation, unless the exclusion is necessary to serve a compelling state interest which cannot be served by a less restrictive action. . . . There is no evidence that CWA's meeting would disrupt or interfere with the general use of the library. Should the contrary prove to be true, library officials may respond by imposing reasonable time, place or manner restrictions on access to the auditorium, provided any regulations are justified without reference to the content of the regulated speech. . . . In the absence of empirical evidence that religious groups will dominate use of the library's auditorium, causing the advancement of religion to become the forum's "primary effect," an equal access policy will not offend the Establishment Clause (citations omitted).

As such, *Concerned Women for America, Inc. v. Lafayette County and Oxford Public Library* affirmed the First Amendment rights of free speech and assembly for a multiplicity of voices in libraries, demonstrating their centrality as public forums, the quintessential venue for democratic expression and debate.

Kreimer v. Bureau of Police for the Town of Morristown

In *Richard R. Kreimer v. Bureau of Police for the Town of Morristown, et al.* (958 F.2d 1242 [1992]), the unresolved social issues raised by homelessness and class bias in America confronted the imperative for public access to information, the right to receive, and the right of libraries to promulgate and enforce reasonable regulations to govern the use of their facilities. Kreimer, a homeless man and frequent patron of the Joint Free Public Library of Morristown and Morris Township, was expelled from the library on several occasions for violating its rules for patron conduct. The library contended that Kreimer often exhibited inappropriate, disruptive, and offensive behavior, such as staring at and following patrons, talking loudly to himself, and a lack of personal hygiene that resulted in an unbearably repugnant odor. In response, Kreimer filed a complaint asserting that the rules were invalid under the First Amendment and the due process and equal protection clauses of the Fourteenth Amendment. Two of the major concerns posed in this litigation were whether the rules unfairly discriminated against homeless people, whose status might prevent them from maintaining the level of personal hygiene required by the library's policy, and the degree to which a library could proscribe conduct on its premises that did not constitute an actual, material disruption incompatible with the library's function.

The United States Court of Appeals for the Third Circuit found that the library's rules were reasonable "manner" restrictions on patrons' constitutional right to receive information and significantly advanced its interest in enabling the optimal and safest use of its facilities. The opinion of the court, written by Circuit Judge Greenberg, explains:

> [The library's] very purpose is to aid in the acquisition of knowledge through reading, writing and quiet contemplation. Thus, the exercise of other oral and interactive First Amendment activities is antithetical to the nature of the Library. These arguably conflicting characteristics, at least in a First Amendment sense, support our conclusion that . . . as a limited public forum, the Library is obligated only to permit the public to exercise rights that are consistent with the nature of the Library and consistent with the government's intent in designating the Library as a public forum. Other activities need not be tolerated. . . . The aim of the [Library] rules . . . is to foster a quiet and orderly atmosphere . . . conducive to every patron's exercise of their constitutionally protected interest in receiving and reading written communications. . . . The Library need not be used as a lounge or a shelter . . . [and] may regulate conduct protected under the First Amendment which does not actually disrupt the Library (internal quotation marks and citations omitted).

Hence, *Kreimer v. Bureau of Police for the Town of Morristown* balanced freedom of expression and the need to preserve order in a democratic society, affirming the right to receive information through the public library while validating library discretion in establishing acceptable use policies.

Conclusion

In summary, the five landmark court cases discussed in this essay present a social history of the application of the First Amendment in libraries. The cases involve some of the most important concerns of librarianship in a democracy: the right of equal access to the public library; the right to receive information; obscenity, freedom of access to library materials, and content-based restrictions on speech; free speech, assembly, and fair access to public library facilities; and public access to information, the right to receive, and the right of libraries to enact and implement acceptable use policies. At the same time, the cases illustrate the constantly changing tableau of American civil society reflected in the societal microcosm that is the public library. The growth and development of the nation, as well as the recurrent cultural and political upheaval characteristic of a democracy, are mirrored in the social struggles evident in the cases we have considered: civil rights; children, school libraries, and book banning; sexuality and culture; political and religious activism; and homelessness and class bias.

In addition to their historical value, these cases are central to the future relationship of the First Amendment, libraries, and democracy. The legal doctrine set out in the cases will have a profound impact on current and future disputes. For example, consider their implications for the present library Internet access controversy. All the cases indicate that libraries have some First Amendment authority to resist attempts to restrict patron Internet access. *Board of Education v. Pico* delineates the constitutional disparity between the removal of materials already in a library's collection as opposed to the failure to acquire items, which is implicated by filtering software. *Pico* also speaks to the right of students to receive unfiltered information. *American Council of the Blind v. Boorstin* suggests that, although libraries themselves and the federal government via the E-Rate are under no obligation to provide public Internet access, once the service exists, it cannot be taken away or limited on a basis that impinges on the First Amendment. *Kreimer v. Bureau of Police for the Town of Morristown* strongly supports the patrons' right to receive all the information that the public library has to offer, including unfiltered Internet access, as well as the library's right to require an acceptable level of behavior in exchange for the privilege.

As institutions in a democracy, libraries derive their mandate and guiding principles from the Constitution, most especially the First Amendment. Whether providing a process for the appeal of decisions or ensuring that rules governing the use of the library and its resources are administered in an equal and fair manner, libraries are charged with providing a space in which everyone's rights of freedom of expression, equal protection, and due process are honored and protected. Yet, as we have seen, frequently our democratic ideals are challenged by our ignoble instincts, such as prejudice and fear. As James Madison observed, "The interest of the man must be connected with the constitutional rights of the place. It may be a reflection on human nature, that such devices should be necessary. . . . But what is government itself, but the greatest of all reflections on human nature?"[2] Consequently, libraries stand at the confluence of our Constitution, our way of life, and our humanity—indeed, they are the cornerstone of our democracy.

Notes

1. Alexis de Tocqueville, *Democracy in America*, rev. ed., 2 vols., tr. Henry Reeve, reprint (New York: Colonial Pr., 1900).
2. James Madison, "The Federalist no. 51," in *The Federalist Papers*, by James Madison, Alexander Hamilton, and John Jay, reprint (London: Penguin, 1987).

Copyright and Democracy

Its Implications for the Public's Right to Know

Siva Vaidhyanathan

At its birth in the British Isles, copyright was an instrument of censorship.[1] In 1557, the Catholic Queen Mary Tudor capped off a 120-year Monarchal struggle to censor printing presses in England by issuing a charter to the Stationers' Company, a guild of printers. Only members of the company could legally produce books. They could only print books that were approved by the Crown.[2]

In contrast, the American copyright system since 1791 has reflected American republican values. While it granted a limited, temporary monopoly to a specific publisher, American copyright embodied four democratic safeguards: a guarantee that all works would enter the public domain once the copyright term expired; a collection of purposes that consumers could consider "fair use," such as limited copying for education or research; the principle that after the "first sale" of a copyrighted item, the buyer could do whatever he or she wants with the item save distribute unauthorized copies for profit; and the concept that copyright protected specific expression of ideas, but not the ideas themselves. Copyright, when well balanced, encourages the production and distribution of the raw material of democracy. But after more than 200 years of legal evolution and technological revolution, American copyright no longer offers strong democratic safeguards. It is out of balance.

The Republican Roots of Copyright

American copyright emanates from the U.S. Constitution, which directs Congress to create a federal law that provides an incentive to create and distribute new works. The law grants an exclusive right to copy, sell, and perform a work of original authorship that has been fixed in a tangible medium. The monopoly lasts for a limited time and is restricted by several provisions that allow for good-faith use by private citizens, journalists, students, and scholars. Copyright was created as a policy that balanced the interests of authors, publishers, and readers. It was not intended to be a restrictive property right. But it has evolved over recent decades into one part of a matrix of commercial legal protections now unfortunately called "intellectual property." Copyright is a "deal" that the American people, through its Congress, made with the writers and publishers of books. Authors and publishers would get a limited monopoly for a short period of time, and the public would get access to those protected works and free use of the facts, data, and ideas within them.

The Role of Copyright

The framers of the U.S. Constitution instructed Congress to develop a statute that would grant an incentive for authors and scientists to create and explore. Without a legal guarantee that they would profit from their labors and creations, the framers feared too few would embark on creative endeavors. If there were no copyright laws, unscrupulous publishers would simply copy popular works and sell them at a low price, paying no royalties to the author. But just as important, the framers and later jurists concluded that creativity depends on the use, criticism, supplementation, and consideration of previous works. Therefore, they argued, authors should enjoy this monopoly just long enough to provide an incentive to create more, but the work should live afterward in the "public domain," as common property of the reading public. A monopoly price on books was considered a "tax" on the public. It was in the best interest of the early republic to limit this tax to the amount that would be sufficient to provide an incentive, but no more and for no longer than that. This principle of copyright as an incentive to create has been challenged in recent decades by the idea of copyright as a "property right." Therefore, many recent statutes, treaties, and copyright cases have seemed to favor the interests of established authors and producers over those of readers, researchers, and future creators. These recent trends run counter to the original purpose of American copyright.

James Madison, who introduced the copyright and patent clause to the Constitutional Convention, argued in *The Federalist* that copyright was one of those few acts of government in which the "public good fully coincides with the claims of individuals." Madison did not engage in "property talk" about copyright. Instead, Madison argued for copyright in terms of "progress," "learning," and other such classic republican virtues as literacy and an informed citizenry.

Copyright fulfilled its role for Madison because it looked forward as an encouragement, not backward as a reward. This fit with the overall Madisonian project for the Constitution. If the federal government were to operate as the nexus of competing interests, each interest would need to approach the public sphere with reliable information. Information could only be deemed reliable if it were subject to public debate. Ideas could only be judged beneficial if they had stood the tests of discourse and experience.[3]

When President George Washington declared his support for the Copyright Act of 1790, he proclaimed that copyright would stabilize and enrich American political culture by "convincing those who are entrusted with public administration that every valuable end of government is best answered by the enlightened confidence of the public; and by teaching the people themselves to know and value their own rights; to discern and provide against invasions of them; to distinguish between oppression and the necessary exercise of lawful authority." In other words, Washington believed that only through free and easy access to information could the public educate itself to be strong enough to resist tyranny and maintain a state that did not exceed its charges. Washington reasoned that copyright encouraged learning, so it would benefit the republic.[4]

Thomas Jefferson—author, architect, slave owner, land owner, and the most important American interpreter of John Locke—had no problems with the laws of the land protecting private property. Yet he expressed some serious misgivings about copyrights. These concerns were based on Jefferson's suspicion of concentrations of power and artificial monopolies. While in Paris in 1788, Jefferson wrote to Madison that he rejoiced at the news that nine states had ratified the new Constitution. "It is a good canvass," Jefferson wrote of Madison's work, "on which some strokes only want retouching." Primarily, Jefferson wanted a Bill of Rights attached to the document. But he also desired an explicit prohibition against monopolies, including those limited and granted by the Constitution: patents and copyright. While Jefferson acknowledged that a limited copyright could potentially encourage creativity, it had not been demonstrated. Therefore, Jefferson wrote, "the benefit of even limited monopolies is too doubtful, to be opposed to that of their general suppression."[5]

The following summer, as Congress was sifting through the proposals that would form the Bill of Rights, Jefferson again wrote to Madison from Paris. This time Jefferson proposed specific language for an amendment that would have allowed copyrights and patents, despite his doubts, but forbidden any other type of commercial monopoly. "For instance," Jefferson wrote, "the following alterations and additions would have pleased me: Article 9. Monopolies may be allowed to persons for their own productions in literature, and their own inventions in the arts, for a term not exceeding _____ years, but for no longer term, and no other purpose." Jefferson lost this battle, as he did many battles before 1800.[6]

Significantly, the founders, whether enamored of the virtuous potential of copyright as Washington was, enchanted by the machinery of incentive as Madison was, or alarmed by the threat of concentrated power as Jefferson was, did not argue for copyrights or patents as "property." Copyright was a matter of policy, of a bargain among the state, its authors, and its citizens. Jefferson even explicitly dismissed a property model for copyright, and maintained his skepticism about the costs and benefits of copyright for many years. Fearing, justifiably, that copyright might eventually expand to encompass idea protection, not just expression protection, Jefferson wrote in 1813, "If nature has made any one thing less susceptible than all others of exclusive property, it is the action of the thinking power called an idea, which an individual may exclusively possess as long as he keeps it to himself; but the moment it is divulged, it forces itself into the possession of everyone, and the receiver cannot dispose himself of it." Jefferson then elucidated the flaw in the political economy of copyright as property. Unlike tangible property, ideas and expressions are not susceptible to natural scarcity. As Jefferson wrote of copyright, "Its peculiar character, too, is that no one possesses the less, because every other possesses the whole of it. He who receives an idea from me, receives instruction himself without lessening mine; as he who lights his taper at mine, receives light without darkening me."[7] Therefore, Jefferson feared, the monopolists could use their state-granted power to strengthen their control over the flow of ideas and the use of expressions. Monopolies have the power to enrich themselves by evading the limitations of the competitive marketplace. Prices need not fall when demand slackens, and demand need not slacken if the monopoly makes itself essential to the economy (like petroleum or computer operating systems). But to accomplish the task of bolstering the value of these monopolies, those who control copyrights would have to create artificial scarcity by limiting access, fixing prices, restricting licensing, litigating, and intimidating potential competitors, misrepresenting the principles of the law and claiming a measure of authenticity or romantic originality. But when Jefferson warned of these potential negative externalities, they were more than a century away. Even in the early twentieth century, jurists considered Jefferson's warnings, and skepticism about idea protection kept monopolists at bay. As Justice Louis Brandeis wrote in a dissenting opinion in 1918, "The general rule of law is, that noblest of human productions—knowledge, truths ascertained, conceptions and ideas—become, after voluntary communication to others, free as the air to common use."[8] Both Jefferson and Brandeis dissented from the conventional wisdom of their times, but nevertheless influenced the philosophy of copyright. So in the early republic and the first century of American legal history, copyright was a Madisonian compromise, a necessary evil, a limited, artificial monopoly, not to be granted or expanded lightly.

The Scope of Copyright

An author can claim a copyright on many categories of creative expression, including literary works, audiovisual productions, computer software, graphic designs, musical arrangements, architectural plans, and sound recordings. According to the Copyright Act of 1976, a work is protected in all mediums and for all possible derivative uses as soon as it is fixed in a tangible medium of expression. This means that as soon as a writer types a story on a computer or typewriter, the work carries the protection of copyright law. Authors need not register the work with the Copyright Office of the Library of Congress unless they plan to pursue legal action against someone for violating the copyright.

The law specifically protects the "expression," but not the facts or ideas that underlie the expression. If one person writes a song that expresses the idea that world peace is desirable, that songwriter cannot prevent others from writing later songs, plays, or novels that use, criticize, or champion the same idea. However, subsequent songwriters should choose different lyrics, chord structures, and arrangements to ensure they do not trample on the original songwriter's copyright. In another example—one that corresponds to a case that reached the U.S. Supreme Court in 1991—it is clear that copyright does not protect "information." One company produced a telephone directory for an area. A second company used that list of names, addresses, and phone numbers, alphabetized by surname, to produce a second and competing directory. The first company sued, claiming copyright infringement. However, the Supreme Court ruled that the 1976 statute and a century of case law clearly stated that copyright only protects original works of authorship, not data. Alphabetization did not count as an "original" method of arrangement. There is a strong philosophical and policy argument for leaving facts, data, and ideas unprotected. The framers of the Constitution realized that for a democracy to function properly citizens should have easy access to information and should be able to debate and criticize without fear of lawsuits.[9]

For the same reason, the framers insisted that Congress be able to grant copyrights for a limited time only. They asserted that after authors had profited for a reasonable amount of time, their works should belong to the public and contribute to the richness of the culture and politics of the nation. For more than 120 years, American authors could enjoy copyright protection for mere 14-year terms, which were renewable for another 14 years. From 1909 through 1978, the term was extended to 28 years, renewable for another 28 years. All works created since 1978 fell under the 1976 revision, which set the term as the life of author plus 50 years, to benefit the author's kin. Most European nations grant copyrights for 70 years past the death of the author, and the U.S. Congress in 1998 extended U.S. copyright to match the European term by passing the "Sonny Bono Copyright Term Extension Act."

Since 1891, the United States has signed a series of treaties that grant reciprocal copyright protection throughout the world, with few exceptions. The 1891 treaty with the United Kingdom protected American authors throughout the English-reading world, and protected British authors within the United States as well. Before this reciprocal treaty, British books sold at a much lower price in the United States than American-written books did, but British authors saw no return from the pirated editions. British authors felt stiffed, and American books could not compete with cheaper British works. Leveling the playing field benefited both groups.[10]

But recent efforts to standardize copyright protection around the globe have been more complicated. Developing nations with weak currencies have spawned thriving black markets for pirated American films, compact discs, and computer programs. In an economy in which a popular American music compact disc might cost a consumer a week's wages, pirated versions offer an affordable choice at a fraction of the price. The U.S. government—on behalf of its software, music, and film industries—has been pressuring developing nations to enforce international treaties that protect copyrights. Meanwhile, European nations and media companies have been urging the U.S. government to abandon many of its copyright principles in favor of maximum protection for authors and producers. European nations have consistently granted a higher level of protection to authors and artists than American laws have. Most European copyright traditions lack the notion that copyright embodies a balance of interests that include the public as well as creators.

Fair Use and Private Use

How can a writer make fun of a television show without borrowing elements of its creative expression? If the writer had to ask permission from the producers of the show, the parody would never occur. No one would grant permission to be ridiculed. Yet parody is an important part of our culture. Without criticism and comment, even ridicule, democracy cannot operate optimally. Without referring to or freely quoting from original works, newspaper editorials, book reviews, and satirical television shows could not do their work. If students had to ask permission from publishing companies for every quotation they used in term papers, education would grind to a halt.

This limited freedom to quote—"fair use"—is an exemption to the blanket monopoly protection that artists and authors enjoy. Fair use evolved within American case law throughout the nineteenth and twentieth centuries, and was finally codified in the Copyright Act of 1976. The law specifically allows users to make copies of, quote from, and refer to copyrighted works for the following purposes: in connection with criticism or comment on the work; in the course of news reporting; for teaching or classroom use; or as part of scholarship or research.

If a court is charged with deciding whether a use of a copyrighted work is "fair" or not, the court must consider the following issues: the purpose or character of the use, such as whether it was meant for commercial or educational use; the nature of the original, copyrighted work; the amount of the copyrighted work that was taken or used in the subsequent work; and the effect on the market value of the original work. So, for example, if a teacher copies three pages from a 200-page book and passes them out to students, the teacher is covered by fair use. But if that teacher photocopied the entire book and sold it to students at a lower cost than the original book, that teacher would probably have infringed on the original copyright. More often than not, however, fair use is a gray and sloppy concept. Commercially produced parodies are frequently challenged examples of fair use. The U.S. Supreme Court has recently granted wide berth for parody, however, as a way of encouraging creative, free, and rich speech.[11]

In addition to fair use, Congress and the federal courts have been unwilling to enforce copyrights in regard to private, noncommercial uses. Basically, courts have ruled that consumers are allowed to make copies of compact discs for use in their own tape players and may record television broadcasts for later home viewing, as long as they do not sell the copies or display them in a public setting that might dilute the market value of the original broadcast. So despite the warnings that accompany all broadcasted sporting events, most private, noncommercial, or educational copying of copyrighted works falls under either the fair use or private use exemptions to the law.[12]

The Clinton administration has agreed to several multinational treaties that would radically alter American copyright law. One provision would establish a new type of intellectual property law to protect data, trumping the Supreme Court ruling that copyright specifically excludes data protection. Another would introduce to U.S. law the concept of an author's "moral rights," which would give authors veto power over proposed parodies of their work. A third provision resulted in a prohibition on attempts to circumvent software that controls access to copyrighted material. Along with the proposal to extend the duration of copyright protection to seventy years past the life of the author, American copyright in the twenty-first century will work very differently from the way it has for the past two centuries.

Abandoning Democratic Safeguards

In the 1990s the Clinton administration championed efforts to undermine the democratic safeguards that used to be built into the copyright system. In addition to signing a twenty-year term extension and pushing for *sui generis* database protection law, the administration and Congress acted on behalf of global media companies by enacting the most egregious example of recent copyright recklessness: the Digital Millennium Copyright Act of 1998, the enabling legislation for the World Intellectual Property Organization (WIPO) copyright treaty. The Digital Millennium Copyright Act (DMCA) has one major provision that upends more than 200 years of copyright law. It puts the power to regulate copying in the hands of engineers and the companies that employ them. It takes the decision-making power away from Congress, courts, librarians, writers, artists, and researchers. The DMCA:

- prohibits the circumvention of any effective technological protection measure installed to restrict access to a copyrighted work;
- prohibits the manufacture of any device, composition of any program, or offering of any service that is designed to defeat technological protection measures;
- orders the Librarian of Congress to conduct rulemaking hearings to judge the effects the law would have on non-infringing uses of copyrighted material;
- specifically allows certain uses such as reverse engineering, security testing, privacy protection, and encryption research;
- makes no textual change to the fair use provisions of the Copyright Law, despite eliminating the possibility of unauthorized access to protected materials for fair use purposes; and

■ limits the liability that online service providers might face if one of their clients were circumventing or pirating.

Before Congressional committees and in hearing held by the Copyright Office of the Library of Congress, public interest advocates such as law professors, electronic civil liberties activists, and librarians outlined some concerns about and objections to the DMCA. These include the possibility that the DMCA makes it possible to levy fees for various uses that might otherwise be "fair" or "free," such as parody and quoting for news or commentary.

In addition, the DMCA erodes the "first sale doctrine." When a work is sold, the copyright holder relinquishes "exclusive" rights over it yet retains "limited" rights, such as restricting copying or public performance. But under the first sale doctrine, the consumer can highlight a book, copy portions for private, non-commercial use, resell it to someone, lend it to someone, or tear it up, without asking permission from the copyright holder. Because the DMCA allows content providers to regulate access and use, they can set all the terms of use. And much like the database protection proposal, the de facto duration of protection under the DMCA is potentially infinite. While copyright law in 2000 protects any work created today for the life of the author plus seventy years, or ninety-five years in the case of corporate "works for hire," electronic gates do not expire. This allows producers to "recapture" works already in or about to fall into the public domain. This also violates the constitutional mandate that Congress copyright laws protect "for limited times." Most dangerously, producers could exercise editorial control over the uses of their materials. They could extract contractual promises that the use would not parody or criticize the work in exchange for access. Many Web sites already do this. Just as dangerous, the DMCA allows producers to contractually bind users from reusing facts or ideas contained in the work. If a user wants to hack through access controls to make legitimate fair use of material inside—perhaps facts, an old film in the public domain, or pieces of the work for commentary or news, that user is subject to civil and criminal penalties under the DMCA.[13]

For most of American history, copyright has not only reflected democratic principles, but also fueled the engines of democracy by rewarding the efforts of both producers and consumers of information and cultural products. Now, as the twenty-first century begins, copyright is tilted to favor the powerful at the expense of the people. But with the spread of digital technology and the popularity of networks that cannot be regulated, such as Napster and Gnutella, the public is once again engaged in discussions of copyright issues. This development offers some hope to the copyright system and democracy itself.

Notes

1. L. Ray Patterson, *Copyright in Historical Perspective* (Nashville: Vanderbilt Univ. Pr., 1968), 2. The accounts throughout this chapter owe their origins to Patterson's early work. For a lighter account of early copyright with a larger historical sweep of recent American copyright changes, see Patterson and Stanley Lindberg, *The Nature of Copyright: A Law of User's Rights* (Athens: Univ. of Georgia Pr., 1991). The most important recent historical revelations about early copyright can be found in a seminal law review article, Howard B. Abrams, "The Historic Foundation of American Copyright Law: Exploding the Myth of Common Law Copyright," *Wayne Law Review* (spring 1983): 1119–89. The best historical rendering of the changes in copyright policy in the United Kingdom is John Feather, *Publishing, Piracy and Politics: An Historical Study of Copyright in Britain* (London: Mansell Publ. Ltd., 1994). Also see Harry Ransom, *The First Copyright Statute: An Essay on an Act for the Encouragement of Learning, 1709* (Austin: Univ. of Texas Pr., 1956). Also see Ransom, *The Theory of Literary Property: 1760–1775* (unpublished doctoral dissertation, Yale University, 1938). Another well written historical account of early copyright debates can be found in Paul Goldstein, *Copyright's Highway* (New York: Hill and Wang, 1994). While Goldstein's recent opinions about the goals of copyright policy are disturbing, he is a talented writer and one of the world's top authorities on copyright law. John Tebbel, *A History of Book Publishing in the United States,* two vols. (New York: R. R. Bowker, 1972), offers a broad but shallow account of early copyright efforts in both the colonies and the early republic, but his bias is toward copyright as a natural or property right, and he evades or misses the anti-monopolistic philosophy that tempered American copyright law for more than a century. Tebbel does not see perpetual monopoly control as a threat to democratic speech. Tebbel's biggest problem, however, is that he seems completely unaware of British copyright law, even of the Statute of Anne of 1709, which clearly inspired the titles and timbre of early American law. A brilliant treatise on British copyright in the seventeenth and eighteenth centuries, from a postmodern perspective, is Mark Rose, *Authors and Owners: The Invention of Copyright* (Cambridge, Mass.: Harvard Univ. Pr., 1993). Rose is inspired by Foucault and other recent theorists, yet does not rely on theory for easy answers. The best account of the struggles for international copyright is still a brilliant dissertation, Aubert J. Clark, *The Movement for International Copyright in Nineteenth Century America* (Washington, D.C.: The Catholic Univ. of America Pr., 1960). Clark's only major flaw is that the dissertation is embedded with Thomistic natural law theories of property rights. Clark's attachment to natural law does not allow him to consider the policy balances and interest group battles that determined copyright policy throughout the century. To his credit, Clark does not, as most publishing historians do, blame resistance to international copyright and expanded copyright pro-

tection on some mysterious "anti-intellectualism" among the American public and its leaders.

2. Abrams, "The Historic Foundation of American Copyright Law," 1135–37. Also Patterson, *Copyright in Historical Perspective,* 65–69.

3. James Madison, "Number 43," in *The Federalist Papers,* Alexander Hamilton, James Madison and John Jay (Cambridge, Mass.: Belknap Pr., 1961), 309.

4. The republican virtues of copyright are best explained by Neil Weinstock Netanel, "Copyright and a Democratic Civil Society," *The Yale Law Journal* (Nov. 1996): 356–86. Washington is quoted in Netanel, "Copyright and a Democratic Civil Society," 357.

5. Thomas Jefferson, "Letter to James Madison, Paris, July 31, 1788," in *The Writings of Thomas Jefferson,* vol. 7 (Washington, D.C.: Thomas Jefferson Memorial Association, 1904), 93–99.

6. Jefferson, "Letter to James Madison, Paris, August 28, 1789," in *The Writings of Thomas Jefferson,* vol. 7 (Washington, D.C.: Thomas Jefferson Memorial Association, 1904), 444–53.

7. Jefferson, "Letter to Isaac McPherson, Monticello, August 13, 1813," in *The Writings of Thomas Jefferson,* vol. 13 (Washington, D.C.: Thomas Jefferson Memorial Association, 1904), 326–38.

8. Louis Brandeis wrote (dissenting) in *International News Service v. Associated Press,* 248 U.S. 215, 250 (1918).

9. *Feist Publications, Inc. v. Rural Telephone Service,* 499 U.S. 340, 111 S. Ct. 1282, 113 L. Ed. 2d 358 (1991).

10. Victor A. Doyno, *Writing Huck Finn: Mark Twain's Creative Process* (Philadelphia: Univ. of Pennsylvania Pr., 1991), 185–98. Also see Aubert J. Clark, *The Movement for International Copyright in Nineteenth Century America* (Washington, D.C.: The Catholic Univ. of America Pr., 1960).

11. *Campbell v. Acuff-Rose Music, Inc.,* 114 S. Ct. 1164 (1994).

12. Paul Goldstein, *Copyright's Highway: From Gutenberg to the Celestial Jukebox* (New York: Hill and Wang, 1994), 129–64.

13. See Julie Cohen, "Lochner in Cyberspace," *Michigan Law Review* (Nov. 1998): 462–562. Also see Siva Vaidhyanathan, testimony at the anticircumvention hearings of the Copyright Office, available at http://lcweb.loc.gov/copyright/1201/hearings.

V. The Library of Congress and Democracy

The Library of Congress and the Democratic Spirit

John Y. Cole

What spectacle can be more edifying or more seasonable than liberty and learning, each leaning on the other for their mutual and surest support?

—*James Madison*

In the epilogue to his *The Epic of America* (1931), historian James Truslow Adams praises the Library of Congress as both a model and "a symbol of what democracy can accomplish on its own behalf." His reasoning is still valid, even though by today's standards his description of the Library is somewhat romantic. Looking down on the Main Reading Room from the Visitors' Gallery, Truslow saw the seats "filled with silent readers, old and young, rich and poor, black and white, the executive and the laborer, the general and the private, the noted scholar and the schoolboy, all reading at their own library provided by their own democracy." To Adams, the Library of Congress came "straight from the heart of democracy" because it was nothing less than "a perfect working out in a concrete example of the American dream," representing the wise appropriation by Congress of "the accumulated resources of the people themselves" and "a public intelligent enough to use" those resources.[1]

In 2000, the Library of Congress commemorated its bicentennial. The past was honored but the focus was on the future, emphasizing new projects and partnerships intended to carry the institution well into the twenty-first century. The Bicentennial Steering Committee, which I co-chaired, spent several months discussing how to make the Library's democratic heritage a meaningful focal point for the commemoration and simultaneously a reminder that all libraries, not just the Library of Congress, are both models and symbols of democracy. Our solution was to adopt "Libraries-Creativity-Liberty" as the major bicentennial theme and the basis for several cooperative projects with the American library community.

169

The democratic roots of the Library of Congress, so admired by James Truslow Adams, are part of the institution's fabric—along with nationalism, optimism, and strong leadership, at least from the Librarians of Congress since the Civil War. Since the 1930s, the size of the Library's collections and staff have increased four-fold, and its annual appropriation has soared from $3 million to more than $450 million. It also has become an international resource of unparalleled dimension. Today the Library's collections of more than 120 million items include research materials in 460 languages and many formats, and are especially rich in manu-scripts, music, maps, photographs, sound recordings, and motion pictures.

Since its creation, the Library of Congress has been part of the legislative branch of the American government, and even though it is recognized as the de facto national library of the United States, it does not have that official desig-nation. Nevertheless, it performs most functions performed by national libraries elsewhere. Its widespread recognition as a symbol of American democracy and learning rests not only in its size and diversity of functions, but also on its physical presence.

The Library of Congress occupies three massive structures on Capitol Hill, near the U.S. Capitol, all named for U.S. Founding Fathers. The Jefferson Building, opened in 1897, is a grand monument to civilization, culture, and American achievement. The functional and classical Adams Building, named for President John Adams in 1980, opened to the public in 1939. The modern and massive Madison Building, completed in 1980, is this nation's official memorial to president James Madison.

How did a library established by the national legislature in 1800 for its own use become such an ambitious, multipurpose place? One point is clear: the growth of the Library's functions derives from the expansion of its collec-tions. Moreover, as James Truslow Adams recognized, the development of the Library of Congress cannot be separated from the history of the democracy it serves. In particular, it cannot be separated from the philosophy and demo-cratic ideals of Thomas Jefferson, its principal founder.

The Jeffersonian Legacy

The Library of Congress was established as the legislature of the young repub-lic prepared to move from Philadelphia to the new capital city of Washington. Members of Congress had used the Library Company of Philadelphia and knew they would need books to support their work once they were established in Washington. On April 24, 1800, President John Adams approved legislation that appropriated $5,000 to purchase "such books as may be necessary for the use of Congress." In 1802 President Thomas Jefferson approved the first law defining the role and functions of the new institution.

A book collector whose personal collection reflected his own wide-ranging interests, Jefferson believed that the power of the intellect should be the driving force in the creation of a free and democratic society. It is not surprising that he took a keen interest in the Library of Congress and its development while he was president of the United States (1801–09). Throughout his presidency, he personally recommended books for the Library, and he appointed the first two Librarians of Congress. In 1814, the British army invaded the city of Washington and burned the Capitol, including the 3,000-volume Library of Congress. By then retired to Monticello, Jefferson offered to sell his personal library, the largest and finest in the country, to the Congress to replace the destroyed collection. The purchase of Jefferson's 6,487 volumes for $23,940 was approved in 1815.

The library that Jefferson sold to Congress not only included more than twice the number of volumes that had been destroyed, it expanded the scope of the Library of Congress far beyond the bounds of a legislative library. Jefferson was a man of encyclopedic interests, and his library contained works on architecture, the arts, science, literature, and geography. It included books in French, Spanish, German, Latin, Greek, and one three-volume statistical work in Russian. Jefferson believed that the national legislature needed ideas and information on all topics and in many languages in order to govern a democracy. Anticipating the argument that his collection might be too comprehensive, he argued that there was "no subject to which a Member of Congress may not have occasion to refer."[2]

The acquisition by Congress of Jefferson's library provided the rationale for the expansion of the Library's functions. The Jeffersonian concept of universality is also the basis for the Library's comprehensive collecting policies. Jefferson and his friend and successor as president, James Madison (1809–17) believed that democracy depended on the mutual support of "liberty & learning." The vast collections and varied and services of the Library of Congress are founded on that belief.

Nationalism, Knowledge, and Democracy

The Library of Congress grew slowly but steadily after the Jefferson purchase, but came upon difficult times in the 1850s. The growing division between North and South hindered strengthening any government institution. Furthermore, in late 1851, the most serious fire in the Library's history destroyed about two-thirds of its fifty-five thousand volumes, including two-thirds of Jefferson's library. Congress responded quickly and generously; in 1852 a total of $168,700 was appropriated to restore the Library's rooms in the Capitol and to replace the lost books. However no plan was set forth for expanding the Library's collection or services. This philosophy was in keeping with the conservative views of Librarian of Congress John Silva Meehan (1829-1861) and Sen. James A. Pearce of Maryland, the chairman of the Joint Committee on the Library, who favored keeping strict limits on the Library's activities.

The person responsible for transforming the Library of Congress into an institution of national significance in the Jeffersonian spirit was Ainsworth Rand Spofford, a former Cincinnati bookseller and journalist who served as Librarian of Congress from the last day of 1864 until 1897. Spofford accomplished this task by permanently linking the legislative and the national functions of the Library, first in practice and then in law through the 1897 reorganization of the institution. He provided his successors as Librarian of Congress with four essential prerequisites for the development of an American national library: (1) firm, bipartisan support for the idea of the Library of Congress as both a legislative and a national library; (2) the beginning of a comprehensive collection of Americana; (3) a magnificent new building, itself a national monument; and (4) a strong and independent office of Librarian of Congress. Spofford had the vision, skill, and perseverance to capitalize on the Library's claim to a national role. Each Librarian of Congress since Spofford has built on his accomplishments, shaping the contours of the institution differently, but never wavering from the belief that democracy depended on the widespread sharing of a comprehensive base of knowledge and information.

Spofford viewed a national library as a unique, independent institution: a single, comprehensive collection of a nation's literature. Congress needed such a collection because, as Spofford paraphrased Jefferson, "there is no work, within the vast range of literature and science, which may not at some time prove useful to the legislature of a great nation." It was imperative, he felt, that such a great national collection be shared with all citizens, for the United States was "a Republic which rests upon the popular intelligence."[3]

Immediately after the Civil War, American society began a rapid transformation; one of the major changes was the rapid expansion of the federal government. Spofford took full advantage of the favorable political and cultural climate and increasing national confidence to promote the Library's expansion. He always believed that the Library of Congress was the national library, and he used every conceivable argument to convince others, particularly the Joint Committee on the Library and other members of Congress.

In the first years of his administration, Spofford obtained congressional approval of six laws or resolutions that ensured a national role for the Library of Congress. The legislative acts were an appropriation providing for the expansion of the Library's rooms in the Capitol building; the copyright amendment of 1865, which brought copyright deposits back into the Library's collections for the first time since 1859; the Smithsonian deposit of 1866, whereby the entire library of the Smithsonian Institution, a collection especially strong in scientific materials, was transferred to the Library; the 1867 purchase, for $100,000, of the private library of books, pamphlets, and manuscripts gathered by archivist and historian Peter Force, establishing the foundation of the Library's Americana and incunabula collections; the international exchange resolution of 1867, providing for the development of the Library's collections of foreign public documents; and the copyright act of 1870, which centralized all U.S. copyright registration and deposit activities at the Library of Congress.

Spofford leaned heavily on nationalistic arguments in making his case. The Peter Force library, for example, should be purchased both for its instrinsic value and to "repair a deficiency," for "it is not creditable to our national spirit to have to admit the fact—which nevertheless is true—that the largest and most complete collection of books relating to America in the world is that now gathered on the shelves of the British Museum."[4] The centralization of copyright at the Library of Congress was important, he maintained, because "we should have one comprehensive Library in the country, and that belonging to the nation, whose aim it should be to preserve the books which other libraries have not the room or the means to procure." This consideration was especially important, he continued, "when it is considered that the Library of Congress is freely open to the public throughout the year, and is rapidly becoming the great reference library of the country."[5]

The centralization of copyright activities at the Library of Congress was Spofford's most impressive collection-building feat. The copyright law of 1870 ensured the continuing development of the Library's Americana collections, for it stipulated that two copies of every book, pamphlet, map, print, photograph, and piece of music registered for copyright be deposited in the Library.

The 1870 copyright law had another lasting effect of great significance: it forced the construction of a separate building for the Library. Spofford foresaw this need immediately, and mentioned it in his 1871 *Annual Report*. The next year he presented a plan for a new building, initiating an endeavor that soon dominated the rest of his career as Librarian of Congress. In the ensuing twenty-five-year struggle to obtain the building, Spofford enlisted the support of many powerful public figures: congressmen, cultural leaders, journalists, and even presidents. The speeches and statements he elicited usually went beyond the need for a building to include endorsement of the Library's anticipated role as an institution that would serve democracy and the American people. Good examples are speeches on the floor of the Senate by two dependable friends and Library users, Senators Justin S. Morrill of Vermont and Daniel W. Voorhees of Indiana.

In March 1879, Morrill proclaimed that:

> we must either reduce the Library to the stinted and specific wants of Congress alone, or permit it to advance to national importance, and give it room equal to the culture, wants, and resources of a great people.[6]

The next year Senator Voorhees asked that the Senate give "this great national library our love and our care," because "knowledge is power, the power to maintain free government and preserve constitutional liberty."[7] Such speeches, plus behind-the-scenes efforts by Morrill, Voorhees, and Spofford, finally resulted in 1886 in authorization for a structure directly across the east plaza from the Capitol. After further delays, construction began in earnest in 1889 and the new building opened to widespread admiration in 1897. It was the largest and costliest library building in the world and immediately hailed as a national monument.

Now called the Thomas Jefferson Building, this elaborately decorated structure is admired as an incomparable symbol of American optimism and cultural nationalism. Its iconography focuses on two themes: the universality of knowledge and the importance of learning to democracy. With regard to the latter, Elihu Vedder's five small paintings, strategically placed at the entrance to the Main Reading Room, are crucial. In the painting above the central door to the Main Reading Room, titled *Government* and representing the ideal state, the figure of Good Government holds a plaque on which is inscribed a familiar quotation from Abraham Lincoln's Gettysburg Address, "A government of the people, by the people, and for the people." Two paintings explaining the practical working of government flank each side of this central image. To the left, *Corrupt Legislation* leads to *Anarchy* (the scroll of learning is burning in Anarchy's right hand and she is trampling on a scroll, a lyre, a Bible, and a book); to the right, *Good Administration* (a youth, educated by the books he is carrying, is casting his ballot into an urn) leads to the fifth painting, *Peace and Prosperity*.

Building Collections and Developing Services

President William McKinley appointed a new Librarian of Congress to supervise the move from the Capitol building and implement a reorganization. He was John Russell Young, who held office briefly, from July 1, 1897, until his death in January 1899. A journalist and former diplomat, Young worked hard to strengthen both the comprehensiveness of the collections and the scope of the services provided to Congress. He honored Jefferson's influence on the Library, bringing Jefferson's library into a special room and commissioning a report on the library that was published in his 1898 *Annual Report.*

Young used his diplomatic ties and experience to enlarge the Library's collections. In February 1898, for example, he sent a letter to U.S. diplomatic and consular representatives throughout the world, asking them to send "to the national library" newspapers, journals, pamphlets, manuscripts, broadsides, "documents illustrative of the history of those various nationalities now coming to our shores to blend into our national life." He also asked for other categories of research materials, broadly summarized as "whatever, in a word, would add to the sum of human knowledge."[8] By the end of 1898, he had received books and other materials from eleven legations and seven consulates.

Herbert Putnam, Young's successor, was appointed by President McKinley in the spring of 1899 and served as Librarian of Congress for forty years, until the autumn of 1939. Asked to characterize the Library as he neared the end of his long career, Putnam penned "Universal in Scope: National in Service." This apt phrase described his entire tenure, for if Spofford's major contributions were the national collections and the building, Putnam was the Librarian who did the most to extend the Library to the American people. He created a systematic program of widespread public use that still exists, opening up the collections to scholars, the public, and to other libraries. The first experienced librarian to serve as Librarian of Congress, Putnam also established a working partnership between the Library of Congress and the American library movement. Rather than serving merely as a great national accumulation of books, a national library should, he felt, actively serve other libraries as well as researchers and scholars.

By 1900, the age of the great library had arrived in America, characterized by huge bookstacks, scientific cataloging and classification, and full-time professional staffs. The Library's new building symbolized this age and, as the first library in the United States to reach one million volumes, the Library of Congress became the leader among American libraries. Putnam's imaginative and decisive actions were approved both by the Joint Library Committee and the professional library community. Under his leadership, in 1901 the first volume of a completely new classification scheme, based on the Library's own collections, was published; access to the Library was extended to "scientific investigators and duly qualified individuals" throughout the United States; interlibrary loan service was inaugurated; and the sale and distribution of Library of Congress printed catalog cards began.

The interlibrary loan system was an especially radical step, for it signaled the institution's transition from a national storehouse of books to a national laboratory or workshop for promoting the use of its collections. It required special legislation by Congress and approval was by no means assured. When asked to defend his view that books should be sent outside the District of Columbia, Putnam explained that the risk was justified because "a book used, is after all, fulfilling a higher mission than a book which is merely being preserved for possible future use."[9] It was a telling statement about the openness of American libraries and the spirit of cooperation that was welding them into a strong community. Moreover, Putnam's extension of the Library's cataloging and classification schemes to the rest of the nation helped "democratize" knowledge, nationally and internationally, for it established bibliographic standards and encouraged cooperative endeavors among librarians and scholars. This sharing of the Library's "bibliographic apparatus," as Putnam called it, helped systematize and communicate information about intellectual activity in America and propelled the Library of Congress into a position of international leadership among research institutions.[10]

The development of the Library's collections into a nationally useful resource took many forms. To aid historical research, Putnam felt the national library "should be able to offer original sources" that described the national life.[11] In 1903, he persuaded his friend and supporter, President Theodore Roosevelt, to issue an executive order that transferred the papers of many of the nation's founding fathers, including George Washington, Thomas Jefferson, and James Madison, from the State Department archives to the Library's Manuscript Division. In 1904, the Library began publishing important historical texts from its collections, such as the *Journals of the Continential Congress*.

As American influence and interests began to expand in the twentieth century, Putnam looked abroad to build the Library's collections, boldly applying Jefferson's dictum that no subject was beyond the possible concerns of Congress or the American people. The Librarian was especially farsighted in acquiring research materials about other countries and cultures. In 1904 he purchased the 4,000-volume Indica collection, explaining in the Library's *Annual Report* that he "could not ignore the opportunity to acquire a unique collection which scholarship thought worthy of prolonged, scientific, and enthusiastic research, even though the immediate use of such a collection may prove meager." In 1906 he acquired the famous 80,000-volume private library of Russian literature owned by G. V. Yudin of Siberia, even sending a staff member to Russia to supervise the packing and the shipping of the books. The Schatz collection of early opera librettos was purchased from a German collector in 1908. Large and important collections of Hebraica and of Chinese and Japanese books were acquired. By

1926, the Library of Congress had obtained appropriated funds to send a permanent representative to Europe, stationed in Paris, to assist with acquisitions and develop contacts with "dealers, collectors, scholars, and learned institutions."

The Library's symbolic role as a cradle of Jeffersonian democracy was enhanced in 1921 when Putnam arranged for the nation's two most precious documents, the Declaration of Independence and the Constitution, to be transferred to the Library from the State Department. In 1924 the Librarian put the documents on permanent public display in a specially designed "Shrine" in the Library's Great Hall. President Calvin Coolidge and other dignitaries took part in the ceremony at which there were no speeches—only the unified singing of two stanzas of "America."

The rapid expansion of the Library's collections and services during Putnam's forty years as Librarian of Congress naturally required more space. Additional bookstacks within the original building were built in 1910 and 1927. Congress approved legislation to acquire land for a second building in 1928, and authorized the Annex Building (today the Adams Building) in 1930. After construction delays during the 1930s, contractors completed the classically simple, rectangular structure in 1938, and it was opened to the public in 1939, the year of Putnam's retirement.

Fortress of Freedom

The Library of Congress as a democratic institution and repository of American cultural traditions was a concept that captured the imagination of Putnam's successor, writer, lawyer, and poet Archibald MacLeish. Appointed by President Franklin Roosevelt in 1939, MacLeish served as Librarian of Congress until the end of 1944, when he became assistant secretary of state. An advocate of U.S. involvement in World War II, MacLeish used the office of Librarian of Congress imaginatively to speak out on behalf of democracy. He urged librarians to "become active and not passive agents of the democratic process," and criticized his fellow intellectuals for their failure to defend American culture against the threat of totalitarianism.[12] He became the most visible Librarian of Congress in the history of the office.

Paying tribute to Thomas Jefferson's concept of liberty and self-government, in 1941 Librarian MacLeish dedicated the South Reading Room in the Library's Adams Building to the Library's principal founder. At MacLeish's request, artist Ezra Winter decorated the Jefferson Reading Room with four murals that drew their theme from Jefferson quotations on the subjects of freedom, the "living generation," education, and democratic government. MacLeish also established a "democracy alcove" in the Main Reading Room, where readers could find the classic texts of the American tradition, including the Declaration of Independence, the Constitution, the Federalist Papers, and other writings of American statesmen. When in 1943 the Library commemorated the bicentennial of Jefferson's birth, MacLeish called Jefferson's definition of liberty the "greatest and the most moving, as well as the most articulate." An annotated catalog of the books in Jefferson's personal library by bibliographer E. Millicent Sowerby was undertaken (it was published in five volumes, 1952–59), and the Library started microfilming its collection of Jefferson papers in the same year.

Librarian MacLeish resigned in 1944 and, in 1945, President Harry Truman named Assistant Librarian Luther H. Evans, a political scientist, as Librarian of Congress. Evans served until 1953. To justify his ambitious proposals in 1947 to expand the Library's collections and services, Evans emphasized Jefferson's "doctrine of completeness and inclusiveness." The challenges of the postwar years meant, to Evans, that "no spot on the earth's surface is any longer alien to the interest of the American people." He felt that the major lesson of World War II was that "however large our collections now may be, they are pitifully and tragically small in comparison with the demands of the nation." He described the need for larger collections of research materials about foreign countries in practical, patriotic terms, noting that in the years leading up to the war "the wants of early issues of the *Voelkische Beobachter* prevented the first auguries of Naziism," while during the war, weather data on the Himalayas from the Library's collection helped the Air Force."[13]

By World War II the Library of Congress was widely recognized as a symbol of democracy. In the early 1950s, Librarian Evans became involved in bureaucratic sparring over the possession of the Declaration of Independence and the Constitution, which had been transferred in 1921 from the Department of State to the Library of Congress. When the National Archives building was constructed between 1933 and 1935, plans were made for the display of these documents and the Bill of Rights in the new building's spacious interior hall. In 1938 the Department of State transferred the Bill of Rights to the National Archives. Librarian of Congress Putnam, however, refused to budge. World War II intervened and it was left to Librarian Evans, who felt the documents indeed should be at the National Archives, to settle the question. Finally, in 1952, the Library reluctantly but gracefully relinquished the two treasures.

"Libraries-Creativity-Liberty"

Historian James H. Billington took the oath of office as the thirteenth Librarian of Congress on September 14, 1987. Convinced that the Library of Congress needed to share its resources more widely throughout the nation, he began several projects to test new technologies that might provide direct access by libraries and schools to the Library's collections and databases. The experimental American Memory Project, launched in 1990, provided electronic copies of selected collections of American history and culture to schools and libraries. The next year the Library began a two-year project to provide the state library agencies online access to its databases.

Envisioning a new educational role for the Library, Billington began strengthening the institution's cultural programs, often using private funds obtained from the James Madison Council, a private-sector support group he established in 1990. In his budget presentation to Congress for 1993, the Librarian emphasized how the Library of Congress was becoming, for the first time, "an important catalyst for the educational, competitive, and creative needs of our nation." New electronic technology, properly organized and supported, should be applied to a Jeffersonian purpose, enabling the Library to "increase the knowledge available to Americans in their local communities—in schools, colleges, libraries, and private sector research enterprises." In this way "even those Americans far from great universities and the most affluent schools and libraries can still have access to the best of the nation's heritage and the latest in up-to-date information."[14]

In 1994, the Library made its bibliographic records and selected items from its Americana collections (mostly manuscripts, maps, photographs, and music) available online, and the institution began establishing what is now a multi-tiered presence on the Web. The same year Congress approved the Library's five-year National Digital Library (NDL) program. Through a combination of private and government funding, the NDL program began collecting digital versions of unique historical materials from more than seventy collections in the Library of Congress and thirty-three other research institutions and made them available, free of charge, on the Library's American Memory Web site.

Thus began a new era in service and accessibility to the Library's collections. Today the Library of Congress is a leader among large institutions in making collections available via the Web. Its Web site, with sections devoted to its own collections, catalogs, and exhibitions, as well as to legislation before Congress and information from the U.S. Copyright Office, is one of the most frequently used institutional sites in the world. The online exhibitions portion of the site, featuring American treasures such as Jefferson's rough draft of the Declaration of Independence (from the Jefferson papers) and two different drafts of Lincoln's Gettysburg Address, is one of the most popular features.

A historian of Russian culture, Librarian Billington had a special interest in using the Library and its resources to encourage the development of democracy in Russia and in Central and Eastern Europe after the collapse of Communism in the early 1990s. Congress approved a special parliamentary assistance program for Central and Eastern Europe (1990–96) and the Soros Foundation supported a Visiting Fellows program that brought Russian librarians to the United States. In 1999 Congress established the Russian Leadership Program (RLP) to bring young Russian civic and political leaders to the United States to observe American democracy and business firsthand. The program was reauthorized by Congress in 2000. Administered by the Library of Congress, by the end of 2000 RLP had brought more than 4,000 Russian leaders to the United States for short visits. In 2000 the program focused on direct legislature-to-legislature exchanges between members of the U.S. Congress and members of the Russian Duma and Federation Council. Leaders from eighty-seven of Russia's eighty-nine regions participated.

The Library of Congress celebrated its bicentennial throughout 2000. The Bicentennial Steering Committee chose "Libraries-Creativity-Liberty" as a major theme because it encompassed the library's key role in promoting creativity in the preservation, organization, and sharing of recorded knowledge and the important role of all libraries—in the Jeffersonian sense—of connecting knowledge and information to responsibilities of citizenship in a democracy. The Library of Congress and the library community developed many joint projects during the bicentennial year, including promotional materials and programs at the annual and midwinter conferences of the American Library Association in 1999 and 2000; a series of projects with the federal library community; second-day issue ceremonies for the Library of Congress Bicentennial postage stamp at more than 200 libraries around the country; poetry readings in dozens of libraries in connection with Poet Laureate Robert Pinsky's "Favorite Poem" project; and "Beyond Words: Celebrating America's Libraries," a national photography contest sponsored with the American Library Association. In addition, three major Library of Congress Bicentennial programs celebrated the "Libraries-Creativity-Liberty" theme: a joint exhibition with the British Library, "John Bull and Uncle Sam: Four Centuries of British-American Relations" (Nov. 16, 1999–Mar. 4, 2000); "National Libraries of the World: Interpreting the Past, Shaping the Future," an international symposium held on October 23–26, 2000; and "To Preserve and Protect:

The Strategic Stewardship of Cultural Resources," a symposium sponsored with the Association of Research Libraries on October 30–31, 2000.

One of the most appropriate and dramatic bicentennial projects aimed to replace the 4,000 books in Jefferson's library that were destroyed in the fire in the U.S. Capitol in 1851. Using funds generously supported by members of the Madison Council, by the end of 2000 all but 800 volumes had been replaced.

Librarian Billington began his 1999 *Annual Report* by thanking Congress for its support, noting that as the Library approached its third century, "Congress can look back with pride at its role as the greatest single patron of a library in the history of civilization." He also stressed the importance of the Library's National Digital Library Program "as the most substantive provider of high-quality, free educational content on the Internet." In October 2000 he announced that the Library had achieved its bicentennial goal of mounting five million digital items on its American Memory Web site by the end of 2000.

Librarian Billington's determination to extend the reach and influence of the Library of Congress is very much in the ambitious tradition of his predecessors. Alone among the world's great libraries, the Library of Congress still attempts to be a universal library, collecting materials of research value in almost all languages and media. Entering its third century, it still is guided by Thomas Jefferson's beliefs that democracy depends on knowledge and that all topics are important to the library of the national legislature—and to the American people.

Notes

1. James Truslow Adams, *The Epic of America* (Boston: Little, Brown, and Co., 1931), 414–15. Unless otherwise indicated, dates and statistics in this article are from John Y. Cole, *For Congress and the Nation: A Chronological History of the Library of Congress* (Washington, D.C.: Library of Congress, 1979). For a recent interpretation of the Library's history, see James Conaway, *America's Library: The Story of the Library of Congress, 1800–2000* (New Haven, Conn.: Yale Univ. Pr., 2000).
2. Jefferson to Samuel H. Smith, September 21, 1814, Jefferson Papers, Library of Congress.
3. Ainsworth Rand Spofford, "The Government Library at Washington," *International Review* 5 (Nov. 1878): 769.
4. U.S. Congress, *Special Report of the Librarian of Congress to the Joint Committee on the Library Concerning the Historical Library of Peter Force, Esq.* (Washington, D.C., Jan. 25, 1867).

5. Ainsworth Rand Spofford to Thomas A. Jenckes, July 9, 1870, Librarian's Letterbook No. 8, Library of Congress Archives.

6. "The Library of Congress. The Capitol and the Grounds," *Speech of the Hon. Justin S. Morrill of Vermont in the Senate of the United States, March 31, 1879* (Washington, D.C., 1879). Pamphlet.

7. "The Library of Congress" (speech delivered by the Hon. D. W. Voorhees of Indiana in the Senate of the United States, May 5, 1880, Washington, D.C.).

8. Report of the Librarian of Congress for the Fiscal Year Ended June 30, 1898 (Washington, D.C., Government Printing Office, 1898), 83.

9. Herbert Putnam, "The Library of Congress as the National Library," *Library Journal* 30 (Sept. 1905): C20.

10. John Y. Cole, "The Library of Congress and American Scholarship, 1865–1939," in *Libraries and Scholarly Communication in the United States: The Historian Dimension,*" Phyllis Dain and John Y. Cole, eds. (New York: Greenwood Pr., 1990), 45–61.

11. Herbert Putnam, "The Relation of the National Library to Historical Research in the United States," in *Annual Report for 1901*, American Historical Association (Washington, D.C., 1902), 120.

12. Archibald MacLeish, "The Librarian and the Democratic Process," *ALA Bulletin* 34 (June 1940): 388.

13. Luther H. Evans, "Library of Congress Records a New Era of World Progress," *The* (Washington, D.C.) *Sunday Star*, Dec. 2, 1945.

14. James H. Billington, Statement before the Subcommittee on Legislative Appropriations, Committee on Appropriations, U.S. House of Representatives, Fiscal 1993 Budget Request, Jan. 29, 1992.

The Library of Congress and the Widening Horizons of Democracy Building

James H. Billington

In 1987, when I took the oath of office as the thirteenth Librarian of Congress, I spoke of the need to move the Library of Congress both out more broadly and in more deeply simultaneously. Despite the seeming contradiction between the two, both of these directions derive naturally from the Library's historical role as a citadel of democracy in America.

Moving out more broadly means making more of the riches of the Library of Congress more available to more people to use in more ways. At the dawn of the twentieth century, this meant opening capacious public reading rooms in the new Jefferson Building and extending our cataloging services to the nation. At the beginning of the twenty-first century, the imperative to reach out has meant using new technologies to distribute the most interesting and important records of the nation's memory through the Internet to people wherever they live.

The Library is also reaching out further into the world to fulfill its unique mission to build collections about all cultures and in all languages on behalf of all our peoples. America itself is a nation of nations, increasingly connected to all the nations of the world. Much of the world's knowledge and information is contained in new formats: ephemera, audiovisual media, digital archives. The Library of Congress must select, preserve, and make accessible the most important items in these categories to sustain its service mission to both the working government of a free people and the scholarly frontiers of all people. It does not serve either well if it simply spreads more information to other places without generating knowledge and wisdom within the Library. We are working hard to preserve and protect our heritage as it is reflected in the Library's remarkable collections and to strengthen our administrative infrastructure. However, we also are making strides in developing programs based on the content and the use of these collections. In order to sustain in our time the great experiment in freedom begun in Philadelphia, we must develop new peaks of intellectual excellence that help our country look beyond the present-minded, advocacy agendas of the political process in our nation's capital. The republic of letters no less than the capital of this republic needs people able and willing to put things together and not just take them apart.

Reaching Out to the World

The Library of Congress is an international institution with a universal collection not limited by subject, format, or national boundary. The Library collects material in more than 460 languages; about two-thirds of the books it acquires are in languages other than English. Its diverse collections include books, pamphlets, manuscripts, music, maps, newspapers, microforms and graphic arts, and other materials totaling 120 million items. The Library's Hispanic American and Arabic collections are larger than exist in Latin America or the Arabic world; the Chinese, Japanese, Korean, Polish, and Russian collections are the largest outside of the countries where these languages are spoken. The map, poster, music, and movie collections are the largest in the world.

Why did this happen? How did a library established in 1800 by the American national legislature for its own use become an international library, universal in scope and service?

Historically, the Library's functions have grown naturally out of the expansion of its collections. The key event in the Library's early history was the purchase by Congress in 1815 of Thomas Jefferson's personal library. As president of the United States from 1801 to 1809, Jefferson had taken a keen interest in the small, initial Library of Congress, recommending books for its collection and appointing the first two Librarians of Congress. When the British army invaded Washington and burned the Capitol, including the 3,000-volume Library of Congress, Jefferson offered to sell his personal library to the Congress to "recommence" its library. His 6,487-volume library was acquired and became much more than a replacement. It included more than twice the number of volumes that had been destroyed, and it expanded the scope of the Library far beyond a legislative reference library of legal, economic, and historical works. Jefferson believed that the power of the intellect should shape a free and democratic society. He had gathered books on all subjects, including architecture, the arts, science, literature, and geography—and in languages that included French, Spanish, German, Latin, Greek, and Russian. Anticipating the argument that his collection might be too wide-ranging, he argued that there was "no subject to which a member of Congress might not have occasion to refer." The Jeffersonian idea that all subjects were important, should be collected, and then made available to both the national legislature and the American people they serve is still the basic rationale for the Library of Congress's comprehensive collecting policies.

Using the theme "Libraries-Creativity-Liberty," the Library of Congress celebrated its Bicentennial in the year 2000. The reconstruction of Jefferson's library, much of which was lost in a fire in the U.S. Capitol in 1851, was a major bicentennial project. Today, the reconstructed library occupies a place of honor in the Library's principal building, which also is named for Jefferson. The Library's adjacent second and third buildings on Capitol Hill also bear the names of founding fathers both of our country and of the Library of Congress. The Adams Building is named for John Adams, the president who signed the bill creating the Library of Congress in 1800; the Madison Building is this nation's official memorial to President James Madison, who, in 1783, first proposed in the Continental Congress the creation of a library for the national legislature. The quotation from Madison carved on the exterior of the Madison Building expresses the strong belief shared by Adams, Jefferson, and Madison alike that "Knowledge will forever govern ignorance, and that a people who mean to be their own governors must arm themselves with the power which knowledge gives."

In spite of the Jeffersonian rationale for expansion, the Library of Congress's international collections did not really begin to grow until the beginning of the twentieth century, a few years after the spacious Jefferson Building opened. Librarian of Congress Herbert Putnam (1899–1939) deserves major credit for stimulating the growth of the Library's research collections in other languages and about other cultures. Putnam believed that the national library should be not just a comprehensive collection of Americana but also a collection "universal in scope which has a duty to the country as a whole." In 1901, he told a group of scholars that the national library had a special obligation to gather and make available the records and publications of the other countries in the Western hemisphere. His sources for acquisitions soon extended to other continents as well, and, by the time he retired in 1939, the Library of Congress owned important special collections of Indica and Hebraica as well as substantial collections of books from Russia, Germany, Spain, Portugal, China, and Japan. In 1926, Putnam obtained appropriated funds to send a permanent Library representative to Paris to make acquisitions and develop contacts with dealers, scholars, and learned institutions. In the same year, Putnam sent James B. Childs, chief of the Library's Documents Division, to Germany, Russia, Lithuania, and

Latvia to establish document exchange programs; in the next year, Childs went to Bulgaria, Greece, Rumania, and Yugoslavia. And in 1928 Putnam established a Chinese Literature Division.

World War II stimulated further development of the Library's international collections and activities. Librarian of Congress Archibald MacLeish (1939–44) extended Jefferson's rationale to foreign materials asserting, in his "Canons of Selection" that the Library should acquire the "written records of those societies and peoples whose experience is of most immediate concern to the people of the United States." MacLeish's successor, Librarian of Congress Luther H. Evans (1945–53) created a mission in Europe to acquire European publications for the Library and other American libraries. In 1945 the Library of Congress organized a reference library in San Francisco to assist participants in the conference that established the United Nations. Two years later, a Library of Congress mission to Japan provided advice for the establishment of the National Diet Library. This early example of a Library of Congress democracy-building project resulted in an institution patterned broadly after the Library of Congress.

Under L. Quincy Mumford, Librarian of Congress from 1954 to 1974, the foreign acquisitions program of the Library of Congress experienced its most dramatic growth. Under the terms of the Agricultural Trade Development and Assistance Act of 1954 (Public Law 480), in 1961 the Library established acquisitions centers in New Delhi and Cairo to purchase for research libraries throughout the United States publications on South Asia and the Middle East, respectively. In 1965, President Lyndon B. Johnson approved a Higher Education Act which, through Title IIC, directed the Library of Congress to acquire, insofar as possible, all current library materials of value to scholarship published throughout the world and to provide cataloging information. This law came closer than any other legislation to making Jefferson's concept of comprehensiveness part of the Library's official mandate. It led to the opening of new acquisitions offices around the world, beginning with London in 1966. Today, overseas offices in New Delhi (India), Cairo (Egypt), Rio de Janeiro (Brazil), Jakarta (Indonesia), Nairobi (Kenya), and Islamabad (Pakistan) collectively acquire materials from more than sixty countries and acquire materials on behalf of some ninety United States libraries participating in the Library's Cooperative Acquisitions Program.

In recent years the Library of Congress has increasingly become involved in programs that support the sharing of people and personal experience as well as collections. The Library of Congress-Soros Foundations Visiting Fellow Program, initiated in 1990, is a prime example. These three-month fellowships for librarians and information specialists in Russia and fifteen other countries, mostly from Central and Eastern Europe, are designed to expose participants from former Communist countries to the workings of libraries in a democracy and the concept of open access to information.

Congressional Support of the Library's Widening Role

The Library of Congress was originally established in 1800 to provide "such books as may be necessary for the use of Congress," and reference and research support for Congress is still the Library's highest priority. Through dozens of laws since 1802, when the president and vice president were permitted to use its library, Congress has approved the expansion of the Library's functions and of the clientele it serves. Few people, in fact, realize that the Congress has, over the years, been the most consistent and generous benefactor of a library in the history of the world.

In 1950, the Library's sesquicentennial year, the eminent librarian S. R. Ranganathan wrote:

> The institution serving as the national library of the United States is perhaps more fortunate than its predecessors in other countries. It has the Congress as its godfather. . . . This stroke of good fortune has made it perhaps the most influential of all the national libraries of the world.[1]

As part of our bicentennial commemoration last year, I had the pleasure of joining with my predecessor as Librarian of Congress, Daniel J. Boorstin, in expressing similar appreciation to the Congress.

In 1914 the Legislative Reference Service was established within the Library as a separate administrative unit devoted solely to fulfilling Congress's need for information about all aspects of the legislative process. Renamed the Congressional Research Service (CRS) in 1970 and given additional analytical responsibilities, CRS provides timely, objective, nonpartisan answers to more than 600,000 Congressional requests annually.

In the 1990s Congress initiated two important democracy-building projects: the Parliamentary Assistance Programs (1990–96) and The Library of Congress Russian Leadership Program (1999–). Each of these special projects took advantage of the Library of Congress's exceptional experience and capabilities to bring "liberty and learning," in Madison's phrase, together in mutual support of free government.

The dramatic sudden collapse of the Communist regimes in the Soviet Union and Central and Eastern Europe prompted Congress to establish parliamentary development programs in twelve emerging democracies of Central and Eastern Europe and the former Soviet Union. The Congressional Research Service administered and implemented the programs. A special House of Representatives Task Force on the Development of Parliamentary Institutions in Eastern Europe provided overall direction, and the House of Representatives Information Systems Office provided automation experts. The Joint Committee on the Library of the U.S. Congress, the Library's oversight committee, authorized the programs in Russia and Ukraine.

Recognizing the Jeffersonian link between access to information and the building of a democracy, the program aimed to develop the capacity to gather objective information and provide independent analysis for the new legislatures. The projects attempted to strengthen parliamentary infrastructure, streamlining work with modern automation and office systems.

The CRS-hosted training programs in both Washington, D.C., and Eastern Europe were funded mostly by the U.S. Agency for International Development but also by foundations that provided computer equipment and books and other library materials. Many Eastern European parliamentary libraries expanded their mission from simply lending books to providing and promoting a broader range of information services. Through the Library of Congress and other Internet resources, they now have international reference resources that can help them find comparative information on policy issues. Intended as a "jump start" and not a permanent program, Congress ended the effort on December 31, 1996, but its influence has been lasting. It is one of the best examples of how the Library of Congress helped stimulate the extension of the democratic ideals upon which it was founded.

The Library of Congress "Open World" Russian Leadership Program (RLP) encourages mutual understanding among U.S. and Russian public policy decision-makers by exposing the emerging new post-Soviet generation of leaders to free enterprise and to American democratic institutions. The program was inspired by the small, but critical, part of the Marshall Plan that brought large numbers of emerging German political and civic leaders to the United States after World War II to gain first-hand experience of the workings of democracy. The U.S. Congress authorized RLP in 1999 and allocated $10 million for its implementation. Because of the overwhelming success of this pilot project, Congress appropriated another $10 million in 2000. In each instance, Senator Ted Stevens of Alaska, chairman of the Joint Committee on the Library, was the chief sponsor of the authorizing legislation.

One of the largest and most inclusive one-time foreign visitation programs ever developed by the U.S., RLP brings delegations of visitors to the United States for short but intensive visits in communities with interests parallel to their own. The Library of Congress awards grants and contracts from Congressional funding to partner organizations such as Rotary International, the American Foreign Policy Council, the Center for Democracy, the Russian Initiative of the United Methodist Church, and Meridian International Center.

In 1999, RLP brought 2,200 of Russia's new and future political leaders to experience America first-hand. The visitors represented forty-one ethnic groups from eighty-three of Russia's regions, and they stayed mostly with American families in their homes in 538 American communities in forty-five states and the District of Columbia. Ten U.S. Senators hosted members of the Federation Council, Russia's upper legislative house, and thirty-two members of the U.S. House of Representatives hosted deputies of the Russian lower body, the State Duma.

The RLP brought 1,605 Russian leaders to the United States in 2000 for a program that had a different character, focusing grants in three categories: (1) the *Duma/Federation Council Program*, which hosted delegations of members of parliament by matching their committee membership with U.S. senators and congressmen. Each delegation focused on a particular issue such as defense, land reform, energy, environment, and the rule of law; (2) a two-day Orientation Program, conducted in Washington, D.C., and in Atlanta, Georgia, provided a basic introduction to the structure of U.S. government at all levels; and (3) an eight-day Local Hosting Program matched Russian participants with host communities and professional counterparts comparable to their own communities and official positions.

Reaching Out More Broadly: The Digital Revolution

Congress has also supported the Library of Congress's efforts, beginning in the 1990s, to share its unique special collections with the nation and the world via the Internet. In 1994, Congress endorsed the Library's five-year National Digital Library (NDL) program, which used both government and private funding to make digital versions of unique historical items from special research collections (mostly manuscripts, maps, photographs, sound recordings, music, and film) available, free of charge, on the Library's Web site. Today, the Library of Congress is a world leader in making high-quality, free material available online through the Web for educational use everywhere. By becoming one of the most important content providers on the Internet, the Library is developing new audiences for its collections beyond the research and scholarly community. Families and young people are the target audience of a new, user-friendly Web site established on April 24, 2000, the Library's 200th birthday. By the end of the bicentennial year, the Library had reached its stated goal of mounting on its Web site five million digital items from its collections of American history and culture. This represents a massive transfer of national treasures to local public schools and libraries all over America.

Congress also helped the Library take the first steps from a National Digital Library towards a global online library. *Meeting of Frontiers*, a project funded by a special appropriation in the Library's FY 1999 budget, enables the Library to create digital copies of unique and rare materials that trace the parallel experiences of the United States and Russia in exploring, developing, and settling their respective frontiers, which met in the Pacific Northwest and Alaska.

The *Meeting of Frontiers* pilot site was unveiled in December 1999 with 70,000 images from the Library's rare book, manuscript, map, photograph, film, and sound recording collections. These collections tell the stories of the explorers, fur traders, missionaries, exiles, gold miners, and adventurers who peopled both frontiers, as well as their interactions with the native peoples of Siberia and the American West. The site is completely bilingual, in English and Russian, and is intended for use in U.S. and Russian schools and libraries and by the general public in both countries. *Meeting of Frontiers* is being expanded with rare additional collections from libraries and partner institutions in the United States and Russia, including the Russian State Library in Moscow and the Russian National Library in St. Petersburg.

Further movement towards a global online library occurred in 2000 when the Library of Congress signed an ambitious agreement with Spain to digitize many of that country's fabulous and rarely seen primary documents about the history of Hispanic America. Digital projects with other nations were discussed in October 2000 at a major Library of Congress conference on "National Libraries of the World: Interpreting the Past, Shaping the Future."

Reaching in More Deeply: The Kluge Center

In October 2000, Senator Ted Stevens, chairman of the Joint Committee on the Library; Representative Bill Thomas, vice chairman of the Committee; and I announced the establishment at the Library of Congress of the John W. Kluge Center and the John W. Kluge Prize in the Human Sciences. The Kluge Center and Prize were made possible by an extraordinary gift of $60 million from Metromedia President John W. Kluge and present a new opportunity to bring the world's greatest minds to delve into the Library's unparalleled resources. The Center will be located in that corner of the Jefferson Building that is opposite the Capitol and Supreme Court.

The Kluge Center will bring scholars from the United States and the world into residence in Washington for limited periods of time. Occupants of five senior chairs and an even larger number of younger scholars will benefit from the Library's worldwide collection strengths and the experience and skills of the Library's expert curators as well as the policy experts in the Library's Congressional Research Service.

Almost all members of Congress have been in the Jefferson Building in recent months for gatherings in the Members Room or other events. This unique building offers senators and representatives a unique opportunity to meet in a scholarly atmosphere yet be able easily to answer a roll call vote in the Capitol across the street.

The type of meeting between thinkers and doers that will develop in the Kluge Center will not duplicate or recycle the many discussions that already occur in the universities and public policy centers in and around Washington. The Center will seek to be catalytic rather than bureaucratic. Meetings will be informal and will try to bring to members of Congress and the public policy community the deeper historical and philosophical perspective of the world's leading thinkers who are widely scattered throughout the world but rarely come to Washington and almost never stay long enough for serious dialog.

Initially, there will be five broadly defined Kluge Senior Chairs: American Law and Governance; Culture and Society of the North, focusing on areas including Europe, Russia, and East Asia; Culture and Society of the South, focusing on the regions of Africa, Latin America, the Middle East, and South and Southeast Asia; Technology and Society; and Modern Culture. The new Center will welcome and accommodate three other distinguished, high-level senior chairs being established at the Library: the Papamarkou Chair in Education, the Henry A. Kissinger Chair in Foreign Policy and International Relations, and the Cary and Ann Maguire Chair in American History and Ethics. Together with the five Kluge chairs, these three broadly defined chairs will assume that there will be a critical mass of the world's leading thinkers in Washington, D.C., at any given time. Their presence will provide an opportunity for a new type of dialog with members of Congress in an authentically scholarly atmosphere.

Finally, in order to celebrate the importance of the human sciences for the public interest, the Kluge endowment will establish in the Library of Congress a unique prize that fills a gap in the firmament of Nobel Prizes and other major, internationally recognized awards. The presentation of the John W. Kluge Prize in the Human Sciences will dramatize America's world leadership in the broad areas of humanistic and social studies and will provide national recognition for a lifetime of achievement in the intellectual arts analogous to Kennedy Center Awards in the Performing Arts.

Conclusion

The Library is using the digital revolution to move materials out more broadly to enrich public education in the nation. The Kluge and other chairs and fellowships will bring the scholarly world to use the multi-medial, multi-linguistic, and human resources of the Library of Congress more deeply and to share scholarly wisdom and perspective directly with our lawmakers. *Meeting of Frontiers* is the Library's first digital project involving international collections and extensive cooperation with foreign institutions to obtain materials for the Library's collections in digital form. Moreover, as the Library's digitization program moves forward, we plan to continue the conversation of unique educational resources that will include important international as well as national materials.

The Kluge Center will be located in the midst of the expanded space for scholars generally in the Library's Jefferson Building—itself a unique tribute to the universality of knowledge and the close relationship between knowledge and democracy. In 1984 Congress generously provided funds for the restoration and renovation of this magnificent structure, and today it houses reading rooms, reference specialists, and collections representing all parts of the world. In 2001 the Library opened "World Treasures of the Library of Congress" in the Jefferson Building's elegant northwest exhibition gallery. It will provide a permanent display, on a rotating basis, of significant items from other civilizations and cultures. It is a companion exhibition to the permanent, rotating exhibition of "American Treasures of the Library of Congress" across the way in the southeast pavilion.

For many of us, however, the most significant exhibition in the Jefferson Building remains the reconstructed library of Thomas Jefferson—arranged for the first time since 1815 in his original classification order. It is the historic core of the Library of Congress and symbolizes America's enduring hopes for the practical uses of knowledge in practicing democracy. In our age of increasing limitations in the physical world, it may be that only in the realm of the mind and spirit can the horizons for our cherished ideal of freedom remain truly infinite.

The pursuit of truth is the highest form of Jefferson's pursuit of happiness. Ours is a society that is properly reluctant to accept answers from those who have stopped asking questions. The ongoing pursuit of truth helps keep us from the pursuit of each other. It enables us to go on pursuing the American democratic dream that, whatever the problems of today, tomorrow can still be better than yesterday.

Note

1. S. R. Ranganathan, "The Library of Congress among National Libraries," *ALA Bulletin* 44 (Oct. 1950): 356.

VI. Library
Advocacy
for Democracy

Advocating for America's Right to Know

Patricia Glass Schuman

As we enter this first year of the twenty-first century contradictory views about America's libraries and librarians abound. Some consider libraries cultural frills at best, or institutions of the past at worst. Others see libraries as threats to morality because they provide access not only to books, but to the Internet. None of these views can simply be dismissed as wrongheaded. In reality, they all represent a danger to a critical precept of American democracy: our right to know.

Although library use is increasing, and libraries and librarians are more necessary than ever, their continued relevance is being questioned. Intense competition for public and institutional dollars makes it more crucial than ever that library advocates help public policy and decisionmakers understand that America's libraries—public, school, academic, and special—are essential in the information age. Other interests have claims that they advocate forcefully in the media and especially in executive chambers and legislative halls. Some are spending megabucks to influence funding and policy. The library community does not have megabucks. What we do have is public support. As special interests make their case in the debate over the shape of cyberspace, library advocates must stand in defense of the public interest and America's right to know.

Our libraries and librarians are a national treasure. Without open and equitable access to information through libraries, America's right to know is at risk: our right to know—and remember—our past; our right to know—and understand—our present; and, our right to know—and evaluate—information that can determine our future. In the early 1990s when libraries were threatened by funding cuts, I chose "your right to know: librarians make it happen" as the focus of my ALA presidency in 1991–92. We planned ALA's first nationwide media campaign to focus on libraries and librarians as crucial to an informed, just, and equitable democratic society. Today's threats are equally as dangerous. Without the right to know, we are far too vulnerable to the power of those who would like to abridge our right to make our own decisions.

Ten years ago, when we began ALA's efforts to train library advocates, we encountered major resistance from some librarians. We also garnered a great deal of support for these efforts. Library advocacy is now accepted as a necessity. ALA has strengthened its Washington efforts and committed to a five-year public awareness campaign. More than 25,000 advocates—librarians, library workers, library supporters—have been trained and are speaking out for their libraries. Our task is to increase that number a thousand-fold.

Privatization of government information, outsourcing, and severe budget slashes taught us that America's libraries are not above politics. Library advocacy has resulted in record high (though not high enough) federal funding, the establishment of the E-Rate, and a new department of library and museum services. Advocacy helped to hold the line on fair use for libraries and educators in the Digital Millennium Copyright Act. It helped designate libraries as universal service providers for electronic information by Congress. In California, the state hardest hit by a weakened economy and taxpayer revolt in the early nineties, it helped launch a major reinvestment in school libraries.

We have also learned that when we fight for the right to know, we can win. Across the nation, cities large and small are reinvesting in their libraries to ensure that every member of their community has access to the Internet and other information technology. But, despite our success, many libraries still remain underfunded, understaffed, and unwired. The fight for fair use of electronic materials is far from over. Censorship has taken on whole new dimensions in cyberspace. Free access to government information in the electronic age is by no means a given. Privatization, a trend in social services and public schools, has now begun to rear its head in public libraries.

Generations of Americans have used libraries and assumed their existence as a natural right. But assumptions are no longer enough. The challenge now is to convince the public and decisionmakers that America's libraries are not institutions of the past. Rather, the demographic, social, economic, and cultural realities of the twenty-first century require well-funded, effective library services—library services easily available to all individuals, where they live, where they study, and where they work.

Librarians were concerned about access to information and information literacy way before the information gap became a digital divide. We have always known the quality of people's lives *depends* on quality information, that more information isn't always better, and that real information power is having the right information you need when you need it. In frontier America, one of the measures by which a community was deemed civilized was the presence (or absence) of a library. Americans need their libraries more than ever to find jobs, to learn to read, to be literate online, to find vital health facts, to research their environment and diets, and to find food for the soul. On the new frontiers of cyberspace, libraries continue to be part of the American dream. The decisionmakers controlling the purse strings and the policymakers setting the legal parameters must get the library message. America's libraries are an important part of the *solution* to the major social problems facing us.

People cannot exercise their right to know unless information is organized and available. None of us can exercise our right to know unless we are intellectually able and psychologically motivated to access and use information. The right to know is much more than free speech. To truly have the right to free expression, people need more than constitutional guarantees; they need societal commitments as well. If you have no job, no education, and no money—your voice will not carry very far. You may have the right to know, but if you don't know how to use it—if you're not aware of it—it will do you no good. Books, magazines, and databases are of little value to people who cannot read. Illiteracy costs this country more than $225 billion annually in lost productivity, welfare payments, crime, accidents, and lost taxes.

America's libraries are not simply a safety net for information "have-nots." Even the information "haves" will lose if they are relegated to simply "buying" whatever information they need from their local bookstore or Internet service provider. They will lose their access to libraries and librarians, to trained knowledge navigators. If we truly believe that information can be used for powerful purposes, we must persuade people that librarians dispense tools for empowerment. We must convince them that the services librarians offer are an essential part of the solution to problems like illiteracy, drugs, poverty, crime, pollution, illness, and unemployment. We must remind them that librarians put a human face on cyberspace while they continue to open doors for millions of immigrants and native-born Americans.

Information itself is not power. The transmission of data, or even facts, must never be confused with the uses people make of them. Information is simply raw material. It is a powerful tool only when processed by the human mind. Salespeople sell information products. Librarians, on the other hand, help people use information to solve problems. Information is like trust, or love. It becomes infinitely more valuable when shared. This sharing is where America's libraries have their greatest potential, their force, their vital impact. They are a critical resource, a public good essential for a humane and just society.

We live in an age where the very idea of public services is under attack, and librarians are being urged to run libraries more like businesses. We must not romanticize the abilities of the private sector. Rather, we must tell the library story by better articulation of the inestimable benefits of libraries as a public service, inherently governmental and community based. We must never forget that the business of librarians is not information. Librarians have no business in business. Librarians have a mission—understanding through knowledge. We help people solve information problems.

Librarians are trained knowledge navigators; professionals ethically committed to the organization and dissemination of information, the dissemination of knowledge, and the tools for empowerment. Our profession is intrinsically bound to the ideals of democracy. Our very existence stands in defense of the First Amendment—and in defense of equality. Librarians are disseminators of information, not merely its guardians. We are often considered society's gate-keepers, but librarians are actually the gateways. Librarianship is the one profession dedicated to ensuring the right to know.

Guarding the right to know means taking leadership. People who know the value of libraries must be leaders who *fight* for libraries. In this current race to shape cyberspace, what actually happens will depend not just on technological innovations, but on our human creativity, ingenuity, vision, advocacy, and commitment. If we truly believe the words carved above the portals of many libraries, "knowledge is power," we must accept responsibility for the exercise of that power. What we ought to be carving above library doorways is "librarians hold the keys to power." We hold information in trust. Libraries are both the first source and the ultimate repository. Librarians deliver the materials and services that undergird the public's right to know by keeping affordable, accessible, and available.

Library budget problems and public policies and laws that infringe on people's right to receive and use information can no longer be silent crises. Protecting the right to know means people must also be aware of the value of libraries and librarians. By using our collective power to influence the press and public policymakers, we can remind decisionmakers that libraries are fundamental to our democracy, that libraries and librarians are essential to a literate and informed citizenry, and that libraries and librarians are as critical to people's lives as hospitals, police, and schools. Public policymakers must recognize that an informed citizenry is a public good that benefits us all. A true information society means that people must not only have access to information, they must be literate enough to use it. We will not truly achieve a true information society, we will not achieve equal opportunity and justice unless—

and until—all people have the library services they need to learn, live, work, participate, and enjoy our democracy.

We can no longer sit back and assume that because our cause is just, the value of libraries and librarians will be recognized. The reality is that even though we know all that librarians can and must do—the American public often does not. Neither, unfortunately, does the pool of talent from which we hope to recruit future librarians. Our information society requires an active professional stance. Even when we effectively promote library buildings, collections, and services—we often forget to tell people about our most powerful resource. The most valuable asset of any library goes home every night: the staff.

This is a critical time for library advocacy. Public policy decisions that will determine how, when, and how much people can exercise their right to know in the twenty-first century are being made at all levels of government *now*. None of us can predict the future. Nevertheless, the library profession can help to influence and invent the future. We are the information experts. We understand both the organization and use of information. Protecting America's right to know requires that we librarians assert ourselves as leaders in meeting society's information needs, as fighters for intellectual freedom and full access to information, as experts in information and communications, as partners in public policymaking, as models for other professionals in recruiting for and service to a pluralistic society, and as professionals working to empower people by teaching them information literacy skills.

Our profession was among the first to recognize the importance of new information technology and to make it available to the public. Our advocacy efforts on behalf of America's libraries are not in our own interest. Speaking up and speaking out for libraries is in the public interest. The library message is a powerful one. Only well-funded, well-stocked, well-staffed, wired libraries will prevent the digital divide from becoming the Grand Canyon.

To capture the public's imagination we need not be concerned with how pretty people think we are—or even how smart. Our challenge is to show them how useful, necessary, and important we are to their everyday lives and work; that librarians are members of a dynamic profession fighting for the right to know. We must articulate our concerns, those of our users, and perhaps more important, the concerns of those who do not use libraries but need our services. Our objective is to excite people about what librarians do, where we do it, and most important—why.

Libraries, librarians, and the right to know cannot be taken for granted. All countries support hospitals, police, and schools. Only free countries support free libraries. What library buildings, their contents, and the people who run

202 LIBRARY ADVOCACY FOR DEMOCRACY

them represent is one of the most fundamental rights we have as American citizens: the right to information, the right to knowledge, the right to all the benefits that knowledge and information deliver—"the right to know." Library advocates must tell the library story at every opportunity if we are to ensure this basic democratic right for the twenty-second century.

Advocacy for Democracy I

The Role of the American
Library Association

William R. Gordon

Those of us attending IFLA represent many countries and many cultures. We represent libraries of all types and all sizes. Our library users are people of all ages, all religions, and all races. We are a diverse group and we represent and serve even more diverse constituencies. We would all agree, nevertheless, that what brings us together is more compelling and more important than any seeming differences. We are librarians. Our common language is the language of information. Our common community is the community of library users—in schools, universities, public libraries, and private industry. Our common work is providing access to information, freely and impartially, to all who seek it. Our common history spans centuries and geography, encompassing everything from the great library of Alexandria to a one-room community library/museum in Hope, Alaska, that won an ALA award for excellence in building design in 1993. Our common future includes the Internet and e-books, digital information and wired communities, virtual buildings, and global information sharing.

Throughout the proud history of our profession, librarians have recognized and championed the power of the printed word in a free and open society. There is no right more fundamental to a democracy than the right of all citizens to information. There is no greater danger to a free society than the loss of freedom that occurs when access to information is restricted. In the turbulent history of recent generations we have seen books burned by those who would deny citizens the right to read.

We have seen newspapers and other media censored by those who would deny citizens the right to know. We face constant challenges from those who would take books off the shelves of our schools and public libraries because the content is seen to be too sexual, too violent, too right-wing or too left-wing,

This paper was first presented at the IFLA Conference in Jerusalem, August 15, 2000.

too religious or too dangerous to religion, to be "safe" for our users. We continue to confront the few who would impose their viewpoints on the many.

We also face challenges as associations from those who would advance their own agendas by misrepresenting our roles and our missions. ALA has been attacked by organizations and individuals who charge that we are sexualizing America's children by exposing them to pornography on the Internet. There are groups that have used their platforms to espouse their points of view and discredit the ALA position on free speech and access to information.

How are we as librarians and association managers to respond? How do we advocate for democracy, for libraries, and for ourselves?

We begin by keeping in mind the importance of associations as advocates for democracy. We provide a forum and a vehicle that allows the voice of librarians to be heard. We create a framework that enables libraries and librarians to increase their effectiveness in empowering the public to participate in a democratic society. We speak out on behalf of our members to promote the free flow of information for all people.

At the American Library Association, our tools are education, legislation and litigation, and advocacy. I'd like to tell you about some of our initiatives in each of these areas.

We educate our members through programming at national and regional conferences, through our publications, and through special initiatives of the association and our member leaders.

Advocacy for democracy will receive particular focus at ALA in 2000–2001. President Nancy Kranich has chosen "Libraries: The Cornerstone of Democracy" as the theme for her presidential year. She has stated, "An informed public constitutes the very foundation of a democracy. Libraries are the cornerstone of democracy in our communities because they assist the public in locating a diversity of resources and in developing the information literacy skills necessary to become responsible, informed citizens who can participate in our democracy." One of Nancy's first initiatives as president was the creation of a tool kit outlining ways that libraries can serve as a resource in the electoral process. The kit was distributed to all of ALA's 59,500 members in the August 2000 issue of our magazine *American Libraries*. It is available on the ALA Web site. If you would like a copy mailed to you also, please contact ALA's Public Information Office.

ALA also extends its educational efforts beyond our membership to the public at large. Our Public Information Office works with regional and national media to disseminate our message and highlight the positive impact of libraries in American communities. We are embarking on a major five-year public awareness campaign as part of our current strategic plan, ALAction 2005. In this plan, we establish ALA as the leading advocate for the value of libraries and librarians in connecting people to recorded knowledge in all forms, and for the public's right to a free and open information society. Democratic values and ideals shape the programs goals, which include increasing support for libraries and librarians by communicating clearly and strongly why libraries and librarians are unique and valuable; serving as the leading voice for equitable access to knowledge and information resources in all formats for all people; becoming a leader in the use of technology for communication with, democratic participation by, and for shared learning among our members; and becoming a leader in continuing education for librarians and library personnel.

One component of ALA's educational mission of which I am particularly proud is ALA's Spectrum Initiative. ALA recognized the need to recruit a diverse professional workforce that is reflective of the communities we serve. In 1997 we announced a three-year program to recruit applicants and award fifty annual scholarships of $5,000 each to students of color to enroll in graduate programs in library and information studies. The success of the Initiative has led to its continuation for a fourth year and a recent commitment by the ALA Executive Board to donate $1 million to an endowment to continue the scholarships into the future. We see this as an investment in libraries, in our communities, and in democracy.

One of the most fundamental components of a democratic society is the legislative process. ALA has become increasingly aware of the impact of legislation on libraries and the public's right to know, as our state and federal governments consider issues ranging from funding to privacy, pornography, and Internet filtering. Our Washington, D.C., office, which was established in 1945, has been strengthened to include an Office of Government Relations and an Office for Information Technology Policy. Together they closely monitor and analyze proposed legislation affecting libraries and information, and they promote the best interests of libraries, library users, and the public at large in a broad and complex range of legislation, regulatory, and public-policy issues.

The Washington Office also sponsors two events that are directly tied to our democratic process. The first is Library Legislative Day. Each year in May, hundreds of librarians and library supporters from all fifty states come to Washington, D.C. They are briefed on current legislative issues and then they fan out to speak with their senators and congressional representatives about the crucial importance of libraries. The twenty-seventh Annual National Library Legislative Day will be held April 30 to May 1, 2001. This year we also sponsored a new initiative, Thank-You Day, a nationwide event during National

Library Week that was created to provide an opportunity for librarians to invite legislators and the press into local libraries to observe library programs and hear success stories made possible through the support of elected officials.

In addition to legislative efforts, when necessary ALA participates in litigation—action undertaken in the courts—in support of libraries. The most compelling example in recent years was ALA's role as lead plaintiff in the Communications Decency Act (CDA) litigation that was heard by the United States Supreme Court in 1997. The CDA legislation was proposed by the U.S. government with the stated goal of removing indecent material from the Internet. The ALA, along with forty-three other organizations including the American Booksellers Association, the Association of American Publishers, and the Freedom to Read Foundation, successfully opposed the legislation as being too vague and putting libraries at risk.

Finally, ALA supports democracy through the efforts of the Office for Intellectual Freedom (OIF), founded in 1967. The OIF performs its role as an advocate for the public's right to information in a variety of ways. The office monitors challenges to library materials and provides support and assistance to librarians as requested. The OIF has a vigorous publications program whose products include the monthly *Intellectual Freedom Action News* and the bimonthly *Newsletter on Intellectual Freedom*. It educates members through programming at conferences and meetings. It also provides special training opportunities, such as the Lawyers for Libraries training institute, which is designed to equip attorneys to counsel and defend libraries, librarians, and library trustees. Each September the OIF cosponsors Banned Books Week to highlight library materials that have been challenged during the preceding year. The message of Banned Books Week, and of all the activities of the OIF, is that we must uphold the freedom of citizens in a democratic society to choose, to read, and to publish, and that we must ensure the availability of unorthodox or unpopular viewpoints to all who wish access to them.

I appreciate this opportunity to highlight the many ways in which the American Library Association advocates for democracy. In closing, I'd like to read a short passage from an article entitled "Of the People, for the People: Public Libraries Serve Democracy," which appeared in the April 2000 issue of *American Libraries*. In this article, the author, David A. Tyckoson, notes that Franklin Delano Roosevelt best articulated the role of the library in a democratic society. During the darkest days of World War II, when the future of democracy was very much in question, he told the nation: "Libraries are directly and immediately involved in the conflict which divides our world, and for two reasons. First, because they are essential to the functioning of a democratic society. Second, because the contemporary conflict touches the integrity of scholarship, the freedom of the mind, and even the survival of culture, and libraries are the great tools of scholarship, the great repositories of culture, and the great symbols of the freedom of the mind."

Advocacy for Democracy II

The Role of the Swedish
Library Association

Joneta Belfrage

What is democracy? There are different definitions. But if you will define a state as a democracy when it is built on the principles of universal and equal suffrage, the democracies of our time are a very modern phenomenon. In Sweden, there has been universal suffrage only since 1918. It was the result of a long struggle based on the work of many popular movements. The start of most of the public libraries in Sweden had the same origin. The people who fought for democracy were aware of the importance of knowledge and free access to information and culture. Therefore they built up libraries within their organizations to be used by their members. Later, when democracy was established, the municipality took over the responsibility for various reasons, including guaranteeing all citizens free access to a library.

For some years now there has been an ongoing discussion in Sweden about the crisis in our democracy. Interest and the participation in political matters and political parties have declined drastically, which makes democracy weaker. There is a gap between the citizens and the elected representatives. The confidence in politicians has declined and a survey made in 1997 to test the credibility of different public institutions showed that the credibility of Parliament, the unions, the municipal council, and the political parties was extremely low. That same year, 1997, the Swedish government set up an official commission to discuss and report on the challenges, problems, and potential for democracy in the twenty-first century.

The report shows that people no longer join the popular movements, that young people are not interested in clubs and associations, and that the confidence in different democratic institutions has declined. The discussion that followed this report has shown that there are different opinions as to what kind

---

This paper was first presented at the IFLA Conference in Jerusalem, August 15, 2000.

of democracy is needed. Some consider it to be sufficient if the citizens vote every fourth year and then leave the rest to the elected representatives. Others find that what the citizens do and say between elections is essential to a living and smoothly functioning democracy. And it is the latter that the authors of the report believe we should fight for.

There have been different explanations given for the current situation as it is. Some say that when the political parties have been a part of the establishment instead of society as a whole the citizens do not feel involved or interested anymore. Others claim that since the real political power has been moved to Brussels, where it is inaccessible, and the national parliament has less to decide, ordinary people have lost interest in political matters.

It is obvious that what has been the core of democracy—discussion, dialogue, and open meetings—has disappeared. And what has replaced all this? It seems to be the media. Today, contacting the media seems to be a better way of making your voice heard than talking directly to an association or a public authority. If you want to influence policy, it is better to use the media than to try to affect a politician.

It is also the media that tell us what the politicians decide. This gives the media great power, and the dialogue between the citizens and the politicians no longer takes place within the political parties or in the popular movements, but elsewhere. German philosopher Jürgen Habermas makes a distinction between authentic opinion and opinion by acclamation. The first arises through discussion, the media create the latter. The important encounter between human beings has vanished. This is a threat to democracy, especially since very few people have the opportunity to be heard in the media. If people think they cannot be heard and that no one pays attention to their opinions, public dialogue ceases to exist and confidence in democracy declines.

Freedom of speech is a cornerstone of democracy. Democracy is based on public opinion and expression. Politicians should encourage freedom of opinion and expression; they should seek opportunities and arenas for this in society. Public libraries are such places, but they seem to be forgotten in the debates and the discussions about reclaiming democracy.

To quote the UNESCO public library manifesto: "Freedom, prosperity and development of society and of individuals are fundamental human values. They will only be attained through the ability of well-informed citizens to exercise their democratic rights and to play an active role in society. Constructive participation and the development of democracy depend on satisfactory education as well as on free and unlimited access to knowledge, thought, culture and information." Public libraries are the guarantors of all this. Freedom of expression cannot exist without access to it. If citizens are to participate and form their own opinions, they must have access to political, social, economic, and other information as well as cultural expression, all of which they can find in good quality libraries.

When the Swedish government began its official investigation into the state of democracy, we felt that it had forgotten to mention public libraries as one of the important conditions for a living democracy. As the chairman of the commission said, "Libraries are so self evident that we do not need to mention them." Unfortunately, this is an opinion that seems to be held by many politicians, which means that the importance of libraries is too seldom mentioned. To bring about a change, in 1998 the Swedish Library Association set up a committee to focus on the importance of libraries in a democratic state. So what has come out of this involvement? We have been in contact with the chairman and other members of the commission, and we have sent them our opinions about libraries and democracy. We have also sought out and spoken with the minister for democracy. We are in the process of writing an opinion about the results of the investigation. Unfortunately, in our opinion, they have still overlooked the libraries. We have attended several seminars and have been invited as lecturers. We have also arranged seminars and invited colleagues and politicians. The committee is now publishing a book about the important role libraries play in a democracy. They have also established ten theses about democracy and libraries that we are circulating all over the country. We have produced them, for instance, as postcards and bookmarks.

These are the ten theses:

1. A temporal and spatial forum.
2. Experience life—living through and with others.
3. Free of charge, free for all—ideas, words and links.
4. A place to learn the basics of participation.
5. An interface for citizenship.
6. Knowledge as the road to empowerment.
7. Outward perspective, inward perspective, insight, opinion.
8. Words, meanings contexts.
9. A safe haven for all.
10. Diversity and potential.

So now we can add the Swedish Library Association's ten theses to UNESCO's Public Library Manifesto and the Committee on Free Access to Information and Freedom of Expression (FAIFE) Declaration on Libraries and Intellectual Freedom.

The discussion about the crisis of democracy certainly has had effects on many people, organizations, and institutions and it has also, of course, been debated in all the media. This has been a good thing in itself, and I think it has strengthened the democratic ideas. What it has also shown is that democratic activities have new forms. Instead of depending on the established political parties in which people have lost confidence, new groups are formed. They get together when there is a question that affects them. It has become more important to make opinions heard through petitions, manifestos, boycotts, and so on. For these forms of direct democracy as for all others it is necessary to have libraries that provide access to information and that serve as gateways to knowledge, thought, and culture. It is also the duty of all libraries to do all what they can to inform the citizens about what they have and what they can offer. Beyond the citizens, the politicians must also remain constantly aware of the importance of the library and what it is. The library and its potential must be campaigned for time and again, ceaselessly.

At the main public library in Gothenburg, where I work, we started a project about a year back to make our information and our media materials about the community, the region, the state, the European Union (EU), the United Nations (UN), and so forth more easily available to our users. We have also put extra effort into access for those who have special difficulties, for example, people whose first language is not Swedish and the disabled. We have gathered all the media and material in one place in the library on PCs with special access to information from different authorities and institutions. We have librarians who have special training in, for example, law media, EU-media, etc. They are available a special day each week for more difficult questions. We also cooperate with local and national politicians and members of the European Parliament (MEPs), as well as with other authorities, institutions, and all forms of educational bodies. We arrange meetings between the citizens and the politicians as well as with representatives of the tax authorities, lawyers, and others.

I hope I have given you an example of the library as the only institution in society that provides "a temporal and spatial forum, a place to learn the basics of participation, and access to knowledge as the road to empowerment" for all.

It has been said that the struggle for democracy provides the best training in democracy. I would like to conclude by saying that, in my opinion, the continuing struggle for library values is the best way to keep libraries and democracy alive.

Contributors

Joneta Belfrage has served as president of the Swedish Library Association since 1998. She has worked in both university and public libraries.

James H. Billington has been Librarian of Congress since 1987. A noted scholar and Russian historian, Billington's most recent book, *The Face of Russia* (1998), is the companion to a three-part television series that he wrote and narrated on public television in June 1998.

Thomas S. Blanton is the director of George Washington University's National Security Archive, which won the 1999 George Polk Award for "piercing the self-serving veils of government secrecy." Series editor for the Archive's microfiche, CD-ROM, and Web publications of declassified documents, he has edited or co-authored books on the White House e-mail case, the Iran-Contra affair, nuclear weapons, and federal open-government laws.

John Y. Cole is the founding director of the Center for the Book in the Library of Congress, which was established by Librarian of Congress Daniel J. Boorstin to stimulate public interest in books, reading, and libraries. His most recent book, co-edited with architectural historian Henry Hope Reed, is *The Library of Congress: The Art and Architecture of the Thomas Jefferson Building* (W. W. Norton, 1997).

Joan C. Durrance is professor at the University of Michigan School of Information (SI) where she teaches, conducts research, and contributes to the literature of information needs and use in community settings, evaluation of information services, and the professional practice of librarians. She is co-principal investigator with her colleague Karen Pettigrew of "How Libraries and Librarians Help," a project funded by the Institute of Museum and Library Services (IMLS). The project will provide librarians with tools for measuring the outcomes of public library community information services.

William R. Gordon is executive director of the American Library Association (ALA). He previously headed the Prince George's County Memorial Library System in Hyattsville, Maryland, from 1977 to 1998.

Anne Heanue is a consultant, having retired in 1998 as associate director of the ALA Washington Office. Heanue authored the award-winning, seventeen-year chronology, *Less Access to Less Information by and about the U.S. Government* (ALA Washington Office, 1981–1998).

Michael Jourdan is a graduate student at the University of Michigan School of Information, working with Joan Durrance on the IMLS-funded "How Libraries and Librarians Help."

Nancy C. Kranich is president of the American Library Association for 2000–2001, on leave from her position as associate dean of libraries at New York University. She has focused much of her professional involvement on advocacy and information policy issues about which she speaks and writes frequently. Her ALA presidential theme, Libraries: the Cornerstone of Democracy, led to the publishing of this book.

Susan B. Kretchmer is a writer and a magazine editor for a publishing company. Her award-winning essay, "Challenging Boundaries for a Boundless Medium: Information Access, Libraries, and Freedom of Expression in a Democratic Society" appears in *The Boundaries of Freedom of Expression and Order in American Democracy*, edited by Thomas R. Hensley (Kent, Ohio: Kent State University Press, 2001).

Elizabeth L. (Betty) Marcoux is director of Certification and Interdisciplinary Programs at the University of Arizona School of Information Resources and Library Science. She has worked as a librarian for over twenty-seven years, especially in school libraries, and was the chair of the American Association of School Libraries/Association for Educational Communications and Technology (AASL/AECT) Vision Committee that wrote *Information Power: Building Partnerships for Learning* (Chicago: ALA, 1998). She was recognized as the 1996 Arizona Librarian of the Year.

Ronald B. McCabe is director of McMillan Memorial Library, Wisconsin Rapids, Wisconsin. He is the author of *Civic Librarianship: Renewing the Social Mission of the Public Library* (Metuchen, N.J.: Scarecrow, 2001).

Kathleen de la Peña McCook is coordinator for community outreach for the College of Arts and Sciences and professor of library and information science at the University of South Florida (USF) in Tampa. She has chaired the American Library Association Advisory Committee for the Office for Literacy and Outreach Services, and is the author of many books and articles, including *A Place at the Table: Participating in Community Building* (Chicago: ALA, 2000).

Paul K. McMasters is the First Amendment Ombudsman at the Freedom Forum, based in Arlington, Virginia. He was a professional journalist for more than thirty years before joining the foundation to help build the First Amendment Center at Vanderbilt University. McMasters writes and lectures extensively on First Amendment issues that arise in Congress, the courts, and elsewhere, and has testified before Congress and governmental commissions on free speech and freedom of information issues.

Karen Pettigrew is assistant professor at the University of Washington Information School and co-directs the IMLS-funded "How Libraries and Librarians Help" at the University of Michigan with Joan Durrance.

Randy Pitman is the editor of *Video Librarian,* the video review guide for libraries. He is the author of *The Video Librarian's Guide to Collection Development and Management* (New York: G. K. Hall, 1992), *Video Movies: A Core Collection for Libraries* (Santa Barbara, Calif.: ABC-CLIO, 1990), *The Librarian's Video Primer* (video, ALA, 1988), and has written numerous articles for various library publications.

Jorge Reina Schement is co-director of the Information Policy Institute and professor of Communications and Information Policy at Pennsylvania State University. Schement conducted the seminal research at the FCC that led to recognition of the digital divide. He has published many books and articles about information policy and has advised leading policymakers, including President Clinton. He is also the author of the Telecommunications Statement of the Congressional Hispanic Caucus.

Karen Scheuerer is a graduate student at the University of Michigan School of Information, working with Joan Durrance on the IMLS-funded "How Libraries and Librarians Help."

Patricia Glass Schuman, president of Neal-Schuman Publishers, is past-president of the American Library Association. She has been a visiting professor at Columbia, Pratt, St. John's, and Syracuse Universities. Her latest book is *Your Right to Know: The Call to Action* (Chicago: ALA, 1993).

Frederick Stielow is a professor and director of the Walter Reuther Library and Labor Union Archives at Wayne State University. He has written extensively on both history and technology and has received numerous awards, including the American Historical Association and Library of Congress's Jameson Fellowship, a Fulbright fellowship to Italy, MCI citation as a "cybrarian" of the year, and the Windsor Prize for library history.

Siva Vaidhyanathan, a cultural historian and media scholar, is the author of *Copyrights and Copywrongs: The Rise of Intellectual Property and How it Threatens Creativity* (New York: New York University Press, 2001). He teaches in the Department of Culture and Communication at New York University.

Index

Printed in the United States
44231LVS00006B/160-231

9 780838 908082